SPOTLIGHT

D1605894

SARASOTA, NAPLES & THE PARADISE COAST

LAURA REILEY

Contents

SARASOTA, NAPLES & THE PARADISE COAST

SARASOTA COUNTY

Want a stiff shot of culture? Sarasota's the place to go. Arts vie with more than 35 miles of dazzling Gulf Coast beaches for top draw. But Sarasota was a slow starter. It took its time becoming the sophisticated, culturally rich city it is today. Centuries after Ponce de León, Panfilo de Narvaez, and Hernando de Soto came through this part of the Gulf Coast, the area went mercifully unnoticed by white settlers. Even after Florida was acquired by the U.S. in 1821, the only white men to linger here were a handful of entrepreneurial fishermen who supplied salted fish and live turtles from the area for export to Cuba. In 1842, William Whittaker homesteaded in the area, planting some orange trees. Not many followed suit, perhaps because the local Seminoles' reputation for fierceness was widely acknowledged.

In fact, it was the brutal seven-year Seminole War that brought Whittaker and a stalwart few to town as part of the Armed Occupation Act, which deeded 160 Florida acres and six months' provisions to any person who agreed to carry arms and protect the land for five years.

Forty years later, as a means for drumming up some new residents, the Florida Mortgage and Investment Company started talking up Sarasota, with a few egregious exaggerations, in Scotland. Sixty Scottish families took the bait, arriving in 1885 to find a water-logged Main Street and a decided lack of amenities. Being Scottish, they promptly built a golf course (possibly America's first) and then got to work making it a real town. Because there was no overland transportation, sailing ships and steamboats were the only connection to

HIGHLIGHTS

◖ Spring Training at Ed Smith Stadium: Take me out to the ballpark. Ed Smith Stadium is the spring-training home of the Cincinnati Reds, with all the Grapefruit League teams cycling through in preparation for the summer season. It's thrilling to see big-league teams in such a small-town setting. Tickets are cheap and the hot dogs are good (page 13).

◖ Marie Selby Botanical Gardens: You don't have to be a master gardener or panting horticulturalist to enjoy a day here. In 11 bayfront acres, the open-air and under-glass museum has more than 6,000 orchids and more than 20,000 other plants, many of which have been collected in the wild by the gardens' research staff. Most impressive is the vast array of otherworldly epiphytes, or air plants (page 17).

◖ John and Mable Ringling Museum of Art: This museum is a must-see for fans of Flemish and Italian baroque art, with room after room of breathtaking canvasses, the most impressive of which is a series by Peter Paul Rubens known collectively as *The Triumph of the Eucharist* (page 17).

◖ Film Festivals: Time a trip to Sarasota to catch one of the city's two film festivals, the Sarasota Film Festival and the Cine-World Film Festival. The former is in April, the latter in November – both are a citywide excuse for a party, in between two-hour popcorn-eating jags at all the city's many movie theaters (page 25).

◖ Siesta Key Beach: Beaches are a central

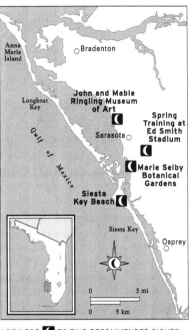

LOOK FOR ◖ TO FIND RECOMMENDED SIGHTS, ACTIVITIES, DINING, AND LODGING.

draw of this area, with a couple of world-class contenders. Siesta Key Beach, with its pure-quartz white sand (it's more like powdered sugar than granulated sugar, so each time you stand up you look like a Greek wedding cookie in a bathing suit), usually gets top honors (page 37).

the outside world. In 1902 came the railroad, which connected Sarasota to Tampa; electricity and paved roads followed not too long after.

An influx of wealthy socialites settled the area starting around 1910, establishing Sarasota as a winter resort for affluent northerners. It was during this time that Sarasota's performing and visual arts institutions were established, to entertain those first hoity-toity tourists. Among the early tourists to be smitten

by the town was circus magnate John Ringling. He scooped up property all around Sarasota, moving the circus's winter home here, building himself a winter residence, art museum, circus museum, and college.

The population doubled in the Florida land boom of 1924–1927—it was Roaring Twenties indeed for Sarasota, with tourist hotels, tourist attractions, and a causeway over the bay sprouting up to accommodate the surge in interest.

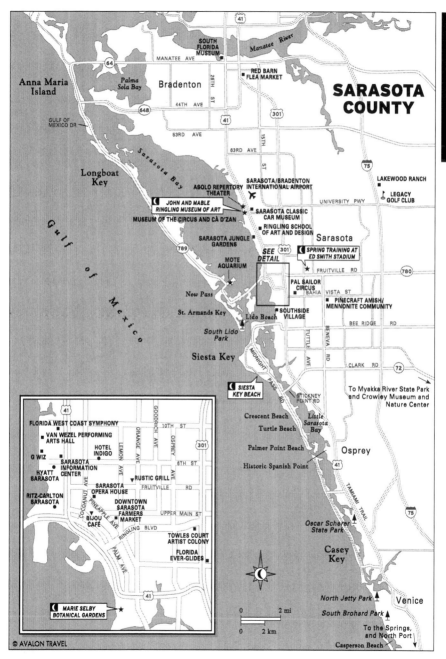

© AVALON TRAVEL

Growth in neighboring towns (Bradenton, Venice, North Port), as well as along the chain of narrow barrier islands (from north to south: Anna Maria Island, Longboat Key, St. Armands Key, Lido Key, Siesta Key, Casey Key) was slower, largely due to limited access. Tourists gradually settled their sights on the keys, noticing the 35 miles of glistening white-sand beaches that fringe their Gulf side.

Because of this head start, the city of Sarasota is the undisputed cultural center of the area, with theater, opera, symphony, ballet, art museums, and restaurants to rival those in much bigger cities. Each of the keys maintains its own identity, with glorious beach access being the central unifying theme. Lido and St. Armands are really just extensions of downtown Sarasota, connected by a causeway, and fairly urban. Started as a quiet fishing village, Longboat Key is now strictly the purview of the posh, with tall resort hotels and condominiums and a glut of golf courses. Siesta Key is much more low-rise, with a personality to match. It's relaxed, laid-back, with a high funk factor. It's the most youthful spot on this part of the Gulf Coast. Casey Key is less of a tourist draw, mostly dotted with single-family homes.

PLANNING YOUR TIME

A typical vacation in this area is about a week. This is partly because there's a week's worth of things to do, and partly because many of the beach houses, condos, etc. rent only by the week, especially in high season. Staying downtown in Sarasota is a little cheaper than staying beachside somewhere. Downtown streets and roads run east–west; avenues and boulevards run north–south. The main street downtown is called, um, Main Street.

From downtown, go east across the John Ringling Causeway to access St. Armands Circle and Lido Key (St. Armands is a shopping and restaurant destination of note). Continue north to Longboat Key, where there's not a lot of draw beyond swanky hotels, golf courses, a few restaurants, and slightly inconvenient beach access and parking. To reach Siesta Key, head south on U.S. 41 (also called the Tamiami Trail), then take a right onto either Siesta Drive or Stickney Point Road—the former takes you to the northern, residential section of the key; Stickney takes you closer to the funky Siesta Village. The public beaches on Siesta Key are among the finest in the state.

The area's peak season begins in February and continues until Easter (average temperatures in the mid-70s F). During that time, prices are hiked and reservations are necessary for accommodations. What travel agents call "the value season" is pretty much all summer in Sarasota, June–September. The Gulf waters are bathwater temperature during much of the summer—and as gentle and safe to swim in as your bathtub, too. On a hot day (in the summer, this means about 90 degrees with a lot of humidity), the water temperatures aren't exactly refreshing, but that's the price to pay for a peaceful, sparsely populated day at the beach. Many of Sarasota's cultural institutions (symphony, ballet, opera, theaters) take a hiatus during the summer months, another drawback to visiting then.

Sarasota

The circus built Sarasota. Sure, a bit of what drew smart and affluent northerners here was the weather (something preposterous like 361 days of sun each year) and the exotic subtropical flora and fauna. But it was when circus impresario John Ringling snapped up real estate that other wealthy, worldly northerners started giving this Podunk orange grove and celery farm another look. And in the 1920s, as Ringling began amassing huge numbers of baroque paintings in his new mansion, Cà d'Zan, so too did Ringling's cohorts begin assembling in all their baroque and even rococo finery for a little winter rest and relaxation. The sunny clime was not enough to entertain for any duration, so cultural amenities like opera, and theater, and symphony orchestras blossomed.

Beyond Ringling's generous bequeathal of house, museums, etc., to the city, the Circus King gave Sarasota a tradition of patronage, a habit of high expectations and connoisseurship when it comes to the arts. Sarasota's population of 54,000, with a little help from twice that number of winter visitors, supports a vast number of arts events, with gusto, along with an equally robust restaurant and shopping scene.

The striking thing is that there's other stuff to do. It's not as if *Die Fledermaus,* or *Swan Lake,* or the comedies of Shakespeare are needed to while away an afternoon or evening in Sarasota. It is home to world-class beaches and all the attendant beach activities, with easy access to notable state parks and outdoor fun. A vacation in Sarasota does not boil down to a dilemma about what to do, just what to do *first.*

SPORTS AND RECREATION
Beaches
North Lido Beach is just northwest of St. Armands Circle, off of John Ringling Boulevard on Lido Key (which really itself is just a 2.5-mile spit of beach from Big Sarasota Pass to New

Siesta Key's sand is powdered-sugar fine and whiter than white — the building blocks of a fantasy sandcastle.

SARASOTA COUNTY

SARASOTA'S GOLF COURSES

BOBBY JONES GOLF COMPLEX
1000 Circus Boulevard, Sarasota,
941/365-4653
6,039 yards, par 71, course rating 68.4, slope 117

HEATHER HILLS GOLF COURSE
101 Cortez Road W., Bradenton,
941/755-8888
3,521 yards, par 61, course rating 58.6, slope 96

IMPERIAL LAKES GOLF COURSE
6807 Buffalo Road, Palmetto, 941/747-GOLF
7,019 yards, par 72, course rating 73.9, slope 136

**LEGACY GOLF CLUB AT
LAKEWOOD RANCH**
8255 Legacy Boulevard, Bradenton,
941/907-7067
Semiprivate, 7,069 yards, par 72, course rating 73.8, slope 130

**THE LINKS AT GREEN FIELD
PLANTATION**
10325 Greenfield Plantation Boulevard, Bradenton, 941/747-9432
6,719 yards, par 72, course rating 72, slope 130

MANATEE COUNTY GOLF COURSE
6415 53rd Avnue W., Bradenton,
941/792-6773
6,747 yards, par 72, course rating 71.6, slope 122

PALMA SOLA GOLF CLUB
3807 75th Street W., Bradenton, 941/792-7476
Semiprivate, 6,264 yards, par 72, course rating 68.4, slope 115

PALMETTO PINES GOLF COURSE
14355 Golf Course Drive, Parrish, 941/776-1375
5,358 yards, par 72, course rating 68.4, slope 92

PERIDIA GOLF & COUNTRY CLUB
4950 Peridia Boulevard, Bradenton,
941/753-9097, www.peridiagcc.net
3,344 yards, par 60, course rating 55.0, slope 76

PINEBROOK/IRONWOOD GOLF CLUB
4260 Ironwood Circle, Bradenton,
941/792-3288
3,706 yards, par 61, course rating 59.9, slope 101

Pass). It's a short walk from shops or restaurants, and fairly secluded. No lifeguards, swift currents, no real amenities. In the other direction from St. Armands Circle, southwest, you'll run into **Lido Beach,** which has parking for 400 cars, cabana beach rentals at the snack bar, playground equipment, and bathrooms. It's a good hang-out-all-afternoon family beach. It's more crowded than North Lido. The third beach on Lido Key is called **South Lido Park,** on Ben Franklin Drive at the southern tip of Lido Key. The park is bordered by four bodies of water: the Gulf, Big Pass, Sarasota Bay, and Brushy Bayou. It has a nature trail, and the beach offers a lovely view of the downtown Sarasota skyline. There's a nice picnic area with grills, as well as volleyball courts. Kayakers use this area to traverse the different waterways.

Golf

Sarasota is Florida's self-described "Cradle of Golf," having been home to the state's first course built in 1905 by Sir John Hamilton Gillespie, a Scottish colonist. The nine-hole course was located right at the center of what is now Sarasota's downtown. That first course is long gone, but there are more than 1,000 holes to play at public, semiprivate, and private courses in Sarasota, at all levels of play and most budgets. Of the top southwest regional courses voted by the readers of *Florida Golf News* (a nice resource, www.floridagolfmagazine.com), many are in the Sarasota area.

Now, I'm not one of those women with the bumper sticker that says, "I got a set of golf clubs for my husband, and I must say, it was a damn good trade!" See sidebar, *Sarasota's Golf*

RIVER CLUB
6600 River Club Boulevard, Bradenton, 941/751-4211
7,026 yards, par 72, course rating 74.5, slope 135

RIVER RUN GOLF LINKS
1801 27th Street E., Bradenton, 941/747-6331
5,825 yards, par 70, course rating 67.9, slope 115

ROSEDALE GOLF AND COUNTRY CLUB
5100 87th Street E., Bradenton, 941/756-0004
6,779 yards, par 72, course rating 72.9, slope 134

SARASOTA GOLF CLUB
7280 N. Lee Wynn Drive, Sarasota, 941/371-2431
6,585 yards, par 72, course rating 72.9, slope 122

TERRA CEIA
2802 Terra Ceia Bay Boulevard, Palmetto, 941/729-7663
4,001 yards, par 62, course rating 67.9, slope 99

TIMBER CREEK GOLF COURSE
4550 Timber Lane, Bradenton, 941/794-8381
9 holes, 2,086 yards, par 27

UNIVERSITY PARK COUNTRY CLUB
7671 Park Boulevard, University Park, 941/359-9999
4,914-7,247 yards, par 72, course rating 67.8-74.4, slope 113-138

VILLAGE GREEN GOLF COURSE
1401 Village Green Parkway, Bradenton, 941/792-7171
2,735 yards, par 58

WATERLEFE GOLF & RIVER CLUB
1022 Fish Hook Cove, Bradenton, 941/744-9771
6,908 yards, par 72, course rating 73.8, slope 145

Courses, for a list of the public, semiprivate, and resort courses recommended to me by golfers, with their top picks indicated. Call for tee times and greens fees, as they vary wildly by time of day and time of year.

◖ Spring Training at Ed Smith Stadium

Sarasota's Ed Smith Stadium has been an exciting part of the Grapefruit League's spring training program for years. The New York Giants arrived back in 1924, followed by the Red Sox and then the White Sox. These days, Sarasota's Ed Smith Stadium (2700 12th St. at the corner of Tuttle Ave., 941/954-4101, box seats $14–16, reserved $12–14, general admission $9) is the spring training home of the Cincinnati Reds (as well as the minor league Sarasota Red Sox of the Florida State League—the Boston Red Sox now train a bit to the south in Fort Myers, and the Pittsburgh Pirates play in nearby Bradenton). To reach the stadium from I-75, take Exit 210, Fruitville Road.

The little 7,500-seat stadium provides intimate access to big-league play in a small-time venue. Cheap tickets and up-close seats—it's a perfect outing on a warm Sarasota spring evening even if baseball's not your sport. Day games start at 1:05 P.M. and night games at 7:05 P.M.; practices begin at 9 A.M. Many spring-training games sell out, so you might want to buy tickets by mail or phone. Send a self-addressed stamped envelope to Reds Tickets, Ed Smith Stadium, 1090 N. Euclid, Sarasota, FL 34237, call 877/647-7337, or visit www.cincinnatireds.com.

Polo

There are scads of spectator sporting opportunities in Sarasota, but polo trumps a fair number of them. Games are enormous fun, the horses racing around tearing up the lush sod of the polo grounds while their riders focus fiercely on that pesky little ball. For a sport with such an effete pedigree, it's amazingly physical and exciting to watch, whether you're in your fancy polo togs (what's with all the hats?) or your weekend jeans. **Sarasota Polo Club** (Lakewood Ranch, 8201 Polo Club Ln., 941/907-0000, 1 P.M. Sun. mid-December–early April, $10, children 12 and under free) is in its 17th year, with professional-level players coming from around the world to play on the nine pristine fields. Bring a picnic or buy sandwiches and drinks once you're there. Gates open at 11:30 A.M. and dogs on leashes are welcome. You can also take polo lessons at Lakewood Ranch. Call Scott Lancaster at 941/907-1122.

Cricket

Polo's not the only game in town for the super fancy-pants Anglophile: Cricket, anyone? The **Sarasota International Cricket Club** (Lakewood Ranch, 7401 University Pkwy., just east of Lorraine Rd., 941/232-9956) was founded in 1983 and has 42 playing members who play about 35 matches a year with clubs from around the Southeast. The season runs weekends from late September through the end of May, and watching is free. Call for game schedule.

Lawn Bowling

Are you starting to see a theme? Lush expanses of perfect grass, a ridiculous number of beautiful sunny days—people in Sarasota clearly need elaborate excuses to spend their days outside. The **Sarasota Lawn Bowling Club** (809 N. Tamiami Trail at 10th St., 941/316-1123, beginning at 9 A.M. weekdays May–Nov., beginning at 12:50 P.M. Nov.–Apr., $2/day to play) is the oldest sporting club in Sarasota, with three greens, *boule* (ball) rentals, and free lessons. Wear flat shoes if you want to play.

Pétanque

Similar to lawn bowling but a little more obscure, pétanque is played at Lakeview Park (7150 Lago St., 941/861-9830, 9 A.M. Sun., free to watch). Players toss and roll a number of steel balls as close as possible to a small wooden ball called the *cochonet,* the piglet. Pronounced PAY-tonk, it's another great spectator sport, especially when accompanied by a wide blanket, a nice bottle of wine, and a tasty picnic. The Sarasota Club de Pétanque has 30 members of all skill levels, from beginners up to the national singles champion, and they bring extra *boules* and are happy to give instructions. Lakeview Park, which is adjacent to Lake Sarasota, also contains a fabulous enclosed dog park—even if Rover stayed at home, visitors find it fun to just watch all that canine enthusiasm (overexuberant dogs have to sit in the "time out" cage). It's open daily 6 A.M. until dark.

State Parks and Nature Preserves

If you want to spend a day out in nature but can't decide how best to engage with the great outdoors, the **Myakka River State Park** (nine miles east of Sarasota, 13208 Hwy. 72, 941/361-6511, 8 A.M.–sunset daily, $5 per vehicle up to eight people) presents pretty unbeatable one-stop shopping. The 28,875-acre park offers hiking, off-road biking, horseback riding, fishing, boating, canoeing, camping, and airboating. Both part of Florida Division of Forestry's Trailwalker Program, the North Loop (5.4 miles) and South Loop (7.4 miles) are fairly easy but scenic marked trails. Beyond these, there are 35 miles of unmarked trails open to hikers, mountain bikers (rentals $15 for two hours, cool four-person quads for $35 for one hour, great for a family), and equestrians (BYOH—that's bring your own horse, but with proof of current negative Coggins test). If you just want to breeze in for an few hours, a ride on the Myakka Wildlife Tours Tram Safari (10151 Sommers Road, Sarasota, 941/377-5797, runs Dec.–May only, $10.00 adults, $5 children 6–12, children 5 and under free if held in lap) takes visitors on a whirlwind tour of the

COURTESY OF SARASOTA CVB

Myakka River State Park is one of Florida's oldest, largest, and most diverse state parks.

park's backcountry, through shady hammocks, pine flatwoods, and lush marshes.

The 14-mile stretch of the scenic Myakka River has fairly easy-to-follow canoe trails (bring your own or rent at the Myakka Outpost; rentals $20 for first hour, $5 each additional hour). Canoes and kayaks can be launched at the bridges, fishing area, other picnic areas, or at the boat ramp. During periods of low water (winter and spring), you'll have to portage around the weir at the south end of the Upper Lake. If you don't want to travel under your own paddle power, the park has a boat tour that runs every hour and a half or so ($8 adults, $4 children, 941/365-0100) and a couple of the world's largest airboats, the *Gator Gal* and the *Myakka Maiden,* are available for guided one-hour tours on the 1-mile-wide and 2.5-mile-long Upper Myakka Lake (serious gator territory).

The park's most unique feature is a fairly new addition. In conjunction with Marie Selby Botanical Gardens, the park opened a Canopy Walkway, the first of its kind in North America: The idea is that you amble along an 85-foot-long observation deck suspension bridge that hangs 25 feet in the air in the midst of a subtropical forest canopy. Perched in the tops of live oaks, laurel oaks, and cabbage palms, your perspective on bird and animal life is unparalleled, if a little vertiginous.

The park offers primitive camping ($4) and more equipped campsites ($22 per night including water and electric), but the neatest option might be one of the five palm log cabins built in the 1930s. They're pretty comfortable, with two double beds, linens, blankets, kitchen facilities, etc. The fee is $60 per night for up to four people (call 800/326-3521 to reserve far in advance).

Adjacent to the state park you'll find the **Crowley Museum and Nature Center** (16405 Myakka Rd., 941/322-1000, 10 A.M.–4 P.M. Thurs.–Sun. May–Dec., Tues.–Sun. Jan.–Apr., $7 adults, $3 children 5–12, children under 5 free), a 190-acre wildlife sanctuary and education center. A couple of hours here dovetails nicely with time spent hiking or paddling in Myakka River State Park—there's a short nature trail, a boardwalk across Maple Branch

HOPE SPRINGS ETERNAL

Sometimes being the driver is good, because you don't need to argue with those in the backseat, you merely set your jaw and direct the car where *you* want it to go. We are going to the **Warm Mineral Springs** (12200 San Servando Ave., North Port, 941-426-1692, 9 A.M.–5 P.M. daily, weather permitting, $20 adults, $14 seniors, $9 students, $8 children 12 and under, $18 AAA members). And it's going to be fun, no matter what the detractors in the backseat are yelling.

Nine million gallons of warm mineral water flow here daily, with a higher mineral content than any other spring in the United States. Eighty-seven degrees year-round. It's thought to be Ponce de León's fabled Fountain of Youth, for crying out loud. How could it be bad?

It wasn't bad exactly, just one of those parallel-universe experiences. First off, North Port isn't exactly a tourist destination. It's a fairly rural, unsexy town that looks like it needs a cash transfusion if the patient is to be saved. The big draw is this natural wonder, an hourglass-shaped sinkhole, 1.4 acres around and 230 feet deep, filled with heavily mineralized water.

We learned quickly upon exiting the car, some of us in a huff, that heavily mineralized water means stink. The sulfurous stink of a really rotten egg. Also, the water's mineral content makes it slimy and viscous-feeling. Also, it's not that warm.

But here's the thing: Russians come from across planet Earth to splash around in this particular sinkhole. Sturdy women in industrial-looking one-piece suits wade in reverently like it's the healing water of the Ganges. English was not a first language for any of the bathers or those relaxing in white plastic patio chairs strewn around the periphery, but lest you think we had merely stumbled upon a large Russian tour group, the snack bar is the proof. It's an all-Russian menu. Goulash, something called Russian ravioli – there were pictures of these things with descriptions beneath, written *in Russian*.

Because the spring contains no dissolved oxygen, organic matter that gets into the springs stays more or less intact. In 1973, a scientist named Wilburn A. Cockrell brought up a nearly complete skeleton of an adult Paleo-Indian male that was dated at 11,000 years old. Dated to nearly the same time period, part of a saber cat was also found. I like the idea that in a few thousand years, divers may pull up an order of Russian ravioli and just scratch their heads and wonder what it was doing here in a rural Florida backwater.

Swamp, and an observation tower overlooking the Myakka River. To give more of a historical context to the area, the Crowley's real core is a pioneer museum tricked out with a rustic one-room cabin, a restored 1892 Cracker house, a working blacksmith shop, and a little sugarcane mill. The museum sponsors Pioneer Days every December, an annual antiques fair, a folk music festival in October, and a yearly stargazing night with high-powered telescopes.

It won't knock your socks off with stunning topography or habitats, but **Oscar Scherer State Park** (1843 S. Tamiami Trail, Osprey, 941/483-5956, 8 A.M.–sundown daily, entrance fee $4 per vehicle) is a local hangout for birders and families who want to spend an afternoon in nature without a lot of hassle. Much of it is a classic Florida flatwoods (scrub pine and sawtooth palmetto, some endangered scrub jays, gopher tortoises, and an indigo snake or two). The park has several marked trails open to hikers and bikers (it's sandy terrain, most suitable for mountain bikes), and kayakers paddle around South Creek (bring your own canoe or kayak or rent canoes from the ranger station: $5/hour, $25/day), launched from the South Creek Picnic Area. Birders may want to join the informal Thursday morning bird walks at 8 A.M., or the Friday morning ranger-led walks at 8:30 A.M., or canoe tours on Wednesdays at 9 A.M. Check in at the park's nature center.

SIGHTS

◖ Marie Selby Botanical Gardens

Much has been written in recent years about the mystery of orchids, bromeliads, and other epiphytes. *The Orchid Thief, Orchid Fever* in the same vein, the more historical *The Orchid in Lore and Legend,* and then a whole bunch of books on monomaniacal plant hunters who scour the globe for their personal botanical holy grail—still, if you're not an enthusiast, the mania may just elude you. Big whoop, you may say.

The word epiphyte comes from the Greek words "epi," meaning "upon," and "phyton," meaning "plant." Beginning their life in the canopy of trees, their seeds carried by birds or wind, epiphytes are air plants, growing stubbornly without the benefit of soil on the branches or trunks of trees. Orchids, cacti, bromeliads, aroids, lichens, mosses, and ferns can even grow on the same tree, a big interspecies jamboree.

And if you want to see some heartbreakingly beautiful and alien epiphytes, spend a long afternoon at Marie Selby Botanical Gardens (811 S. Palm Ave., 941/366-5731, 10 A.M.–5 P.M. daily, $12 adults, $6 children 6–11, children under 6 free). The nine-acre gardens on the shores of Sarasota Bay are one of Sarasota's absolute jewels. Marie Selby donated her home and grounds "to provide enjoyment for all who visit the gardens." Meandering along the walking paths through the hibiscus garden, cycad garden, a banyan grove, a tropical fruit garden, and thousands of orchids—there's a lot of enjoyment to be had. The botanical gardens also host lectures and gardening classes, and have a lovely shop (beginners should opt for a training-wheels phalaenopsis—very hard to kill—or an easy-care bromeliad) with an exhaustive collection of gardening books (80 on orchids alone). Spend an hour gazing at epiphytes in the tropical greenhouse and you'll never say "big whoop" again. Caveat: Kids get fairly bored here, with a brief flurry of interest around the koi pond and butterfly garden. I would tend not to bring them unless they're very mature or stroller-bound.

◖ John and Mable Ringling Museum of Art

John Ringling's lasting influence on Sarasota is remarkable, but the John and Mable Ringling Museum of Art makes it simply incontrovertible (5401 Bay Shore Rd., 941/351-1660, www.ringling.org, 10 A.M.–5:30 P.M. daily, $19 adults, $16 seniors, $6 students and children 6–17, Florida teachers and students $6 with ID).

In 2007, the museum completed a six-year, $140 million master plan marking the completion of one of the most extraordinary transformations of any museum in North America. It's now one of the 20 largest art museums in North America. Since 2006, the Ringling Museum has opened four new buildings, the Tibbals Learning Center, the John M. McKay Visitors Pavilion, The Ulla R. and Arthur F. Searing Wing, and the Education/Conservation Building, as well as opening the restored Historic Asolo Theater.

The whole museum complex is spectacular,

The Cà d'Zan (House of John) mansion was John and Mable Ringling's winter residence in the 1920s.

The Ringling estate consists of several buildings including Cà d'Zan, the Museum of the Circus, and the original art museum building.

but the art museum is definitely worth its fairly hefty admission price, having been built in 1927 to house Ringling's nearly pathological accretion of 600 paintings, sculptures, and decorative arts including more than 25 tapestries. The Mediterranean-style palazzo contains a collection that includes a set of five gargantuan paintings by Peter Paul Rubens, lots of wonderful Spanish work (soulful El Grecos, Velázquez's portrait of King Philip IV of Spain, etc.), and the music room and dining room of Mrs. William B. Astor (Ringling bought all this in 1926 when the Astor mansion in New York was scheduled to be demolished). The permanent collection is opulent, stunning, with Van Dycks, Poussins, and lots of other baroque masters, but there are shows such as a recent one on surrealism and another on the photos of Ansel Adams and Clyde Butcher that enter beautifully into at least the 20th century.

But wait, that's not all. (Do I sound like that old Ginsu knife commercial?) The complex also houses the **Museum of the Circus,** a peek into circus history. It achieves a certain level of hyperbole in the interpretive signs when it parallels the ascendance of the circus with the growth of the country more generally. Still, the museum's newspaper clippings, circus equipment, parade wagons, and colossal bail rings make one nostalgic for a time and place one probably never knew.

The single most impressive thing about the museum, the thing that caused rampant loitering and inspired commentary like, "Whoa, cooool," is the Howard Bros. Circus model. It takes up vast space—the world's largest miniature circus, after all—and is a three-quarter-inch-to-the-foot scale replica of Ringling Bros. and Barnum & Bailey Circus when the tented circus was at its largest. The model itself takes up 3,800 square feet, with eight main tents, 152 wagons, 1,300 circus performers and workers, more than 800 animals, a 57-car train, and a zillion wonderful details.

Fully restored and reopened in 2002, John Ringling's home on the bay, **Cà d'Zan** (House of John) is also open to the public, an ornate structure evocative of Ringling's two favorite Venetian hotels, the Danieli and the Bauer Grunwald. Completed in 1926, the house is 200 feet long with 32 rooms and 15 baths (a comfort to those of us with small bladders). All kidding aside, there's something about the quality of light much of the year in Sarasota that seems utterly appropriate as host to such a magnificent Venetian Renaissance-style mansion.

Sarasota Classic Car Museum

What's your dream car? DeLorean? Ferrari? Mini Cooper? The Sarasota Classic Car Museum (5500 N. Tamiami Trail, 941/355-6228, 9 A.M.–6 P.M. daily, $8.50 adults, $7.65 seniors, $5.75 children 13–17, $4 children 6–12, children under 6 free) has examples of everyone's favorite wheels. A recent facelift has added some pizzazz to the collection of more than 100 vehicles, from muscle to vintage to exotic cars. You'll see a rare Cadillac station wagon, one of only five ever made, and the gift shop has collectibles for most automotive preoccupations. The museum rents out some of its cars if you want to make a grand entrance somewhere, and the cars are also available for photo ops.

Historic Spanish Point

History buffs may want to visit Historic Spanish Point (337 N. Tamiami Trail, Osprey, 941/966-5214, 9 A.M.–5 P.M. Mon.–Sat., noon–5 P.M. Sun., $9 adults, $8 Florida residents, $8 seniors, $3 children 6–12), operated by Gulf Coast Heritage Association. Bordered on its western edge by Little Sarasota Bay and by pine flatlands to the east, the 30-acre site tells the story of life in the greater Sarasota area going back many generations. Interpretive markers and an "Indian village" show how early Floridian natives fished and hunted here, building middens, or shell mounds, and a burial mound (an archaeology exhibit in the main hall gives you the background on this). Then there's a pioneer home and chapel that have been restored, revealing the story of the early white settlers here, the Webb family. After that, you'll stroll the gardens of heiress Bertha Matilde Honore Palmer's winter estate on Osprey Point. More recently, the site opened a butterfly garden to add to the mix, showing the larval and nectar plants for monarch, zebra longwing, swallowtails, and other butterflies native to the area. Slightly incoherent to the outsider, this National Register historic site has clear support from stalwart local boosters and zealous volunteers.

South Florida Museum

The South Florida Museum (201 10th St. W., Bradenton, 941/746-4131, 10 A.M.–5 P.M. Mon.–Sat., noon–5 P.M. Sun., $15.95 adults, $13.95 seniors, $11.95 children 4–12) is worth a short drive north to Bradenton for the history buff. I'll be honest, I thought the admission fee was pretty steep for some rooms of Ice Age dioramas with animals and natural history exhibits that trace the state's ancient history. The Spanish explorers are covered with nice detail, and the museum houses the Tallant Collection of artifacts, an assemblage of booty from Floridian archeological sites.

Tours

I went to Disney World and couldn't ride the best ride. It wasn't that the ride was sold out, or that I didn't meet the height requirements, it was that the ride wasn't open to the public. It was only for Disney employees (they're known by a euphemism—cast members? honorary rodents?). The people who directed your car to its final resting place in the Disney theme park parking lots were riding the coolest vehicles ever, called Segways. You can rent a Segway Human Transporter of your very own in Sarasota, however, with **Florida Ever-Glides** (200 S. Washington Blvd., Ste. 11, 941/363-9556, tours 9 A.M.–11:30 A.M. and 2 P.M.–4:30 P.M., $65, no kids under 13) and take a 2.5-hour guided tour of downtown Sarasota along the bayfront and arts community. The two side-by-side wheels (as opposed to a bike or motorcycle, in which the two wheels are in a line) are self-balancing, and you stand above the wheels on a little platform and steer the electric-powered vehicle with the handlebars. With speeds of up to 12 mph, they can be used in pedestrian areas and are a perfect way to cover serious ground at a pace slow enough to really appreciate things. Plus, you look really cool. Tours are limited to 12 people and there are weight limitations.

If your passion is architecture, you won't need to be told that Sarasota is the birthplace of a certain strain of American modernism. (If this is news to you, pick up a copy of the excellent *The Sarasota School of Architecture, 1941–1966,* by John Howey.) The **Sarasota Architectural Foundation** (P.O. Box 3678, Sarasota, FL 34230-3678, 941/365-4723, www.saf-online.org) hosts architectural tours, educational events, film screenings, exhibits, and parties for architecture lovers who travel to Sarasota to see its architecture up close and personal. A list of tours is posted on their website.

After indulging in several of Sarasota's effete cultural attractions, you need to clear your head and take a **Walk on the Wild Side** (3434 N. Tamiami Trail, Ste. 817, 941/351-6500, $30–65). The very friendly tour providers tailor trips, taking small groups kayaking, canoeing, day hiking, backpacking, camping, auto touring, bird-watching, or wildlife-viewing, according to people's interests and mobility. You don't need prior canoeing or kayaking experience (they instruct you, but you still have to be fairly fit to work that paddle) for them to take you out on the area's bays, estuaries, and rivers, pointing out birds, dolphins, gators, and manatees along the way. You can choose where you go and for how long (half day, full day, or overnight), but the most romantic is the sunset canoe outing with wine and cheese.

Several companies offer boat tours on Sarasota Bay and into the Gulf of Mexico. **Enterprise Sailing Charters** (2 Marina Plaza, 941/951-1833, 8 A.M.–8 P.M. daily, $40 for two hours, $55 for three hours, $70 for four hours, group and child discounts) takes people out on a tall-masted three-sail ketch.

Key Sailing (2 Marina Jack, Bayfront Plaza, 941/346-7245, two-, three-, and four-hour sails daily, $45–150) offers charters and sailing instruction aboard a pretty 41-foot Morgan Classic II. **LeBarge Tropical Cruises** (U.S. 41 at Marina Jack, 941/366-6116, 9 A.M.–6 P.M. daily, $18 adults, $13 for children 4–12) offers two-hour cruises of Sarasota Bay, either a dolphin watch narrated by a marine biologist, a narrated sightseeing cruise, or a tropical sunset cruise with live entertainment.

Farmers Market

Despite the fact that Florida is a huge agricultural state (citrus, sugarcane, tomatoes, strawberries, etc.), much of the Gulf Coast doesn't have a dense enough concentration of foodies and gourmands to support serious farmers markets. Sarasota is an exception. Every Saturday morning year-round you'll find all the sights and smells that are unique to the breed: stacked produce; the cookie lady; an earnest band of musicians passing the hat;

The downtown farmer's market is fun even if you're not buying — lots to see and lots of free tastes.

COURTESY OF SARASOTA CVB

babies in strollers, smiling around a mouthful of gummed peach; wind chimes and handicrafts hawked by dreadlocked waifs; and bromeliads, orchids, and cut flowers festooning the bulging bags of nearly every shopper. The **Downtown Farmers Market** has been going on for 30 years, the tents and tables of 50 or so vendors erected Saturday mornings by 7 A.M. and broken down around noon. It used to be located on South Pineapple Avenue, but now it sets up each week on Lemon Avenue at the intersection of Main Street.

Family-Friendly Attractions

My favorite family attraction in Sarasota is **Sarasota Jungle Gardens** (3701 Bay Shore Rd., 941/355-5305, 9 A.M.–5 P.M. daily, $14 adults, $13 seniors, $10 children 3–12, children under 3 free), but then I'm a sucker for quirky Old Florida attractions. Once part boggy banana grove, part universally agreed-upon "impenetrable swamp," the subtropical jungle was purchased in the 1930s by newspaperman David Lindsay. He brought in tropical plants, trees, and bird species. It opened in 1940 as a tourist attraction, and it puttered along through a couple of ownership changes until it ended up in the hands of the Allyn family. Every elementary student within 100 miles has made the trek by school bus to sit and watch the short birds of prey show (there's also a show that features animals linked only, I think, by their universal repugnance to human beings—things like giant Madagascar hissing cockroaches, I kid you not), and then wander along the paths through the lush formal gardens, the farmyard exhibit, the tiki gardens, and the majorly stinky flamingo area. The zoological gardens are home to about 100 animals, many of them abandoned pets, so it's an odd assortment. (I spent about half an hour trying to get two former pet myna birds to say, "Put a sock in it" to the next person to speak to them.) The most peculiar part of the park, however, has nothing to do with plants or animals. In one back corner of the park there's something called the Gardens of Christ. It's a series of eight two-dimensional dioramas

by Italian-born sculptor Vincent Maldarelli depicting the most important events in the life of Jesus Christ. So, to review, Sarasota Jungle Gardens: tropical plants, hissing cockroaches, large colorful birds, and the life of Jesus Christ.

The **Mote Marine Laboratory and Aquarium** (1600 Ken Thompson Pkwy., City Island, 941/388-2451, 10 A.M.–5 P.M. daily, $17 adults, $16 seniors, $12 children 4–12, children under 4 free) is a pleasant small aquarium that also serves as a working marine laboratory. For kids, the coolest parts are the 135,000-gallon shark tank, the "immersion cinema" state-of-the-art theater with a 40-foot wide, high-definition screen with Dolby Surround sound. Visitors get their own interactive console that changes the outcome of the game or movie on the screen. Children will also like the underwater microphone in the Marine Mammal Center, which allows visitors to hear the resident manatees chirping at each other and methodically munching the heads of romaine lettuce that bob at the top of their tank. There's a touch tank, where you'll see parents cajoling their small ones to feel up a sea urchin, starfish, horseshoe crab, or stingless stingray, as well as nicely interpreted exhibits of eels, puffer fish, sea horses, and extraterrestrial-looking jellies.

The more impressive part of the Mote is not really open to the public—the Mote Marine Laboratory is known internationally for its shark research and more locally for its research on red tides, or algal blooms that occasionally adversely affect Sarasota's summer beach season with these yucky floating plants that wash ashore with all the fish they've killed.

Sarasota Bay Explorers (941/388-4200) works in conjunction with Mote Marine Laboratory and runs their science boat trips out of the facility. They offer several wonderful styles of ecotours, all perfect for a fun, yet educational family outing. There are narrated **Sea Life Encounter Cruises** (for $35 you get aquarium admission, too; $28 children), backwater **guided kayak tours** ($50 adults, $40 children), and private charters aboard the 24-foot Sea Ray Sundeck *Miss Explorer* ($295 for a three-hour trip, $4,455 for a five-hour trip).

If fate hands you a foul-weather day during your visit, a lovely family afternoon can be had at **G. WIZ** (1001 Boulevard of the Arts, 941/309-4949, 9 A.M.–7 P.M. Mon.–Thurs., 9 A.M.–10 P.M. Fri.–Sat., 10 A.M.–8 P.M. Sun., $22 adults, $20 seniors, $17 children 3–18). It stands for the Gulf Coast Wonder & Imagination Zone, but it could best be summarized as a 33,000-square-foot facility of interactive science-focused exhibits. There are traveling shows (most recently that controversial Bodies Revealed exhibit that has made the rounds, probably much to the consternation of the spirits of the Chinese indigents whose bodies were filleted for our benefit), and the permanent exhibits are compelling. Kids can fly, be free, as they zoom through the EcoZone (snakes, box turtles, and other native Florida creatures), the EnergyZone (with exhibits on electricity, sound, light, and neat building materials made out of magnets), the TechZone (where you can design a robot or create an animated video), and the BodyZone (exhibits on human anatomy, strength, endurance, and flexibility). Which is handy, as parents will need some strength and endurance of their own to keep up with their scampering progeny. The G. WIZ also offers programs for school groups and summer day camps.

Sarasota has a pleasant paint-your-own-pottery center, **S'Platters Pottery Painting Place** (2110 Gulf Gate Dr., 941/926-3070, 11 A.M.–6 P.M. Tues., Wed., and Sat., 11 A.M.–9 P.M. Thurs. and Fri., noon–5 P.M. Sun., prices start at $7, most pieces $12–25, which also includes paint, time, and firing), another satisfying bad-weather family activity. S'Platters has jumped on a couple of current trends in kids' entertainment, offering a build-your-own-teddy bear option, a bead-painting option so you can make your own beaded jewelry, and some neat mosaic-making kits. You can also take your favorite photo from your family vacation and have it fired onto a ceramic piece as a keepsake of your trip.

ENTERTAINMENT AND EVENTS

Sarasota describes itself as the "cultural coast" of Florida. And as Mohammed Ali said back when he was Cassius Clay, it ain't braggin' if it's true. It starts getting monotonous when you enumerate all the professional arts options in Sarasota, but I suppose I'm getting paid to do so.

Theater

Celebrating 48 years of professional theater in Sarasota, the **Asolo Repertory Theater,** until 2006 called the Asolo Theatre Company (5555 N. Tamiami Trail, 941/351-8000, www.asolo .org, curtain times generally 2 P.M. and 8 P.M., Asolo Rep Nov.–June, prices vary), is a professional company that performs primarily in the 500-seat Harold E. and Esther M. Mertz Theatre at the Florida State University Center for the Performing Arts, a theater originally built as an opera house in 1903 in Dunfermline, Scotland. There's a second, smaller 161-seat black-box Jane B. Cook Theatre on-site for performances of the conservatory season and smaller productions of the Asolo. Students also present a series of original works known as the LateNite series, and the FSU School of Theatre presents a variety of other special events and performances. Recently, the Asolo Rep and the Conservatory perform one show each in the Historic Asolo Theater, located in the Ringling Museum's Visitors Pavilion. All of this means more shows and more variety for Sarasota's theatergoers. This means that in a single season you might see John Patrick Shanley's riveting *Doubt,* followed by Peter Shaffer's *Equus* (sorry, no Daniel Radcliffe in this production), Mamet's *Speed the Plow,* and a play adapted by Steve Martin called *The Underpants.*

Because the Florida State University Conservatory for Actor Training's graduate-level program yields so many newly minted thespians in Sarasota, the whole theatrical playing field has been elevated. Worthwhile community and professional theater troupe efforts include the contemporary dramas and comedies at **Florida Studio Theatre** (1241 N. Palm Ave., 941/366-9000) where I saw a nice

COURTESY OF SARASOTA CVB

The Asolo's resident equity company performs in rotating repertory on the historic mainstage, and the FSU/Asolo Conservatory presents a season of productions on a second, smaller stage.

production of *Moonlight and Magnolias* about the making of *Gone with the Wind*, mostly Broadway musicals at **Golden Apple Dinner Theatre** (25 N. Pineapple Ave., 941/366-5454), six annual musical productions with **The Players of Sarasota** (838 N. Tamiami Trail, 941/365-2494), dramas in the summer with **Banyan Theater Company** (at the Asolo's Jane B. Cook Theatre, 941/358-5330), the more avant-garde readings of **Infinite Space** (different locations, 941/330-8250, www.infinite-space.org), and even the little community productions on two stages of the **Venice Little Theatre** (140 W. Tampa Ave., Venice, 941/488-1115).

Music and Dance

The oldest continuously running orchestra in the state of Florida, **Florida West Coast Symphony** (Van Wezel Performing Arts Hall, 709 N. Tamiami Trail, box office 941/953-3434, www.fwcs.org, prices and times vary) offers a wide array of more than 75 symphonic and chamber music concerts in a 37-week annual season and is host to the internationally recognized Sarasota Music Festival each June (an intense three-week event of chamber music, master classes and concerts, with the coaching and performance of chamber music as its primary priority). Seven Masterworks programs are presented by the symphony throughout the season, as well as a four-concert Composer's Series and a set of six Great Escapes programs of light classics and pops on Thursday, Friday, and Saturday evenings and Friday mornings. The symphony also occasionally presents Symphonic Pops concerts with special guests. The orchestra, under the current direction of artistic director Leif Bjaland, has experienced a period of real growth and international accolades.

But even if you're not a huge symphonic music fan, it's a good excuse to check out Sarasota's most distinctive landmark, the **Van Wezel Performing Arts Hall** (777 N. Tamiami Trail, 941/953-3368, www.vanwezel.org, times and prices vary). Designed by William Wesley Peters of the Frank Lloyd Wright Foundation, the building riffs on a seashell found by Frank Lloyd Wright's widow, Olgivanna, near the Sea of Japan. It has an eye-popping lavender/purple color scheme, and it looks accordioned, like a scallop shell (supposedly to maximize the space's acoustical possibilities). Love it or hate it, the Van Wezel presents a wonderful range of Broadway productions, world-class dance, music, comedy, and popular acts, as well as being the home base for many of the local arts organizations.

For instance, the **Sarasota Ballet of Florida** (5555 N. Tamiami Trail, 941/351-8000, www.sarasotaballet.org, times and prices vary) splits its performances between the Van Wezel and the Asolo, offering a combination of treasured classical works and contemporary and modern dance. The ballet was founded as a presenting organization in 1987 by Jean Allenby-Weidner, former prima ballerina with the Stuttgart Ballet. Through community support, it became a resident company in 1990. The ballet often works collaboratively with other local arts organizations on productions—in 2005 they staged a ballet with Circus Sarasota that tells the story of John Ringling's life, complete with aerialists, clowns, and such. (The Sarasota Ballet also runs the Sarasota Ballet Academy; The Next Generation, an award-winning scholarship program for youth at risk; and an international summer school.)

The **Sarasota Opera** (61 N. Pineapple Ave., 941/366-8450, ext. 1, www.sarasotaopera.org) has similar youth outreach, its Sarasota Youth Opera receiving all kinds of plaudits for its productions. The acorn doesn't fall far from the tree: The Sarasota opera presents concerts year-round, but its much-anticipated (often sold out) repertory season is every February and March, housed in the beautifully restored 1926 Mediterranean Revival–style Edwards Theatre. The opera house underwent an extensive renovation in 2007.

It's a stamina event, one that takes grit, fortitude, and a good pair of opera glasses. The Sarasota Opera's Winter Opera Festival draws opera buffs from all over the country for a compact season of four productions, which can be enjoyed nearly at one sitting for the especially stalwart.

"Usually we try to open with a very popular opera," explains Sarasota Opera's director of marketing, Richard Russell. "We open with one and the following week we open the second opera, then we take a week's break before opening the third opera, so the first one has the most performances."

The festival is hardly devoted to staging only the big crowd-pleasers, however.

"We have two programs that we've been running since 1989," says Russell. "With the Masterworks Revival Series, we try to look for important works that may not be done often, or pieces that were popular in an earlier time but have been neglected more recently. Our other initiative is the Verdi Cycle, with the aim of producing every piece of music he wrote. We're about two-thirds of the way through that."

In 2008, that meant Verdi's *Rigoletto,* Puccini's *La rondine,* Verdi's *I due Foscari,* and Mozart's delicious comedy *Così fan tutte,* all sung in their original language with real-time English translations projected above the stage. And while you're hanging around in the gorgeous art deco lobby during intermission, look up: The chandelier is from the movie *Gone with the Wind.*

Sarasota also has an annual chamber music festival each April, **La Musica International Chamber Music Festival** (rehearsals in Mildred Sainer Pavilion of New College of Florida, performances in the Edwards Theatre, 61 N. Pineapple Ave., 941/366-8450, ext. 3, www.lamusicafestival.org, 8 P.M., $35 single tickets, $50 pass to all the rehearsals). The public is welcome to watch rehearsals for $10 each, to see the musicians work their way through complicated pieces by Tchaikovsky, Schubert, Mendelssohn, Prokofiev, Brahms, Mozart, and others. Before the actual evening performances there are short lectures about the pieces.

Circuses

Five of the seven sons of August and Marie

Salomé Ringling of Baraboo, Wisconsin, ran away and joined the circus. Or, rather, they invented their own. In 1870, they premiered their show and charged a penny admission, building it year by year from a modest wagon show (its first "ring" a strip of cloth staked out to form a circle) to a major national show that traveled via rail from town to town. Meanwhile, circus titans P. T. Barnum and James A. Bailey teamed up in 1888 to create "The Greatest Show on Earth," blowing away all the competition with their glitz, animals, and death-defying acts. It was Bailey's untimely death in 1906 that led the "Greatest Show" to be bought out by the Ringling brothers. The two circuses ran separately until 1919, when they were joined to form the mega-huge **Ringling Bros. and Barnum & Bailey Circus,** and the rest is history.

In the 1920s, John Ringling and his wife Mable built a stunning Venetian-style estate on Sarasota Bay, called Cà d'Zan (House of John in Venetian dialect). In order to house their bursting-at-the-seams collection of works by Peter Paul Rubens, 17th-century Italian paintings, and Flemish art, they built an art museum. But it was in 1927 when Sarasota became an official circus town—the Ringling Bros. and Barnum & Bailey Circus's winter quarters were moved here, giving the sedate Florida town an indelible whiff of the oddity, eccentricity, and glamour that is the circus.

Many of the circus performers who acted in the *Wizard of Oz* and that ultimate non-PC film *Terror of Tiny Town* (a musical western starring all little people) called Sarasota home, with specially built homes in a section of town called, unsurprisingly, **Tiny Town** (you can tour this area on the Ever-Glide guided tours, see *Tours*).

Today visitors get a sense of Sarasota's circus history at the **Museum of the Circus** on the Ringling grounds, but during February and March the circus comes alive with **Circus Sarasota** (8251 15th St. E., 941/355-9335, ringside $40, section C $20). Founded in 1997 by Ringling Bros. alums, Pedro Reis and Dolly Jacobs (an aerialist, she's a second-generation

circus performer—her father was the famous clown Lou Jacobs), it's a single-ring, European-style circus that changes every year. Reis and Jacobs often perform an aerial pas de deux, and there are tightrope acts, trained horses, aerial acrobats from China, clowns, tumbling, contortionists, and so forth, all performed in an intimate setting.

Despite the fact that Ringling Bros. circus now makes its winter home to the north in Tampa, Sarasota is still training the next generation of circus performers. **PAL Sailor Circus** (2075 Bahia Vista St., 941/361-6350, 11:45 A.M. and 7 P.M., $10–14) has been thrilling audiences for more than 50 years, educating kids 8–18 in the circus arts and then letting them put on a show. In 2004, the program was on the verge of closing. With the assistance of Sheriff William F. Balkwill, the Police Athletic League took over the Sailor Circus as one of its after-school programs. About 90 students participate in the twice-annual training sessions, where they learn circus skills like clowning, tumbling, high-wire and flying trapeze, unicycling, juggling, rigging, and costuming. Then, in March and the end of December, the students perform for the public in an exciting four-ring circus.

◖ Film Festivals

Sarasota supports not one, but two film festivals. By far the more famous of the two is the **Sarasota Film Festival** every April (multiple venues, box office is located in the Main Plaza at 1991 Main Street, Suite 108A, adjacent to the Regal Hollywood 20 Theatre, 941/366-6200, www.sarasotafilmfestival.com). The fastest-growing film festival in the country, it showcases 200 independent features, documentary, narrative, and short films; throws lavish parties to which the celebrities and filmmakers actually come; and uses the opportunity to watch sedate Sarasota carouse with great diligence. The event usually includes a Shorts Fest, a couple of family-oriented events, and lots of panel discussions with industry leaders and symposiums with guest stars. And every November there's the Sarasota Film Society's 10-day **Cine-World Film Festival** (Burns Court Cinemas,

CLOWNING AROUND

"Snakes don't bond."

I'm getting a lesson in reptile psychology from T.M., The Gator Guy, one of the acts in the 132nd edition of Ringling Bros. and Barnum & Bailey Circus. The T.M. stands for Ted McRae, and while he talks to me by cell phone, McRae is on the world's largest privately owned train, the Ringling Train, stretching one mile and 53 cars long. Cellular service from this train stinks.

He keeps calling me back to say things like: "Reptiles are totally alien. Mammals do certain things that you are familiar with, but reptiles might as well be from another planet. An alligator might sit there for three days without moving. It is an ambush-type predator. It's waiting to kill something. And their eyes don't give anything away."

The Gator Guy is a crusader of sorts, a promoter of human-reptile relations who travels with his trusty pet python and his savannah monitor lizard, Jake. He rode the wave of interest prompted by the late Steve Erwin, the Crocodile Hunter.

"Thank you, Steve Erwin. I was in the right place at the right time – people are fascinated. And it's a good thing, because *all* animals are being pushed aside in their natural habitats, not just the cute, fuzzy ones. The ones that scare you and are dangerous, they're getting pushed aside as well."

The animal-rights activists that are a fixture outside the circus might not agree with his reasoning – that the circus gives visibility to endangered or ignored animals' plights – but McRae certainly seems like an enthusiast. He places his entire head into the open mouth of a 10-foot alligator, wraps himself with his beloved 200-pound python, and soothes his cold-blooded wards into stillness.

The Gator Guy is one of several acts to anchor the ever-changing circus. Ringling Bros., the oldest – in addition to being the greatest – show on earth, reinvents itself every two years, with two totally different traveling units. The Red Unit and the Blue Unit each tour North America 11 months out of the year for two years before going back to winter quarters (now in Tampa, but historically here in Sarasota) and preparing a new edition. The Red Unit presents the odd-numbered editions, the Blue Unit presents the even-numbered editions (so, for instance, if you see the 138th edition Blue Unit this year, you'll see the 139th edition Red Unit next year).

So one year the show's centerpiece might be the Living Carousel, an assemblage of 105 people, 27 animals, and more gold lamé than a Liberace concert, with something like two million rhinestones and elephant blankets inset

---

506 Burns Ln., 941/955-3456), which showcases Florida film artists in addition to presenting the best of the preceding Toronto, Cannes, New York, and Telluride film festivals.

Festivals

February's not a bad month to visit, because you can catch the month-long annual run of the European-style **Circus Sarasota.** Sarasota is the self-described "circus capital of the world," after all. Music lovers may want to come in February or March for the repertory season of the **Sarasota Opera,** although in April there's **La Musica International Chamber Music Festival** (and also in April

you'll encounter the weeklong **Florida Wine Fest & Auction**).

If you're coming to the area strictly for the white, powdery sand, you might think of coming in May for the cutthroat pro-am **Sand Sculpting Contest** on Siesta Key Beach (also, the Fourth of July fireworks over the Gulf are wonderful from the vantage spot of Siesta Key Beach).

NIGHTLIFE
Bars

Downtown has a few of the kind of nightspots that feel like the epicenter of something big. **Zoria** (1991 Main St., 941/955-4457,

with 81,000 mirrors turning the whole arena into a disco-ball fantasy.

Or it's the Globe of Steel, a 16-foot steel globe, into which ride eight members of the Torres Family (five brothers and three cousins), riding a complicated routine of loops around the interior, reaching speeds of 65 mph, and then someone gets in and stands there, daring one of them to flub up. Talk about extreme sports.

Or maybe sixth-generation circus performer Taba, no last names please, the "tiger whisperer," who gently coaxes four different types of Bengal tigers to romp around the center ring. Then there are always the high-wire acts, the elephant poop-scooping guys, the classic Clown Alley, and a live band performing the swelling circus music.

But in some ways, the movies are ruining the circus. Ringling Bros. and Barnum & Bailey Circus comes to town in this new millennium with its usual splash, pageantry, and death-defying acts, and audiences sit in stony, underwhelmed silence. Audience members are no longer able to mentally separate the wheat (high-wire acts without a net) from the chaff (computer-generated explosions and disembowelments).

The Gator Guy explains why we should have respect for the performers under the bigtop.

"Circus performers do things that are very difficult, almost impossible. We try it, and then we practice it, and then we present it to you. You have so much fun, and you think, 'There's gotta be a trick.' Well, there is no trick. It's real, and that's the magic of the circus."

To get a sense of how much the magic used to mean, you need only to visit the **Museum of the Circus** (5401 Bay Shore Rd., 941/351-1660, 10 A.M.-5:30 P.M. daily, $19 adults, $16 seniors, $6 students and children 6-17, $6 Florida teachers and students with ID). It was John Ringling who brought the circus to Sarasota, moving the winter quarters of the Ringling Bros. and Barnum & Bailey Circus from Bridgeport, Connecticut, to Sarasota in 1927 – thus changing this part of Florida forever. The museum documents, preserves, and exhibits the history of the circus with props, rare handbills, parade wagons, tent poles, and memorabilia.

As for me, I wanna join the circus. Maybe my act will be something modest like one I saw performed by Svetlana Shemsheeva's, an exotic woman who trained Persian cats to walk tightropes and cavort with doves. She even got a bird to land on a cat's back, and neither one seemed disgruntled. Sure, it's not a planet exploding or an alien birth, it's just a little piece of reality that makes up the greatest show on earth.

11 A.M.–2 P.M. Mon.–Fri., 5–10:30 P.M. Mon.–Sat., bar menu 10:30 P.M.–midnight, 5–9 P.M. Sun., $19–31) deserves a fairly lavish restaurant description, but its vital bar scene is its most notable quality, young professionals drawn by the globetrotting by-the-glass wine list.

For a more rarefied experience, head to the **Cà d'Zan Lounge** at the Ritz-Carlton (1111 Ritz-Carlton Dr., 941/309-2000, 4 P.M.–midnight Sun.–Thurs., until 2 A.M. Fri. and Sat., $10–25). Overstuffed couches, clubby leather chairs, gleaming hickory wood walls, and a specialty martini menu that will shake *and* stir you.

Beyond these, there are refreshing drinks and engaging conversations to be had nearly everywhere here—the **Beach Club** (5151 Ocean Blvd., Siesta Key, 941/349-6311, www.beachclubsiestakey.com, 2:30 P.M.–2 A.M. daily) in Siesta Key Village and **Blu 1266 Lounge** (1266 Old Stickney Point Rd., 941/346-1711, 10 P.M.-2 A.M. Thurs.–Sun.), on the south side of Siesta Key; **Sharky's** (1600 Harbor Dr S., Venice, 941/488-1456, 11:30 A.M.–10 P.M. Sun.–Thurs., until midnight Fri. and Sat.), beachfront on the Pier in Venice; the **Sports Page** (1319 Main St. Sarasota, 941/365-0469, 11:30 A.M.–2:30 A.M. daily), and **Findaddy's** (935 N. Beneva Road, Suite 601, Sarasota Commons Shopping Center, 941/953-6356,

4 P.M.–midnight Mon., 11 A.M.–midnight Tues.–Sat., noon–midnight Sun.), in Sarasota for watching the big game, and **8 Ball Lounge** (3527 Webber St., Sarasota, 941/922-8314, noon–2 A.M. daily), for when you feel like working on your own game.

Dance and Music Clubs

For when you're ready to rev the engine a little, the **Five O'Clock Club** (1930 Hillview St., 941/366-5555, www.5oclockclub.net for concert schedule, happy hour noon–8 P.M. daily, small cover charges change nightly depending on band) in Southside Village has what the mechanic ordered. There's live music seven nights a week, with national and local rock/blues/whatever bands taking the stage at 10 P.M. The 5-O draws a 30s and 40s crowd, and just a smattering of college kids. The **Gator Club** (1490 Main St., 941/366-5969) is another longtime nightlife haunt for the fully adult (read: those who are secretly somewhat flattered when they still get carded). Again, there's live music every night, often of the Jimmy Buffet–cover variety, pool tables upstairs, and an impressive single-malt selection.

For something totally different and un-booze-centric, track down the **Siesta Key Drum Circle** on Sunday evenings, a drop-in party in which everyone adds their own beat. It all gets underway about one hour before sunset just south of the main pavilion between lifeguard stands 3 and 4.

SHOPPING

The shops of **St. Armands Circle** on Lido Key have been a primary retail draw in Sarasota for a long time, historically known for high-end boutiques. These days the shops cover familiar ground—chains like **Chico's** (443 St. Armands Circle, 941/388-2926), **Tommy Bahama** (300 John Ringling Blvd., 941/388-2888), **Fresh Produce** (1 N. Boulevard of the Presidents, 941/388-1883), and **The White House/Black Market** (317 St. Armands Circle, 941/388-5033)—and a paltry handful of upscale, independently owned boutiques. You'll have better luck noodling in the circle's novelty and giftware shops: **Fantasea Seashells** (345 St. Armands Circle, 941/388-3031), **Wet Noses** (pet stuff, 472 John Ringling Boulevard, 941/388-3647), or **Kilwin's** (ice cream and fudge, 312 John Ringling Blvd., 941/388-3200).

Towles Court Artist Colony (Adams Ln. or Morrill St., downtown Sarasota) is a collection of 16 quirky pastel-colored bungalows and cottages that contain artists working furiously and the art they've been working furiously on. You can buy their work and watch them in action 11 A.M.–4 P.M. most Tuesdays through Saturdays, or visit Towles Court on the third Friday evening of each month for Art by the Light of the Moon.

Palm Avenue and **Main Street** downtown are lined with galleries, restaurants, and cute shops, and historic **Herald Square** in the SoMa (south of Main St.) part of downtown on Pineapple Avenue has a fairly dense concentration of antiques shops and upscale housewares stores. Also on Pineapple you'll find the **Artisan's World Marketplace** (128 S. Pineapple Ave., 941/365-5994), which promotes self-employment for low-income artisans in developing countries worldwide by selling their baskets, clothing, and handicrafts.

Westfield Shoppingtown Southgate (3501 S. Tamiami Trail, 941/955-0900) is a pretty standard mall, with several anchor stores (Saks Fifth Avenue, Dillard's, Macy's) and many of the usual suspects (Ann Taylor, Talbots, Pottery Barn, Banana Republic, Gap, Gymboree, The Disney Store). For when you need to make those credit cards sizzle, you have to head north on I-75 to the **Prime Outlets** in Ellenton (5461 Factory Shops Blvd., Ellenton, 941/723-1150). There are more than 130 stores (Ralph Lauren, Gap, Geoffrey Beane, Tommy Hilfiger, Nike, Off Fifth) with deep, deep discounts.

And if your mantra is "reduce, reuse, and recycle," you'll find lovingly used doodads of all stripes at the more than 400 covered booths of the **Red Barn Flea Market** (1707 1st St. E., Bradenton, in Manatee County to the north, 941/747-3794). Go on the weekend for the greatest number of vendors and the widest variety of things, from collectibles to antiques to out-and-out junk.

ACCOMMODATIONS

There are scads of condos and beachfront rentals in the greater Sarasota area, but most of these rent only by the week. If that's your time frame, the weeklong rentals often are a more financially prudent choice. Try giving **Argus Property Management** (941/927-6464) a call, or visit **Vacation Rentals by Owner** (www.vrbo.com). There are also golf resort condo communities such as **Heritage Oaks Golf and Country Club** (4800 Chase Oaks Dr., 941/926-7602) and **Timberwoods Vacation Villas & Resort** (7964 Timberwood Cir., 941/923-4966) that rent by the week. If you're only in for a few days, hotels and motels run the gamut from moderately priced and no-frills to truly luxurious. Generally speaking, beachside places are pricier than mainland or downtown accommodations, and winter rates are highest, dropping down usually by a third to summer rates. Listed here are Sarasota and Lido Key accommodations—Longboat Key, Siesta Key, Venice, etc., are covered in *The Keys* section of this chapter.

Under $75

The **Cadillac Motel** (4021 N. Tamiami Trail, 941/355-7108, $42–58) is a no-frills, clean, single-story motel. It's a bit away from all the action of downtown (about a mile), but there's a sweet little pool and shuffleboard to entertain you. For a simple room, efficiency, or apartment, rented by the day or by the week, try **Southland Inn** (2229 N. Tamiami Trail, 941/954-5775, rooms starting at $50). Rooms have been recently remodeled, most with kitchens, and there's a large heated pool. Near the Ringling School of Art and Design.

$75-150

The three-story **La Quinta Inn & Suites Sarasota** (1803 Tamiami Trail N., 941/366-5128, $129–299) is not far from Ringling School of Art and Design, a few

minutes' drive from downtown. Rooms are midsize, some with sofa beds, and those on interior hallways have desks. There's a serviceable outdoor pool, a pleasant complimentary breakfast, free parking, and pets under 30 pounds are accepted.

Business travelers enjoy **Springhill Suites by Marriott** (1020 University Pkwy., 941/358-3385, $149–189), a moderately priced all-suites approach fairly close to the airport. All rooms have a king or two double beds with separate sleeping, eating, and working areas. There's also a pullout sofa bed, a pantry area with minirefrigerator, sink, and microwave, and a big desk with fancy chair and two-line telephones with data port. The free continental breakfast isn't an afterthought, with items like sausage, eggs, oatmeal, and make-your-own waffles.

Courtyard by Marriott (850 University Pkwy., 941/355-3337, $149–199) is a mostly business, recently renovated three-story hotel directly across from the airport. It's convenient to both Bradenton and Sarasota. Great hotel for business trips or family vacations. There's wireless high-speed Internet throughout the hotel, and a hot breakfast buffet.

Over $150

It was controversial when it opened, but the **Ritz-Carlton Sarasota** (1111 Ritz-Carlton Dr., 941/309-2000, reservations 800/241-3333, www.ritzcarlton.com, $410–719), a 266-room, 18-story luxury hotel right downtown, has managed to blend in beautifully, as if it has always been here. Ritz-Carlton's signature service (warm, efficient, but seldom verging on obsequious), spacious rooms with balconies and marble baths, and great amenities make it the top choice among business and high-fallutin' travelers. The downtown location is convenient to restaurants (although there are two laudable ones on-site) and attractions; there's a lovely pool, and the wood-paneled Cà d'Zan Bar & Cigar Lounge is always hopping.

The Ritz has a spa open to guests and members only, and the Members Golf Club located 13 miles from the hotel offers a Tom

Fazio–designed 18-hole championship course. It is a par 72, located on 315 acres of tropical landscape with no real estate development.

Lido Beach Resort (700 Benjamin Franklin Dr., 941/388-2161, $209–449), formerly a Radisson, is a favorite among families vacationing in the area. Recently remodeled and doubled in size—the north building being older, cheaper, and less elegant than the 12-story south tower of one- and two-bedroom suites with kitchens. The hotel has two gorgeous free-form pools and three hot tubs all right on the beach, and one of Sarasota's few beachside tiki bars. It's a brief walk out the door to Lido Beach and St. Armands Circle shopping/dining area, 10 minutes to downtown, and 15–20 minutes to the airport. The hotel offers beach volleyball, a free shuttle to St. Armands, dry cleaning, laundry, business services, and meeting rooms.

At the end of April 2008, the 12-story **Hyatt Sarasota** (1000 Boulevard of the Arts, 941/953-1234, $229–439) completed a $22 million transformation, with a full makeover of guestrooms, lobbies, corridors, meeting space, fitness center, business center, restaurants, and bars. It's a big convention hotel right downtown with easy access to Van Wezel Performing Arts Hall, the Municipal Auditorium, and other attractions. It's right in the downtown business district, but waterside, with its own private marina, a floating dock, and a beautiful lagoon-style pool. The 294 guest rooms all have a view of the bay or marina, most with little balconies.

One of the most attractive hotels to open in recent years is the ◖ **Hotel Indigo** (1223 Boulevard of the Arts, 941/487-3800, $199–233), a sweet boutique job with a canny use of vibrant colors and whimsical design elements. Guest rooms have wall-size murals and wonderful fabrics in rich blues and greens—altogether it's a fun, contemporary alternative, right in the thick of things. The onsite café is called the Golden Bean, there's a little wine bar called Phi, and a fitness studio called, well, Phitness Studio. Still, I'd spend my time in one

of the cushioned Adirondack chairs or out on the lovely patio.

If for you small is beautiful, you may want to take a gander at **The Cypress, a Bed & Breakfast Inn** (621 S. Gulfstream Ave., 941/955-4683, $180–279), with only four distinctly decorated rooms. Set in a 1940s tin-roofed cypress home, the four suites are kitted out with American and European antiques, paintings, and artifacts, and the house's common space is lovely (but not precious). Room rates include an extravagant breakfast and an afternoon social hour with hors d'oeuvres and refreshments. The inn is across the street from Bayfront Park and down the block from Marie Selby Botanical Gardens. No children, no pets.

FOOD

Strips of chain restaurants pop up on the Gulf Coast of Florida like so many noxious mushrooms after the wet season. In fact, many chains (Outback, Hooters, etc.) call the Gulf Coast home, and new chains are often market tested first in the urban areas along this part of Florida. Why, I ask myself? It's demographics. In an area that still has a fairly dense concentration of retirees, the newest growth segment is young families. And what do the elderly and young families have in common? They like to eat out, but they want things to be familiar. They want to go to Chili's and eat the same thing they ate last time. They don't want food that is spicy, weird looking, hard to eat, or intellectually or emotionally challenging. They want the sauce on the side, all vegetables recognizable, and to be able to count on the regular, soothing presence of ranch dressing.

Before you get insulted by my gross overgeneralization, you need to know I resemble that remark. I have a 12-year-old who is, as is common to the species, a creature of habit. Change is met with fear and loathing. Thus, chain restaurants provide her a modicum of control over her world. An auteur's mercurial whim, evidencing itself as a daily-changing menu or serendipitous food marriages—that stuff is lost on her.

TABLE HOPPING

In the off-season, Sarasota's many culinary pearls are yours for the plucking – and during June that plucking gets all the more delicious with a 10-day **Savor Sarasota restaurant week.** In a city with one of the highest concentrations of *Zagat*-rated restaurants in Florida, dozens of restaurants have banded together to offer the public value-priced, three-course, prix fixe menus.

"We're offering our prix fixe lunch for $15, $25 for dinner," says Jeremy Saccardi, chef de cuisine at the Ritz-Carlton Sarasota. That's right, I said the Ritz-Carlton. "For us in particular it's a chance to see some people who wouldn't normally come into the restaurant, who would consider us out of their budget. We were so busy during the restaurant week last year that we had to extend it another week."

Alright, it's a bargain, but what's in it for the restaurants? According to Michael Klauber, proprietor of Michaels on East and one of the instigators of the restaurant week, "The original idea came from the local convention and visitor's bureau. They got a few of us restaurateurs together to talk about it. We thought this would be a great way to showcase the restaurants, and it gives the restaurants an opportunity to explore something different with a special menu. I hope it can become a destination event, and that hotels and resorts will see an influx of people."

Some restaurants include interactive cooking demonstrations, others feature live music. Many of the restaurants offer several choices for appetizer, entrée, and dessert, some with suggested wine pairing flights. At core, though, it's not complicated: Pick a participating restaurant, make a reservation, dine, pay ($15 for lunch, $25 for dinner). Repeat. For more information about participating restaurants, events and pricing, visit www.savorsarasota.com.

Well, Sarasota restaurants are fighting the creeping encroachment of chains. Twenty-eight independent restaurants in town joined together not long ago to build public awareness about the importance of the community's unique cuisine. They formed the Sarasota Originals, the first Florida Chapter of the Council of Independent Restaurants of America (CIRA). For the visitor, this is good news. The city has a superabundance of fairly stylish restaurants and the sophisticated diners who love them.

Downtown

I'll start with the heavy hitters. A new addition to the Sarasota culinary landscape, **Derek's Culinary Casual** (514 Central Ave., 941/366-6565, 11:30 A.M.–2:30 P.M. Tues.–Fri., 5–10 P.M. Tues.–Sat., until 10:30 P.M. Fri. and Sat., until 9 P.M. Sun., $19–29) is the brainchild of chef/owner Derek Barnes, former chef at 5-One-6 Burns. In a much larger, high-ceilinged space, he has brought exciting,

contemporary American cuisine (complete with a glossary on the back of the menu) to Sarasota's Rosemary District. Tuna gnocchi, pork confit with monkfish medallions, and duck "two ways" (a seared breast paired with crispy pecan-crusted leg confit, German spaetzle and bitter greens) all aim to bring a new level of sophistication to classic French/Italian/Californian dishes. The wine list is similarly ambitious and fairly priced, but small. While it is still the reservation to nab in Sarasota, service has been known to bobble.

Located in the historic Florida Citrus Exchange, newcomer **Rustic Grill** (400 N. Lemon Ave., 941/906-1111, 5–10 P.M. Sun.–Thurs., until 11 P.M. Fri. and Sat., $24–34) has blown the socks off Sarasota with its stunning Tuscan villa interior and luxurious array of art and antiques. Chef Clinton Combs' open kitchen and wood-burning grill have met the expectations such a gorgeous interior prompt, in an inventive array of small plates and large plates. The waiters need stamina to explain each dish: Grilled local grouper comes with baby fennel confit, haricots vert, calamata tapenade, roasted tomatoes, English pea emulsion, and a blistered red pepper coulis. Whew. Grilled meats are the star of the show, from the bone-in strip loin to a smoky pork tenderloin.

Sarasota's **C** **Bijou Cafe** (1287 1st St., 941/366-8111, 11:30 A.M.–2 P.M. Mon.–Fri., 5–9:30 P.M. Mon.–Thurs., until 10:30 P.M. Fri. and Sat., until 9 P.M. Sun., $19–36) has been a local sparkling jewel since 1986, making everyone's top 10 list and garnering lots of drippy adjectives from *Zagat, Bon Appetit* and *Gourmet*. It's what you'd call Continental-American fare, presided over by chef Jean-Pierre Knaggs and his wife, Shay. Located a couple blocks from Ritz-Carlton Sarasota in a 1920s gas station turned restaurant, the vibe is special-occasion or big-time-business dining. A fairly recent renovation (after a fire) has yielded a new bar, lounge, private room, and outdoor dining courtyards. The wine list is unusual, with a fair number of South African wines (Knaggs is South African), and the menu contains dishes like velvety shrimp and crab bisque, crispy roast duck napped with orange-cognac sauce, or luscious crab cakes with Louisiana rémoulade. All hail the crème brûlée.

Opened in 2003, **Mattison's City Grill** (1 N. Lemon Ave., 941/330-0440, 11 A.M.–11 P.M. Mon.–Thurs., until midnight Fri. and Sat., until 10 P.M. Sun., $17–25) has added a little vim and vinegar to the downtown dining scene. It's casual, hopping, with Italian-ish small plates and pizzas and lots of pretty people. It feels more urban than many of the other downtown restaurants, with great outdoor seating, cool wine events and cigar dinners, and live jazz nightly. It's been so successful that owner Paul Mattison has a virtual empire in the area now: Mattison's Riverside, Mattison's Steakhouse at the Plaza, Mattison's Forty One, and a catering business—all fun, all gastronomically progressive.

Another longtime downtown favorite has nightly live music but a totally different feel. **Marina Jack's** (2 Marina Plaza, 941/365-4232, 11:30 A.M.–1 A.M. daily, main dining room closed 2–5 P.M., $8–36 depending on which dining room you choose) is all about waterside dining for the masses, with a few different ways to consume your comestibles with the water in view. Choose from the second-level Bayside Dining Room, the Portside Patio, or a cocktail at the Deep Six Lounge and Piano Bar. If you still don't feel aquatic enough, there's the *Marina Jack II* yacht, which wines you and dines you in the bay (nothing cutting-edge about the food, but it's fairly decent prime rib, lemon sole, and such). Back on land, the menu leans to crowd-pleasers like crab-stuffed mushrooms, conch fritters, steaks, and grilled grouper.

In a similar idiom (fun, casual, seafood-centric American cuisine), but with no water views, **Barnacle Bill's** has had a recent makeover in its downtown location (1526 Main St., 941/365-6800, 11:30 A.M.–9 P.M. daily, with a small-plate menu only 4–5:30 P.M., $12–24). The Main Street location is the chain's white-tablecloth establishment, still a little bare bones if you ask me, but people don't notice as they decimate an order of crab cakes, fried popcorn shrimp, or stuffed flounder. Other locations: 3634 Webber St., 941/923-5800 (this one was just renamed Chef D's Italian Fisherman); 5050 N. Tamiami Trail, 941/355-7700; and 8383 S. Tamiami Trail, 941/927-8884.

It's not exactly downtown, but just slightly south. Still, any list of important downtown restaurants has to include **C** **Michaels On East** (1212 East Ave. S., 941/366-0007, 11:30 A.M.–2 P.M. Mon.–Fri., 5:30–10 P.M. daily, $18–31). It's won best-of-Florida accolades from nearly everyone since its opening at the beginning of the 1990s—and it's kept up with all the newcomers, consistently pushing the envelope and wowing diners with its "New American" take and opulent decor. During the day it's a power-lunching crowd enjoying Wendy's warm chicken salad with dried cranberries, goat cheese, and candied pecans in honey-lemon-basil vinaigrette and a big bottle of bubbly water; at night, romantic dinners à deux include a grilled duck breast paired with Bermuda onion and shiitake fondue, and fig and pecan risotto, all flavors elegantly showcased with a gorgeous big-ticket burgundy or California pinot noir.

For when you're tired of fish, **❮ Patrick's** (1400 Main St., 941/952-1170, 11 A.M.–midnight daily, $9–18) gets top honors for Sarasota's best burger. It's another casual spot, with no reservations accepted, but with more of a patina of glamour. The crowd is a little hipper, the bar scene is fun.

Located just a few steps from the Burns Court Cinema, with a monumental banyan tree marking the sweet little Old Florida cottage, **5-One-6 Burns** (516 Burns Court, 941/906-1884, 11:30 A.M.–2 P.M. Mon.–Fri., 5:30–10 P.M. daily, $12–28) is a locals' favorite. The tree is beloved—a single, romantic table is set beneath its impressive canopy—the location divine, but this solid newcomer is prized primarily for its innovative American bistro fare. The menu waltzes through the cuisines of many countries, never making a misstep, from sweet and sour shrimp broth redolent of lemongrass, with shrimp, shiitake mushrooms and scallions; to grilled Alaskan halibut with grilled peach, preserved lemon and mint salsa. The wine list is ambitious, focusing on lesser-known producers and boutique wineries.

Just want a quick, inexpensive bite, no fuss, no muss? Head to downtown's **Cafe Epicure** (1298 N. Palm Ave., 941/366-5648, 11 A.M.–10:30 P.M. Mon.–Fri., 9 A.M.–10:30 P.M. Sat. and Sun., $5–25). It's a cool bistro/deli/market, an easy place to hang out on the terrace and write postcards while sipping a nice wine by the glass and enjoying an addictive *insalata di polpo con patate e fagiolini* (octopus salad with potatoes and string beans).

Best breakfast? It's a chain, but this location is without a doubt the best of the breed. **First Watch Restaurant** (1395 Main St., 941/954-1395, 7:30 A.M.–2:30 P.M. daily, $5–12) serves Sarasota's finest quick, no-fuss, inexpensive breakfasts with bottomless coffee and cheery service. Investigate the Greek Fetish omelet (roasted red peppers, feta cheese and spinach, topped with black olives and

red onions) or the cranberry nut pancakes. Lines can be long, but they move quickly. If you just can't wait, walk south along Central Avenue and stop into one of the sidewalk coffeehouses.

St. Armands Circle and Lido Key

In 1893, a Frenchman named Charles St. Amand bought a little mangrove island off Sarasota, homesteading in the usual way with fishing, hunting, and growing a little produce. In the land deeds his name was misspelled, so it stuck when circus magnate John Ringling bought the property in 1917 (well, it's rumored he won it in a poker game). He planned for St. Armands Key to be a residential and shopping development laid out in a circle, bringing people over first by steamer and then via the John Ringling Causeway completed in 1926 (the major lifting done by circus elephants). The area has had a fairly consistent commitment to all that is posh since Ringling wheedled it away from old Charles St. Amand. It's often compared to Rodeo Drive and other famous shopping districts.

Here's the thing: The shopping isn't so great these days. My rule of thumb is, if there are more than two shops that sell fudge and saltwater taffy, and if there are more than two boutiques in which you can buy T-shirts with cats and funny feline slogans on them, then you're in a tourist trap. St. Armands is such a place. However, some of the city's best restaurants line up around the circle. So, buy your fudge, smirk at the T-shirts, and go to dinner.

Two of the oldest on the stretch are **Café L'Europe** (431 St. Armands Circle, 941/388-4415, 11:30 A.M.–3 P.M. and 5–10 P.M. daily, Sun. brunch 11:30 A.M.–3 P.M., $23–40) and the **Columbia Restaurant** (411 St. Armands Circle, 941/388-3987, 11 A.M.–11 P.M. Mon.–Sat., noon–10 P.M. Sun., $8–28). Close together, both feature beautiful dining rooms and wonderful sidewalk dining, but the food's better at Café L'Europe. The Columbia opened in 1959, making it the oldest restaurant in Sarasota. (Its sister restaurant in Tampa goes one better, being the oldest restaurant in the state of Florida.) The Cuban food is pretty bland and dated, and even its "world-famous" dishes—the 1905 Salad with chopped cheese, olives, and a ho-hum vinaigrette; the sangria; the red snapper Alicante—don't thrill the way they used to. The black bean soup and pompano in parchment seldom disappoint, though. As for Café L'Europe, it's a sophisticated stew of culinary influences that's hard to pin down: The kitchen does an equally adept job with shrimp pad thai, veal cordon bleu with luxe chanterelle mushroom risotto, and a Mediterranean chicken Kavalla that pairs chicken breast with feta, spinach, and crab.

15 South Ristorante Enoteca (15 S. Boulevard of Presidents, 941/388-1555, 4–11 P.M. nightly, open for lunch during high season, nightclub 7 P.M.–2 A.M. nightly, $14–34) seems to be the place to go in the area for sophisticated northern Italian, and the upstairs **Straight Up Night Club** features an excellent martini bar and equal-opportunity music nightly (Latin acts, belly dancing, Caribbean tunes, a big band, you name it). The restaurant's menu will be familiar, but the execution of dishes like classic carpaccio, grilled veal chop topped with gremolata, or a plate of zingy-with-garlic bruschetta is exceptional.

It's a chain of sorts, so I hesitate to praise it too vociferously, but **Tommy Bahama Tropical Café & Emporium** (300 John Ringling Blvd., 941/388-2888, 11 A.M.–10 P.M. weekdays, until 11 P.M. weekends, $20–33) is just plain fun, the food is excellent, and the drinks too good for common sense to kick in. The store downstairs carries its signature mix of tropical leisurewear and strangely hip housewares—you have to take a flight of stairs off to the side to reach the upstairs restaurant, which has huge windows that look out on the circle. Salads and cocktails are fairly pricey, but worth it. A key lime martini managed to marry so elegantly with a tropical chicken salad that it hovers in my taste memory like a beautiful mirage.

Oh, and **Cha Cha Coconuts** (417 St. Armands Circle, 941/388-0325) is a good place for a drink, as is **Hemingway's Restaurant & Bar** (325 John Ringling Blvd., 941/388-3948,

11:30 A.M.–4 P.M. daily, 4–10 P.M. Sun.–Thurs., until 11 P.M. Fri. and Sat., $15–22), but **Cork & The Bottle Shop** (29 N. Blvd of the Presidents, 941/388-2675) is strictly for the serious oenophile. **Blue Dolphin Cafe** (470 John Ringling Blvd., 941/388-3566, 7 A.M.–3 P.M. daily) is where to go for cheap, diner-style breakfasts with a twist (lobster Benedict, raspberry pancakes), and, finally, when you're ready for that fudge, head to **Kilwin's** (312 John Ringling Blvd., 941/388-3200).

Southside Village
You may drive right through Southside Village and before you have time to ask, "Hey, why are there all these beautiful young professional types drinking glasses of red wine at sidewalk tables on the middle of a Tuesday afternoon," you've passed right through it on your way downtown. Visitors don't hit this little shopping/restaurant area with frequency, which is a shame. A few of Sarasota's most contemporary, most gastronomically forward-thinking restaurants are right here. Southside Village is centered on South Osprey Avenue between Hyde Park and Hillview Streets, about 15 blocks south of downtown.

Perhaps the best place in Sarasota to pick up the ingredients for a picnic is in the same block. **Morton's Gourmet Market** (1924 S. Osprey Ave., 941/364-2283, 8 A.M.–8 P.M. Mon.–Sat., 10 A.M.–5 P.M. Sun.) has the kind of fresh salads, deli items, fancy specialty sandwiches, and cooked entrées that make you press your nose up against the glass case, leaving an embarrassing smudge. Most items are fairly cheap, and you can eat on the premises or take it all out.

Pacific Rim (1859 Hillview St., 941/330-8071, 11:30 A.M.–2 P.M. Mon.–Fri., 5–9 P.M. Mon.–Thurs., 5–10 P.M. Fri. and Sat., $7–15) takes you on a very pleasant pan-Asian romp, from Thai curries redolent of basil and galangal to expertly rolled tekka maki sushi and beyond. You can play chef here and select your combinations of meats and veggies to be grilled or cooked in a wok.

Nearby **Hillview Grill** (1920 Hillview St., 941/952-0045, 11 A.M.–10 P.M. Mon.–Sat.,

5–9 P.M. Sun., $13–29) traffics in another melding of cuisines, this time Cajun and Creole with a dollop of several other ethnic influences. It's more of a neighborhood joint, with easier prices and a relaxed setting. Its more high-flying flights of fancy aren't always successful, but if you stick with dishes like roast chicken with red bliss potatoes or New Zealand lamb chops with apple-mint salsa, you'll be satisfied.

And nearby **The Table** (1934 Hillview St., 941/365-4558, 11:30 A.M.–2:30 P.M. Mon.– Fri., 5:30–9:30 P.M. Mon–Sat., $13–28) is one of my favorites, where chef/owners Rafael Manzano and Pedro Flores do what they call Atlantic Rim cuisine, traipsing through South America, the Caribbean, Eastern America, and a hint of Spain in a delicious way.

International District at Gulf Gate

So far I've focused on fairly high-end eats-but if your tastes run a little thriftier, you're in luck. The **Gulf Gate neighborhood** is a tiny international district that spans a three-block area from Gulf Gate Avenue to Superior Avenue, Mall Drive around the block to Gateway Avenue. It's where to go to get a quick meal on the fly, takeout, or just something that won't break the bank. There are big sandwiches at the **Italian Village Deli** (6606 Superior Ave., 941/927-2428). Around the corner on Gateway Avenue you'll come upon the little French bistro **Le Parigot** (6551 Gateway Ave., 941/922-9115), **Pontillo's Pizza** (6592 Superior Ave., 941/921-0990), and **Rico's Pizzeria** (6547 Gateway Ave., 941/922-9604). After all that pizza, and for something totally different, try

the pierogies at **Lucy's Polish Delicatessen** (6542 Gateway Ave., 941/926-8980). Then you'll need a beer at **Paddy Wagon** (6586 Gateway Ave., 941/925-2344). And once you hit Gulf Gate Drive, there are a couple of Chinese and sushi takeout places, a Russian joint, and a British tearoom.

Pinecrest and Beyond

Amish cuisine. If that looks like a typo sitting there, you'll need to adjust to the fact that Sarasota is a huge Amish and Mennonite winter resort. Both groups come down from Pennsylvania and the Midwest looking for sun and good Amish food, with luck on both counts. The locus of Amish activity here is in Pinecrest, where you'll see the bearded men in suspenders and wide straw hats, the women in long skirts and bonnets, all enjoying the Florida weather. What do they do while here? Go to **Yoder's** (3434 Bahia Vista, 941/955-7771, 8 A.M.–8 P.M. Mon.– Sat., $6–14) to find out. It's been a Sarasota institution since 1975, with wholesome, rib-sticking country ham and corn fritters, turkey and gravy, meatloaf and mashed potatoes, and pies, pies, pies. Note especially the peanut butter cream pie. **Troyer's Dutch Heritage** (3713 Bahia Vista, 941/955-8007, 6 A.M.–8 P.M. Mon.–Sat., $5–12) is even more venerable, dating back to 1969, with sturdy, accessible buffet-style meals and a gift shop on the second floor. Another one people seem devoted to is **Sugar and Spice Family Restaurant** (4000 Cattleman Rd., 941/342-1649). All of them are closed on Sunday and serve no alcohol.

The Keys

The northernmost of Sarasota's stretch of keys, Longboat Key is a 12-mile barrier island for the wealthy who *vant to be alone.* What you can see of the posh residences is showy enough, but I have a sneaking suspicion that the really jaw-dropping manses are down all those long drive-ways and behind those tall hedgerows. There are only about 8,000 full-time residents, but in high season (Dec.–Mar.), Longboat Key is where the rich and/or famous come to play a little golf and get a little sun away from the prying eyes of the hoi polloi. If you are, like me, one of the hoi polloi with prying eyes, hang around at the **Longboat Key Club** or on the golf courses to catch a glimpse of Robert DeNiro or Tom Selleck or Bill Cosby or that guy in Aerosmith.

The island hasn't always been so swanky. It was the Arvida Company that laid the foundation in the late 1950s (literally, enabling construction to occur on previously loose, shifting soil) for the development of the island. Generally speaking, visitors stay in the imposing high-rises that line the impeccably groomed Gulf of Mexico Drive; residents live on the bayside in discreet, shielded estates.

Siesta Key is something else again. It's a similar eight-mile-long barrier island with even more gorgeous beaches, some insist. But Siesta is for the proletariat—it's family-owned accommodations, none outlandishly fancy, easy access to the beach from anywhere, fishing, boating, kayaking, snorkeling, scuba diving, and sailboarding. And at night, unlike on Longboat, these people like to party. Siesta Village has the area's most lively nightlife.

Farther south, Casey Key is eight miles long, stretching from Siesta Key on the north to Venice at the southern tip. It is almost exclusively single-family homes (getting fancier and pricier by leaps and bounds), with just a few low-rise Old Florida beach motels. Two bridges provide access to the key, including a cool, old "swing bridge" dating back to the 1920s. Parts of the key are only 300 yards wide.

The town of Venice is more like a real place

COURTESY OF SARASOTA CVB

Open wide at the annual Shark's Tooth and Seafood Festival in Venice.

than a tourist destination, in good and bad ways. The residents seem to be mostly retirees, very chummy, very active, with keen civic pride. The downtown is quaint—a handful of boutiques and galleries, a couple of restaurants, a place to get ice cream, a couple of coffee shops, and a good wine bar. There's a little community theater, of which the residents are inordinately proud. Really, the biggest draw in Venice is teeth.

Every August, the Venice Area Chamber of Commerce holds the **Shark's Tooth and Seafood Festival,** with arts, crafts, food stalls, and lots of little pointy black fossils. It seems that sharks of all species shed their teeth continually. They have 40 or so teeth in each jaw, with seven other rows of teeth behind that first one waiting in the wings, as it were, to mature. The average tiger shark produces 24,000 teeth in 10 years. In order to find them when they wash up on Venice beaches, stop by one of the gift shops downtown and ask for a shark tooth shovel. And once you've found a few, visit www.veniceflorida.com/shark.htm to identify the species.

SPORTS AND RECREATION
C Siesta Key Beach

We have a winner of the international whose-beach-is-better smackdown. In 1987 scientists from the Woods Hole Oceanographic Institution in Woods Hole, Massachusetts, convened to judge the Great International White Sand Beach Challenge, with more than 30 entries from beaches around the world. To this day, Siesta Key Beach remains the reigning world champ, with all other beaches too cowed, or too chicken, to demand a rematch. Its preeminence has long been known—supposedly in the 1950s a visitor from New York, Mr. Edward G. Curtis, sent a pickle jar of Siesta's sand to the Geology Department of Harvard University for analysis. The report came back: "The sand from Siesta Key is 99 percent pure quartz grains, the grains being somewhat angular in shape. The soft floury texture of the sand is due to its very fine grain size. It contains no fragments of coral and no shell. The fineness of the sand, which gives

it its powdery softness, is emphasized by the fact that the quartz is a very hard substance, graded at 7 in the hardness scale of 10."

The real test can't be done with sand in a pickle jar. You need to lie on the sloping strand, run the warmed granules through your fingers, sniff the salt air, and listen to a plaintive gull overhead. That way, too, Siesta Key Beach wins—it's been named America's Best Sand Beach and ranked in Florida's Top Ten Beaches multiple years on the Travel Channel. Dr. Beach named it in his top 10 beaches in America again in 2007 (it's made it into the top 10 numerous times); *National Geographic Traveler* has also named Siesta One of America's Best Beaches. The list goes on.

Other Beaches

The greater Sarasota area has lots of beaches to recommend. The beaches described here run from north to south.

Longboat Key has 10 miles of white, powdery beach, but most of it is accessible only to those who live there or are staying in a resort or condo. **Longboat Key Beach** is accessible at several points—at Longview Drive, Westfield Street, Mayfield Street, and Neptune Street. It's mostly underpopulated and often offers incredible sand dollar collecting. **Beer Can Island Beach,** at the very north end of Longboat Key and accessible by boat or from North Shore Road off Gulf of Mexico Drive, attracts a fair number of anglers and sun worshippers.

Then there's the aforementioned Siesta Key Beach, on the north side of Siesta Key (it is contiguous with another favorite beach called Crescent Beach—good snorkeling off this one), with white sand so reflective it feels cool on a hot day. Scientists estimate that the sand on this beach is millions of years old, starting in the Appalachians and eventually deposited on these shores. The water is shallow, the beach incline gradual, making it a perfect beach for young swimmers. There are 800 parking spots, which tend to fill up, and the lifeguard stands are painted different colors (as points of reference, so you don't lose your way). The Siesta Key beaches south of a rock outcropping called

ANNA MARIA ISLAND

Stand at the northern end of Longboat Key and look north. You'll see another long, seven-mile strip of sandy barrier island that couldn't be much different from Longboat. Manatee County's Anna Maria Island is an island both literally and metaphorically – it is far enough south of Tampa to be removed from the city's urban hubbub, and it's far enough north of Sarasota to escape being just another feather in that city's cap. It's the northernmost of the string of barrier islands that extend down to the Florida Keys, with three distinct towns spread along its length. There's the town of Anna Maria at the northern end, Holmes Beach in the middle, and Bradenton Beach at the southern end – all of them linked by their sweet, laid-back atmosphere. Three drawbridges access the island, one from Longboat Key and two from the mainland (Hwy. 64 and Hwy. 684).

Really, the little island community owes its very existence to the Fig Newton. The inventor of the "oo-ee, gooey, rich and chewy" Newton, Charles Roser, sold the recipe to Nabisco, made a fortune, and then bought up Anna Maria land and started building. (Actually, to pick some nits, the island probably owes its existence to James Henry Mitchell, who invented the *apparatus*, a kind of funnel within a funnel, that supplies the necessary steady stream of fig jam while outside it there's a tube-like stream of dough. But, enough with the Newtons already.)

These days, there's an active year-round community as well as a robust tourist trade (for some reason you'll encounter more Danish, German, British, and Australian visitors than Americans). Tourists come for the outstanding boating, sailing, scuba, snorkeling, and fishing. Parking is the only hassle on the island, so park your car where you're staying and walk across to the beach – Holmes Beach, Anna Maria Beach, Coquina Beach, Cortez Beach, and Manatee Beach are all equally lovely stretches of white sand and blue green water. (Manatee has the most parking and a nice picnic area.) None have lifeguards or restrooms.

It's the kind of island on which it's easy to do nothing – not because there's nothing to do, but because the pace is such that you feel entitled to stuporous, languorous, slack-jawed relaxation. If your puritan work ethic forces you to do *something*, I recommend a sunset sailing cruise with **Spice Sailing Charters** (departures from next to Rotten Ralph's Restaurant on Anna Maria Island, 941/704-0773, $25/person). Our captain had a wealth of information about Florida history, fishing, and the area's recent environmental challenges.

Also worth checking out, Bradenton Beach has a newly revitalized municipal pier complex (closed since Hurricane Charley). It includes a restaurant, 220-foot floating dock for free day docking, a bait house, and public bathing facilities. The 660-foot fishing pier and boater-related facilities sit at the bayside end of Historic Bridge Street in Bradenton Beach. Visitors can take advantage of watercraft transportation to the dock, but new bike lanes, sidewalks, a multiuse nature path along the beach, and a free trolley system add some other options for navigating the area.

Point of Rocks are not as white and soft, the sand being shellier and grayer. Still, **Turtle Beach,** on Midnight Pass Road near the south end of Siesta Key, is another popular beach, prized for its more private feel, large picnic shelter, and good shelling opportunities.

There used to be a small inlet that separated Siesta Key from Casey Key, an inlet called Midnight Pass that, amongst great controversy, was filled in in 1983. There are unpleasant environmental consequences to this choice, but for the visitor it means you can walk all the way on **Palmer Point Beach** from Siesta Key to Casey Key. The northern part of the beach was the former home of Mote Marine Laboratory. These days it's a quiet dune-backed beach, populated mostly by people trudging with determination at the

ACCOMMODATIONS

Palm Tree Villas (207 66th St., 888/778-7256, www.palmtreevillas.com, $115-195) is an inviting, warm, boutique-style haven, whether it's for honeymooning couples or families. The low-rise Old Florida–style motel has been lovingly refurbished, the nicely appointed units clustered around a central courtyard and swimming pool. There's a great packet of literature in each villa, and the warm owners, Peggy and Ashok Sawe, are serious boosters of the area.

Another favorite on the island is **Harrington House Beachfront Bed & Breakfast** (5626 Gulf Dr., Holmes Beach, 941/778-5444, www.harringtonhouse.com, $139-359), a converted 1925 coquina-brick beachfront house. Most rooms feature French doors opening onto balconies that overlook the heated swimming pool, the beach beyond, and beyond that the Gulf. The breakfasts here are legendary (many recipes are featured in *From Muffins to Margaritas – Visit the Kitchens of Florida's Finest Inns*), there's a sweet little beach gazebo from which you watch the sunset, and the common living room is a sure-fire place to start lively conversation with total strangers.

FOOD

Beach Bistro (6600 Gulf Dr., Holmes Beach, 941/778-6444, www.beachbistro.com, $15-40) beats much fancier restaurants in Sarasota, Tampa, and beyond for best restaurant on the Gulf Coast, according to *Zagat, Wine Spectator,* and numerous other publications. The place is quirky and cozy, with the kind of charm that comes of an independent (noncorporate) culinary vision. The food is largely excellent, and they've recently annexed space to make a more casual bar/café on one side (my pick, for a stellar burger enjoyed while listening to the virtuoso nightly piano player). The more formal dining room, its ceiling draped with luxurious raw silk, is stunning, with long single roses adorning the center of each table. Geared toward romantic dining, the Beach Bistro still extends real warmth and care to visiting children. For a restaurant of this caliber it isn't outlandishly pricey if you opt for the "small plates," which are certainly ample if you have an appetizer as well.

My other favorite restaurant on the island is **Oma's Pizza** (201 N. Gulf Dr., Bradenton Beach, 941/778-0771, $8-15), a seriously delicious pie, big and cheesy with a thin crust and those black bubbles you get with good New York pizza. The lasagna is pretty good, too. For more everyday dining, it's hard to go wrong with the barbecue at **Mr. Bones** (3007 Gulf Dr., Holmes Beach, 941/778-6614, $6-14), and it also has fairly good Indian food; go figure. And you pick your beer from a coffin in the reception area. Then there's the newly refurbished **Rotten Ralph's** for fish 'n' chips and an excellent blackened grouper sandwich. You can pull your boat up to the dock and place your order.

For more information about the island, contact **Anna Maria Island Chamber of Commerce** (5313 Gulf Dr. N., Holmes Beach, Florida 34217, 941/778-1541) and they'll send you a great packet of information and maps.

water's edge. No lifeguards, no facilities. Casey Key also has **Nokomis Beach** directly west of the Albee Road Bridge, a pleasant but unremarkable beach, and **North Jetty Park** at its southernmost tip. North Jetty Park is one of the few Gulf Coast spots that draws surfers, and fisherfolk seem to congregate here, too. Boats pass through the jetties from the Intracoastal Waterway to the Gulf.

South from here you enter into the beaches of Venice, rightfully known as the place to go when you're hunting shark's teeth. So, now you might be worried that there are loads of sharks lurking offshore waiting to gum you to death. The shark's teeth that wash up on the beach are fossilized, floating in from a shark burial ground a few miles offshore, a deep crevice where these cold-blooded predators once went to die. In addition to these gray/black teeth, fossilized bones of prehistoric animals like camels, bison, and tapirs sometimes wash up on this beach. In local shops you can rent or buy a shark-tooth scooper, a wire rake with a mesh box that sifts the sand and shell fragments at the water's edge, leaving the teeth behind in the basket. **Venice Beach** (so different from the beach of the same name in California) is at the west end of Venice Avenue not that far from town. **Brohard Park,** at the southernmost part of Venice, is the beach of choice among anglers, with a 740-foot fishing pier on the property for public use. (Dogs are also allowed at **Paw Park** at South Brohard Park, with a fenced area, a small dog beach, and dog showers.) Farther south, near Venice's little airport (which houses Huffman Aviation, the flight school where, unfortunately, terrorists responsible for 9/11 were trained to fly), **Casperson Beach** is really the locus of shark's teeth mania. Truth is, it's harder to find teeth than it used to be, partly because city boosters have replenished the sand on the beach with sand from an offshore sandbar. It's a very pretty beach left in its natural state, with people surf casting and red-shouldered hawks swooping above the shorebirds.

Golf

In the early 1920s, John Ringling purchased major acreage on the south end of the Longboat Key. He constructed a golf course and planted Australian pine trees along Gulf of Mexico Drive, along with the construction of a luxurious Ritz-Carlton, which he eventually abandoned. With this legacy, the **Longboat Key Golf Club** (301 Gulf of Mexico Dr., 941/383-9571, resort courses, greens fees $42–142) offers several remarkable golfing experiences to guests (and their guests' guests). Opened in 1960, the Bill Mitchell–designed Islandside Course (par 72, 6,792 yards, course rating 73.8, slope 138) features 18 holes of crisp, up-and-down shot-making through a 112-acre bird sanctuary filled with more than 5,000 palm trees and flowering plants. Water appears on 16 of its 18 fairways.

With a more country-club feel (and where more of the private members play), the resort also has three 9-hole courses, played in three 18-hole combinations: blue/red (par 72, 6,709 yards, course rating 72.6, slope 130), red/white (par 72, 6,749 yards, course rating 72.7, slope 131), white/blue (par 72, 6,812 yards, course rating 73.1, slope 132).

Fishing

Venice is a fairly well-known fishing destination—you'll see people wetting a line at the Venice jetties, Sharky's Pier, or Caspersen Beach. If you try your hand, expect to catch snook, redfish, Spanish mackerel, sheepshead, sea trout, and flounder, depending on the time of year. There are also lots of charter companies willing to take you deep-sea fishing out in the Gulf (grouper and snapper most of the year; kingfish, cobia, greater amberjack, and mahimahi seasonally). At the end of East Venice Avenue on the Myakka River, **Snook Haven Fish Camp** (5000 E. Venice Ave., 941/485-7221) has a fun riverside restaurant, boat rides, and fishing. **Reel Fast Charters** (941/650-4938, $75 sunset cruise, $425 for four hours, $600 for six hours, $725 for eight hours) takes groups out fishing as well as on nonfishing sunset cruises. And **Triple Trouble Charters** (941/484-3225, rates vary) takes small groups out from the Dona Bay Marina in Nokomis, just minutes from the Venice Inlet, on a 25-foot custom-rigged Parker for inshore and offshore fishing.

Waterway Park

Halfway completed, the **Venetian Waterway Park** (daylight hours, admission free) in Venice is a 10-mile-long mixed-use linear park with trails through some of the area's least developed land along the east bank of the Intracoastal Waterway, ending on Caspersen Beach, one of the prettiest on the Gulf. It's a long, winding, wheel-friendly park, good for rollerbladers, bikers, even jog strollers. Rent bikes at **Beach Bikes & Trikes** (127 Tampa Ave. #10, Venice, 941/412-3821, $10/day, $25/week).

While in Venice, visit the recently renovated **Venice Train Depot** (303 E. Venice Ave., depot tours are free) downtown. The Mediterranean-style depot was constructed in 1927 and is listed on the National Register of Historic Places.

SHOPPING

Shopping on Longboat Key is fairly limited: On the lush, tropically landscaped Avenue of the Flowers there's a little shopping center (525 Bay Isle Pkwy.) where you'll find a larger Publix grocery and a drugstore; at the **Centre Shops** (5370 Gulf of Mexico Dr., 941/387-8298) about mid-island, you'll find a small collection of boutiques (tourists' T-shirts, resortwear, and such), galleries, and little restaurants.

On Siesta Key there are two main shopping areas, **Siesta Key Village** on the northwest side of the key about one block from the Gulf, and **Siesta South shopping area** beginning at the Stickney Point Bridge and going south along Midnight Pass Road. Both have the ubiquitous T-shirt-'n'-sunglasses shops, the shell-themed beachy giftware shops, and a few useful stores. Neither area boasts much in the way of high-end merchandise (fine-art galleries, antiques, clothing), but that's just fine.

ACCOMMODATIONS
Longboat Key

Longboat Key is mostly dotted with swishy high-rise condos and resort hotels that loom over the beaches. If you like a more modest scale, the **Wicker Inn** (5581 Gulf of Mexico Dr., 941/383-5562, www.wickerinn.com, cottages $980–2,996 per week) is on a more human scale. There are 11 breezy Key West–style cottages set around an inviting pool and festooned with purple hibiscus and oleander. There's a private beach just steps away and a 16-acre public park.

Colony Beach & Tennis Resort (1620 Gulf of Mexico Dr., 941/383-6464, www.colonybeachresort.com, from $275) has been patronized over the years by George W. Bush,

Walk or bike to Siesta Key Village, a collection of friendly stores and sidewalk cafés, with live music and casual shopping.

Tom Brokaw, Dustin Hoffman, and countless other luminaries. It's the area's oldest beach resort, with 235 luxuriously large suites, a relaxed atmosphere, two popular restaurants, private beach access, and 21 tennis courts (with 10 pros on staff). It's considered by many to be the nation's top tennis resort, but there are plenty of other distractions such as a lovely beachfront pool and luxury spa.

The other big gun in town is **C The Resort at Longboat Key Club** (301 Gulf of Mexico Dr., 941/383-8821, www.longboatkeyclub. com, from $311). Serious golfers come for the 45 holes of the private Longboat Key Club, but there are lots of other reasons to settle into one of the 210 suites (with full kitchens) or one of 20 hotel rooms. There's a fine restaurant on-site, 38 tennis courts, bike and beach rentals, great pools, and a private stretch of white-sand beach with lovely cabana rentals and beachside service. Despite the fact that this is luxury with a capital L, the people who work here are friendly and personable, never lapsing into the kind of obsequiousness that gives me the heebie-jeebies. (Speaking of heebie-jeebies, this site was once owned by John Ringling, where in the 1930s he built a Ritz-Carlton. The hotel was never completed because of the Great Depression, and it sat abandoned until it was demolished in 1963. Locals called the hulking shell the "Ghost Hotel," spreading all the requisite apocryphal tales of horror, ghost sightings, and untimely death.)

Another big, but less expensive, favorite on Longboat is the **Hilton Longboat Key Beachfront Resort** (4711 Gulf of Mexico Dr., 941/383-2451, $270–495). The large, recently renovated rooms are decorated in jewel tones with contemporary furniture, all rooms with either two queen beds or one king. It sits adjacent to a private stretch of white-sand beach. The hotel provides free shuttle service to the shopping on St. Armands Circle.

Siesta Key

There are not too many chain hotels and no huge resorts on Siesta Key—which is fine, because you're more likely to have a memorable

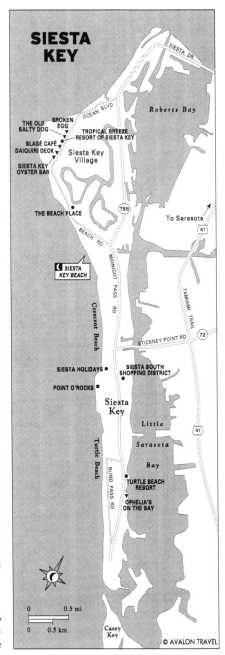

time in one of the modest mom-and-pop house rentals or small hotels. The warm, independent spirit of many of these hoteliers is apparent in the relaxed decor and their easy beachside pleasures. Many accommodations on Siesta Key adopt an efficiency approach, with little kitchens, essential for keeping vacation costs down (snarf a bowl of cereal in the morning, then prepare yourself a great picnic lunch for the beach).

Rented by the week, the tropical garden beach cottages of **The Beach Place** (5605 Avenida Del Mare, 941/346-1745, www.siestakeybeachplace.com, $500–1,700/week) make a nice romantic or family beach getaway. There's a pool (but the beach is 30 seconds away), a tiki cabana with wet bar, beachside barbecue facilities, lounge chairs, beach cruiser bikes, and free laundry. The cottages themselves are modest but recently repainted and pleasant, whether it's the one-bedroom Coquina, the one-bedroom Seahorse, the two twin-bed Starfish, the large one-bedroom Sand Dollar, or the huge studio cottage called the Dolphin.

Siesta Holidays (1017 Seaside Dr., 941/312-9882, www.siestaholidays.com, $425–1,450/week, depending on the season and unit) is a similar place, with two options. It has the Siesta Sea Castle directly on Crescent Beach, consisting of a large two-bedroom, two-bath apartment, and four one-bedroom efficiency apartments. The ground-level units have patios directly on the beach. Then there's the Siesta Holiday House, a little farther from the beach, with two one-bedroom apartments on the ground floor (with a big private screened pool) and two two-bedroom, two-bath apartments on the second floor. Pets are allowed in the Holiday House.

The **Tropical Breeze Resort of Siesta Key** (5150 Ocean Blvd., 800/300-2492, www.tropicalbreezeinn.com, $169–365/night) also offers a range of choices, spreading across four blocks of a cute neighborhood between the village and the shoreline. There are one-, two-, and three-bedroom efficiencies and suites located directly on the beach as well as more

privately located units in lush tropical gardens. Each building comes with its own pool, and the property has a centrally located yoga deck. Everything is within walking distance of Siesta Key Village.

On the south end of the island, **Turtle Beach Resort** (9049 Midnight Pass Rd., 941/349-4554, www.turtlebeachresort.com, doubles from $250) is one of the area's best-kept secrets, only now the secret's been blabbed by lots of travel magazines. Reservations are harder to come by, but the 10 clapboard cottages, each individually decorated with its own porch and hot tub, are worth waiting for. With views of Little Sarasota Bay, Turtle Beach is a short walk away, and guests have free use of bikes, hammocks, canoes, kayaks, paddleboats, and fishing poles. Eat at Ophelia's next door. Pets welcome.

Venice

If you've come to the Sarasota area with the express purpose of collecting shark's teeth, then it makes sense to stay in Venice. Otherwise, Venice lacks a lot of the amenities of Sarasota, Lido Key, Longboat Key, or Siesta Key, and the downtown pretty much closes up at night. There's a fairly inexpensive **Inn at the Beach** (725 West Venice Ave., 941/484-8471, $98–159) and a **Best Western** (400 Commercial Court, 800/611-7450, $149–199), both perfectly fine.

FOOD
Longboat Key

One of Sarasota's most long-term love affairs has been with **Euphemia Haye** (5540 Gulf of Mexico Dr., 941/383-3633, $22–43). Hours vary by dining locale here: 5:30–10 P.M. Sunday–Thursday, 5–10:30 P.M. Friday and Saturday in the restaurant; 6–10 P.M. daily in the dessert room; 5 P.M.–midnight in the HayeLoft. Opened in 1975 on Longboat Key, the restaurant has marched to the beat of its own drum, serving wildly sophisticated and far-reaching food in a lush garden setting. It always wins top honors from local magazines and national food mags as well, and you need only

AWESOME, BABY!

It was 7:40 A.M. and I should have been up. Drifting in the last delicious, guilty minutes of sleep, I gradually became aware that a man was speaking loudly from my office down the hall. Not speaking, really, but commentating. In my fog, I was convinced Howard Cosell's voice boomed from the vicinity of my guest bathroom. Or was it John Madden? Distinctly, I heard, "It's phenomenal, baby!" And then it all came into sharp focus.

Dick Vitale – Dickie V. to some – was leaving me a message, enumerating his list of beloved Sarasota institutions. It was no small list. The famous ESPN sports broadcaster has called the greater Sarasota area home for the past 19 years, his successes and enthusiasms inextricably knit into the fabric of this vital community. If you don't believe it, take a trip to the Dick Vitale Sports and Fitness Gym at the Boys and Girls Clubs of Sarasota County and see where he stands outside in lustrous bronze ("My grandkids get such a kick out of that," Vitale laughs.).

In fact, it was his daughters' sports interests that drew Vitale and family to the area – the girls came to The Nick Bollettieri Tennis Academy, which is now part of the 300-acre multisport training and educational facility called IMG Academies, for which Vitale has nothing but praise. Still, it didn't manage to make his top 10 list, but the competition was fierce:

1. Siesta Key Beach

"I love walking that beach. I bring a lot of people there and it blows their mind – love the white sand!"

2. Sarasota Restaurants

"From Fleming's to Ruth's Chris Steakhouse to the Le Colonne Restaurant to the Café L'Europe," Vitale lists thoughtfully, splitting his faves between tried-and-true chains and some of the area's independent eateries.

And what does Dick Vitale eat at Sarasota's wealth of stylish restaurants? "I'm not a red meat guy – I try to watch it by staying away from red meat and cheeses. I eat a lot of fish dishes, a lot of salmon, maybe chicken marsala, or pasta with marinara and veggies."

3. The Broken Egg in Siesta Key and Lakewood Ranch

Sure, it's another restaurant, but as Vitale notes, "It's my office away from home, five minutes from my house. I sit there for hours, doing all my work, my DickVitale.com articles, reading all my newspapers, and just having a blast with all the people." Sometimes ensconced for a couple hours at a time, Vitale is known to do radio shows and TV interviews from the hangout where he is, he jokes, "the mayor of The Broken Egg." And when he gets hungry? The Dickie V turkey burger, of course.

4. Lakewood Ranch Country Club

The area was once owned by the founders of Schlitz Brewing Company, long given over to cattle ranching, turf farming, and citrus. In 1994, after much wrangling with the city, ground was broken on a new luxury residential development set squarely between Sarasota and Bradenton. It bears the distinction of being the largest master-planned community in the state to achieve the designation of Green Community by the Florida Green Building Coalition.

"It's a whole new area, growing by leaps and bounds," enthuses Vitale. "It's gorgeous, just a great place that's going to be a total city. I live in the country club, and I play tennis every day when I'm home. I play singles with the ladies in the neighborhood. I'm the envy of all the guys there!"

5. Spring training with the Cincinnati Reds

"The Reds are going to be here for a number of years," Vitale explains. "It's great to get up close." The little 7,500-seat stadium provides intimate access to big-league play in a small-time venue. Vitale takes his grandkids, but he adds, "The building of a new, modern park has been approved, but they're going to keep the Ed Smith."

6. Van Wezel Performing Arts Hall

"All the seats are great because it's so small, and it's got great sound," insists Vitale. The Van Wezel presents a wonderful range of Broadway productions, world-class dance, music, comedy, and popular acts, as well as being the home base for many of the local arts organizations. "Whether it be The Temptations, Vince Gill, or Tony Bennett, it's just phenomenal. I'm going there Wednesday night to see Frankie Valli and the Four Seasons. It's so great to know you have a place that close."

7. Main Street in Sarasota and Lakewood Ranch

"Both are special places to walk around, with restaurants and shops and lots of activities and music on the weekends," says Vitale. Lakewood Ranch's version dates back as recently as 2005, but still has an appealing range of boutique-style stores and eateries. More established, Sarasota's is lined with galleries, restaurants, and cute shops, and nearby historic Herald Square in the SoMa (south of Main Street) part of

downtown on Pineapple Avenue has a fairly dense concentration of antique shops and upscale housewares stores.

8. St. Armands Circle

"A tourist's delight," notes Vitale. While it's often compared to Rodeo Drive and other famous shopping districts, Vitale's affection for it is a little less highbrow: "Kilwin's ice cream is just phenomenal. I take a lot of people there. Since I try to stay away from fats, I go for the yogurt. It's romantic to walk to Lido Beach from there. Keeps your marriage going – I've been married 35 years!"

9. The Ritz-Carlton Sarasota and the Beach Club

The 266-room, 18-story luxury hotel right downtown has managed to blend in beautifully, as if it has always been here on the Sarasota scene. Ritz-Carlton's signature warmth and personality appeals to Vitale: "It's a great, great asset to the area. We love going there for dinner and going to listen to the great bands they have on the weekend."

10. Boys & Girls Club of Sarasota County

Vitale's commitment and enthusiasm on this topic are infectious: "My buddies and friends and I raised over $1 million to help build the Lee Wetherington Boys & Girls Clubs. It's always special to see young kids getting an opportunity in their lives."

Vitale's voice quiets a little as he says, "I've been lucky enough in my life to have opportunities to help kids chase their dreams. To bring a smile to a kid's face is really something."

I'd say it's phenomenal, baby.

MAMA MIA

Quick, who said: "If the definition of poetry allowed that it could be composed with the products of the field as well as with words, pesto would be in every anthology"?

Longboat Key's one and only **Marcella Hazan.** She's the mother of Italian cooking in this country, the author of The Classic Italian Cookbook, Marcella Says, Marcella Cucina, Marcella's Italian Kitchen, and a few other Marcella books in the same vein. She introduced balsamic vinegar to this country (by way of Chuck Williams, of Williams-Sonoma), and just as Julia Child's Mastering the Art of French Cooking was a book that many Francophile cooks slept with under their pillows, so too was Hazan's first book in 1973 the kind of cookbook that serious students of Italian cuisine eventually had to replace with a fresh copy (too much sauce gumming up the pages).

Hazan's in her 80s now and this native of Cesenatico, Italy has called Florida home for the past nine years. Having moved countless times ("four times across the ocean," in her words), she's feeling settled.

"Our son moved here to Florida. My husband and I only knew the East Coast of Florida and we didn't like it, so we were surprised by his move. We were in Italy, and we came down to cheer him up and we found that this place was completely different from the East Coast. We love to be near the water – we lived for 20 years in Venice with water all around – and we like the beach and the warm weather."

Hazan herself didn't cook a lick before she got married. But she learned fast. She got her start in culinary education in the 1950s, just teaching her friends the fundamentals of Italian cooking from her New York apartment kitchen. Americans were woefully ignorant of real Italian cuisine, despite the five million southern Italians that poured into country by the end of the first World War. If it wasn't Franco-American canned spaghetti or Kraft parmesan cheese in the ubiquitous green shaker, we didn't know much about it.

"I was also teaching how to eat," Hazan remembers. "In Italy, people don't eat just a dish of pasta and a salad. They have different courses, but the courses are small. That was the first thing my students learned. I was teaching menus. Every menu was different,

---

to try the smoked salmon on buckwheat crepes, fried green tomatoes, or pistachio-crusted Key West snapper to see why. The wine list is broad, with good depth at every price point. As far as the food, prices are high and dishes are rich in the restaurant, so you can try the lighter/cheaper fare upstairs in the HayeLoft if you feel inclined. Chef/owner Raymond Arpke also offers cooking classes at the restaurant.

The other Goliath on Longboat Key is clearly the **Colony Restaurants** (1620 Gulf of Mexico Dr., 941/383-5558, $8–38) at the 36-year-old Colony Resort, partly for the sheer range of choices, and partly because so many local chefs cut their chops here. There's the fancy continental Colony Dining Room (opt for the skillet-seared snapper "Colony" with sun-dried tomatoes and lump crabmeat), the more casual Monkey Room and Bar, or the outside Monkey Room Patio and Bar. The Monkey Room is a must for party animals, the drinks tall and goofy (screaming yellow monkey, anyone?), the views stunning, and the island-inflected cuisine pleasant (although I'd take the plain old burger before the jerk chicken or froufrou Caribbean lobster tails). Live entertainment nightly. It's open 11:30 A.M.–9:30 P.M. daily with Sunday brunch in the dining room; breakfast and dinner in the Monkey Room, no lunch; 11:30 A.M.–1 A.M. in the bar.

Located mid-key on the bay side of Longboat Key is a wonderful find, **Pattigeorge's** (4120 Gulf of Mexico Dr., 941/383-5111, 6–9:30 P.M. nightly, $16–28). Chef Tommy Klauber experiments with an East-West fusion style that somehow never seems precious or contrived (he formerly owned a restaurant in Aspen called Gieusseppi Wong, a purveyor of Italian/

with different ingredients, so I took the students to the market, so they could see what it was they were going to use. It was very simple recipes with very few ingredients – people think it's such a production to make a meal. It was important for me to teach the feeling and the taste. I never tried to teach them presentation of a dish. That's not important to me – you have to eat it, not look at it."

It was Craig Claiborne of *The New York Times* who gave Hazan's vital and incisive spin on Italian cooking its big break in the early 1970s. Her classes became so popular that she began writing all of it down, a project that eventually became *The Classic Italian Cookbook*.

All of her books lay out the principles of Italian cooking in no-nonsense, understandable prose, and the most recent (2004), *Marcella Says*, is filled with the wisdom – and the passion – she's shared at her culinary classes for more than three decades.

It's as she says: "Music and cooking are so much alike. There are people who, simply by working hard at it, become technically quite accomplished at either art. But it isn't until one connects technique to feeling, turning it into the outward thrust of that feeling, that one becomes a musician, or a cook."

Never at a loss for an opinion, when asked which of her books Hazan favors, she seems stumped but quickly regroups.

"That's like asking which of your children you like best . . . *Essentials of Classic Italian Cooking* is more like a textbook, with home-cooking dishes that most people who like Italian food know about or have heard about. That book is still going very well, sold all over the world."

These days, though, Hazan isn't teaching Americans to cook, or working on a cookbook at all. She's writing her memoir. She once said, "I cook for flavor. Like truth, it needs no embellishment." We can rest assured that her memoir will be full of both truth and flavor.

Look for her books in Sarasota's Main Street bookstores, such as **Sarasota News & Books** (new books, nice café, 1341 Main St., 941/365-6332), **Main Bookshop** (four stories of remainders, 1962 Main St., 941/366-7653), or **Book Bazaar** (used and out-of-print books, 1488 Main St., 941/366-1373). She also occasionally does book signings at these places.

Chinese cuisine). Pattigeorge's has been around since 1998, making it another old-timer on the island. The dining room is comfortable but upscale and the views are nice—still, the main attraction is dishes like crackling five-spice calamari with orange blossom honey-mustard, or Thai green curry grouper, or maybe a Thai chicken pizza.

Siesta Key

Like everything else on Siesta Key, restaurants are mostly more casual there than on Longboat Key. Ocean Boulevard runs through Siesta Village, which is lined with loads of fun, laid-back, beachy bars and restaurants. Most places have outdoor seating, and many have live music at night.

For when you need a little romance, though, only one place on Siesta Key will do.

🄲 **Ophelia's on the Bay** (9105 Midnight Pass Rd., 941/349-2212, 5–10 P.M. daily, $20–29), at the southern tip of the key, has a waterfront terrace that I swear the moon favors with an extra luminous show over Sarasota Bay and the mainland. The interior of the restaurant is elegant, but you just gotta sit outside. The chef seems smitten with sweet-and-salty combinations that marry meats with fruits (coconut-and-cashew-crusted grouper with papaya jam) and salty meats with fish (black sea bass and cockle clams pan roasted with applewood smoked bacon and leeks). It's a distinctive and memorable palette of flavors that is complemented by a quirky wine list. Try the macadamia nut torte for dessert. (Oh, and the oyster bar next door to Ophelia's is a wonderful place to kill a little time, and appetite, if you have to wait for a table at Ophelia's.)

The Siesta Key restaurant that thrills me the most is **Siesta Key Oyster Bar** (5238 Ocean Blvd., 941/346-5443, 11 A.M.–midnight daily, $6–15), but that's because the acronym on the sign out front is SKOB. It's the exact onomatopoeic word that would be elicited by an oyster going down the wrong way. But then, I'm immature that way. Their sandwiches are, in fact, called skobwiches, which is just gross. Still, the swordfish skobwich or the crab cake skobwich is mighty fine washed down with a house margarita while listening to a live rock band. Margaritas seem to find their foothold in Siesta Key, reaching their volatile tequila effulgence here in the white powdery sand under the hot sun. But if rum's more your poison (and, unfortunately, sometimes that feels literal), right down the way you'll enjoy the **Daiquiri Deck** (5250 Ocean Blvd., 941/349-8697, 11 A.M.–1 A.M. daily, $6–17). The most sophisticated drink is the Grateful Deck, a mélange of Bols raspberry liqueur, light rum, gin, vodka, raspberry juice, and sour mix. Tangy, yet sweet, yet boozy. Lots of other mad-scientist brews are powered by grain alcohol, something no one over 22 or so should wittingly consume.

Beer batter–dipped hot dogs. I kid you not. And they're pretty good. **The Old Salty Dog** (5023 Ocean Blvd., 941/349-0158, 11 A.M.–midnight Mon.–Thurs., until 1 A.M. Fri. and Sat., noon–midnight Sun., $5–15) is an institution among locals, who come for that particular gastronomic challenge or a bowl of clam chowder and a beer. It's open-air, with great views, good burgers, saucy waitresses. The beer bar is fashioned from the hull of an old boat, which adds a little nautical tilt to every drinker's voice. There's another location with the same hours at 1601 Ken Thompson Parkway (941/388-4311).

Best breakfast? That's the easiest call on Siesta Key. Anyone in town will promptly steer you to the brand new◖ **The Broken Egg** (140 Avenida Madera, 941/346-2750, 7:30 A.M.–2:30 P.M. daily, $5–9), now located one block down from it's original location. The place is such a cheery mob scene most mornings that they opened a second location in 2005 at Lakewood Ranch. It's no accident that their website plays the theme song from *Cheers*—it is the kind of place "where everybody knows your name," even if you've only been there a couple of times to dispatch a Scram Sam (three eggs scrambled with smoked salmon and chives, served with tomatoes, onion, cream cheese, and a bagel) or banana-nut-bread french toast. The verdant patio is the place to sit, despite the crusty white molded plastic patio chairs.

Blasé Café (5263 Ocean Blvd., 941/349-9822, 9 A.M.–9:30 P.M. daily, $7–23) gives The Broken Egg a run for its money, with expertly prepared egg dishes and a fine burger at lunch. Be sure to ask for outside seating on the wooden deck with the big palm tree in the middle (but if you're just stopping in for a drink, the beautiful bar is the seat of choice).

Casey Key

On Casey Key, the place to go is **Casey Key Fish House** (801 Blackburn Point Rd., 941/966-1901, 11:30 A.M.–9 P.M. daily, $5–15). Despite Hurricane Charley's best efforts back in 2004, this shambling restaurant-and-tiki bar still does a brisk business with people who navigate peel-'n'-eat shrimp while watching the sunset over picturesque Blackburn Point Marina. Casual seafood is the mainstay, but fancier white wine–steamed mussels and almond snapper are wonderful.

Venice

Along Nokomis Avenue (the main drag downtown) you'll find shops, diners, coffeehouses, and lunch spots—the best of which is **Venice Wine and Coffee Co.** (110 Nokomis Ave. S., 941/484-3667), a coffee shop by day and wine bar at night. To find Venice's Old Florida dining possibilities, all fun, all casual, you'll have to go farther afield. The **Crow's Nest, Marina Restaurant and Tavern** (1968 Tarpon Center Dr., 941/484-9551, 11 A.M.–11 P.M. Mon.–Thurs., until midnight Fri. and Sat., $13–32) has been feeding locals since 1976, with a fun tavern and pretty views of the marina,

Venice Inlet, and the Intracoastal Waterway. The wine list is incongruously sophisticated for this fried oysters–fried shrimp–steamed clam, friendly kind of menu. Happy hour in the tavern is 4–6 P.M. Marina hours are 8 A.M.–7 P.M. daily.

The **Snook Haven Restaurant and Fish Camp** (5000 Venice Ave. E., past River Rd., 941/485-7221, 11 A.M.–9 P.M. daily, $9–20) has a similar vibe, only more downhome and bayou-style, right on the Myakka River (rent a pontoon boat or kayak before you eat). The burgers are good and you can count on some entertaining fellow customers and occasional live entertainment.

Sharky's on the Pier (1600 S. Harbor Dr., 941/488-1456, 11 A.M.–11 P.M. Mon.–Thurs., until midnight Fri. and Sat., $12–24) is closer to civilization, with beach views and the day's catch offered broiled, blackened, grilled, or fried. Sit outside on the veranda and enjoy a Bait Bucket margarita that's finished off with triple sec and blue curaçao for that irresistible Windex look.

Information and Services

Sarasota and vicinity are located within the **Eastern time zone.** The area code is **941.**

Tourist Information

The **Sarasota Convention & Visitors Bureau** (official Sarasota Visitor Information Center, 701 North Tamiami Trail, a.k.a. U.S. 41, 941/957-1877, www.sarasotafl.org, 10 A.M.–4 P.M. Mon.–Sat., noon–3 P.M. Sun.) and the **Sarasota Chamber of Commerce** (1945 Fruitville Rd., 941/955-8187, www.sarasotachamber.org, 8:30 A.M.–5 P.M. Mon.–Fri.) both offer heaping piles of reading material on the area. The former has more useful material and a more central location.

Sarasota has its own daily newspaper, the **Sarasota Herald-Tribune,** with multiple zoned editions serving the area, along with a 24-hour television news station, S NN. Local weekly publications include the **Longboat Observer,** Siesta Key's **Pelican Press,** and a business newspaper, the **Gulf Coast Business Review.** Nine magazines cover different aspects of Sarasota County, from business to the arts and the social scene.

Police and Emergencies

In any emergency, dial 911 for immediate assistance. If you need the police in a nonemergency, Sarasota's Police Department Headquarters

Building is at 2050 Ringling Boulevard (941/954-7025). For medical emergencies, or problems that just won't wait until you get home, the nicest facilities are at the emergency care center at **Sarasota Memorial Hospital** (1700 S. Tamiami Trail, 941/917-8555).

Radio and Television

Ten radio stations are located within Sarasota County, with 40 more stations in neighboring counties, including all major affiliates. Tune to **WFLA 970 AM** for news and talk radio; **WDDV 92.1 FM** is easy favorites (think Englebert Humperdinck's "After the Lovin'"). You'll find National Public Radio at **89.7 FM.**

On television, **WFLA Channel 8** is the NBC affiliate, **WTVT Channel 13** is the FOX affiliate, and **WWSB Channel 7** is the ABC affiliate. There are additional public television and local news channels.

Laundry Services

One of the perks of renting a beach house is the reliable presence of non-coin-op laundry facilities on-site. Big resort hotels in Sarasota and on Longboat Key invariably offer laundry services. If you absolutely need a launderette, there are several in Sarasota, such as **All Star Laundry & Dry Cleaning** (2241 Bee Ridge Rd., 941/921-1258).

Getting There and Around

BY CAR

Sarasota is along I-75, the major transportation corridor for the southeastern United States. Sarasota County is south of Tampa and north of Fort Myers, 223 miles from Miami (about four hours' drive time), 129 miles from Orlando (about two hours' drive time), and about 5–6 hours from the Florida–Georgia line. If you prefer I-95, take it to Daytona Beach, then follow I-4 to I-75 before heading south.

U.S. 301 and U.S. 41/Tamiami Trail are the major north–south arteries on the mainland; the Gulf-to-Mexico Drive (County Road 789) is the main island road. The largest east–west thoroughfares in Sarasota are Highway 72 (Stickney Point Road); County Road 780, University Parkway; and (to the islands) Ringling Causeway, which takes you right to Lido Beach.

BY AIR

Sarasota-Bradenton International Airport (SRQ) (6000 Airport Circle, at the intersection of U.S. 41 and University Pkwy., Sarasota, 941/359-2770) is certainly the closest, served by commuter flights and a half dozen major airlines or their partners, including Continental, Delta, Northwest, AirTran, and US Airways. Another option is to fly into **Tampa International Airport** (813/870-8700), which offers more arrival and departure choices, and often better fares on flights and even rental cars. Tampa International Airport is just 53 miles north of Sarasota County via I-75 or I-275. Also check flights through **St. Petersburg-Clearwater International Airport** (although usually they aren't as often or as cheap as through the Tampa airport). Private planes can use the **Venice Municipal Airport** in the City of Venice, just down U.S. 41 from Sarasota.

Alamo (800/327-9633), **Avis** (800/831-2847), **Budget** (800/527-0700), **Dollar** (800/800-4000 domestic, 800/800-6000 international), **Enterprise** (800/736-8222), **Hertz** (800/654-3131), and **National** (800/227-7368) provide rental cars from Sarasota-Bradenton International Airport. **Diplomat Taxi** (941/355-5155) is the taxi provider at the airport.

BY BUS AND TRAIN

Sarasota County Area Transit, or **SCAT** (941/316-1234), runs scheduled bus service 6 A.M.–7 P.M. Monday–Saturday. A 75-cent fare will take you to stops in the city and St. Armands, Longboat, and Lido Keys. **Greyhound** (575 N. Washington Blvd., Sarasota, 941/955-5735) offers regular bus service to Sarasota from Fort Myers and points north, and Miami to the southeast; and **Amtrak** (800/872-7245) provides shuttle buses between the Tampa station and Sarasota.

LEE COUNTY

The area between Sarasota and Naples was inhabited for 2,000 years by the fierce, tall, and agriculturally impaired Calusas. No matter, because the fishing was good and the shell-fishing was better. For a while Lee County had a slick ad campaign that read: "Ancient cultures once used shells as currency. Guess this place must have been Fort Knox." They seem to have retired the campaign, but the fact remains: The long lengths of beaches in this area are spectacular for their sand, their birds, their sunsets, and, most strikingly, for their shells. You could stub a toe on a lightning whelk (an anomaly in the mollusk world, opening to the left and not the right) or strain your sciatic stooping for perfect Florida fighting conch along the water's edge.

Gold-seeking Spanish conquistadores all but wiped out the Calusa and then never really settled here with any impressive numbers. The nearly unpopulated barrier islands became a hideout for pirates, most famously José Gaspar, the "last of the buccaneers." Whether apocryphal or not, in 1783 Gasparilla, as he called himself, commandeered a Spanish ship, the *Floridablanca,* and roamed the Gulf Coast waters plundering treasure and capturing beautiful women (his "captives," it is said, were warehoused on "Captiva" Island).

The area, called the Beaches of Fort Myers and Sanibel, (its county, Lee County, was named after Confederate general Robert E. Lee), was the site of one of the southernmost land battles of the American Civil War. It was fought in Fort Myers on February 20, 1865, with both sides claiming victory (the confusing event is celebrated annually in North

HIGHLIGHTS

◖ **Lovers Key State Park:** Lee County beaches are ranked some of the best in the nation for shelling, with more varieties found here than anywhere else in North America. Lovers Key State Park gives you the widest range of recreation options, including shelling the 2.5-mile stretch of beach and 5 miles of bike trails (page 57).

◖ **Edison & Ford Winter Estates:** Thomas Edison, who spent 46 winters in Fort Myers, is considered to be the most inventive man who ever lived, holding 1,097 patents for everything from light bulbs, cement, and phonographs to the natural rubber he made from goldenrod. His estate and that of his buddy Henry Ford are fascinating (page 59).

◖ **J.N. "Ding" Darling National Wildlife Refuge:** Occupying more than half of Sanibel Island, this refuge is home to a tremendous array of birdlife (page 74).

◖ **Bailey-Matthews Shell Museum:** It's a crash course in Neptune's treasures, a must if you want to know which species you're painstakingly unearthing along the shoreline (page 74).

◖ **Palm Island:** If you have the resources of time and money, a day or two on Palm Island is good for the soul, and most other parts, too. It's an unbridged barrier island paradise (page 85).

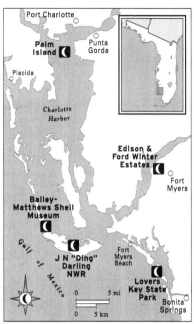

LOOK FOR ◖ TO FIND RECOMMENDED SIGHTS, ACTIVITIES, DINING, AND LODGING.

Fort Myers with a battle reenactment during its Cracker Festival). The county was named after the war, when it separated from nearby Monroe County in 1887.

Lee County's draw for the visitor is sheer variety. The city of **Fort Myers,** in large measure due to its most famous residents, Thomas Edison and Henry Ford, is culturally rich, with attractions spread along the banks of the Caloosahatchee River. It is the oldest and largest city in southwest Florida, and as such, dense with history. Nearby, the barrier islands offer tropical island getaways.

The most well known of this group of islands are **Sanibel** and **Captiva.** Once connected to

each other at what is now Blind Pass, the siblings bear a family resemblance but have vastly different personalities. Both cater to affluent winter visitors, but Sanibel is more accessible (financially, physically, metaphorically), with miles of bike paths, low-rise independently owned inns and teeny hotels. Living here is casual; a tremendous wildlife refuge takes up nearly half of the island, with white-sand beaches on the Gulf side and picturesque mangrove forests on the eastern side. Captiva, to the north and connected by a causeway, is the playground of the even more affluent. Many people own homes on Captiva (you won't see it, but artist Robert Rauschenberg had an unassuming

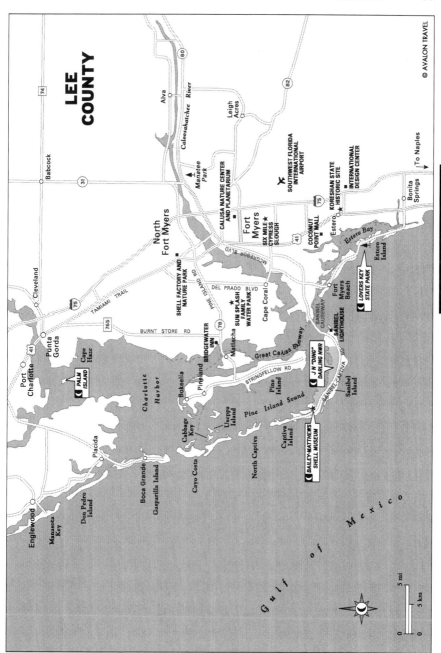

LEE COUNTY

© AVALON TRAVEL

white, beachfront mansion and studio on the island), most tucked down driveways shielded from prying eyes by lush foliage. There's less to do on Captiva, there are fewer places to stay, fewer tourist amenities. But that's how people on Captiva like it.

Then there are the other barrier islands, each with its own character. Fort Myers Beach is on the long strip of coast-hugging land known as Estero Island. It's the closest thing this area has to a spring break–type beach, with affordable motels and crowded, family-friendly beaches. Gasparilla Island has made a name for itself as the tarpon capital and host to American presidents and a wide array of fish-seeking celebrities. Its town of Boca Grande is worth the quick boat ride or slightly longer car ride (you've got to go north and then out a causeway) to see. Cabbage Key, North Captiva, and Useppa are accessible only by boat but make a lovely day trip. And Pine Island is the largest of the barrier islands in this area, mostly residential, with the charming maritime towns of Matlacha, Bokeelia, Pineland, and St. James City. Anglers know it for its "Fishingest Bridge in the U.S."

PLANNING YOUR TIME

The area could entertain the troops for a week or more. The budget traveler will make his or her home base in Fort Myers or Fort Myers Beach, slinking over the very expensive causeway ($6) to Sanibel and Captiva for a day of rejuvenating beach therapy. The Edison & Ford estates in Fort Myers will occupy much of a day, as will the J. N. "Ding" Darling National Wildlife Refuge on Sanibel. The rest of the area's attractions are more fleetingly entertaining

(although the beach never gets old). Families will spend a fair amount of time at the kids' water park and attractions to the north in Cape Coral; history buffs will likely occupy themselves at one of several Calusa museums; the outdoors enthusiast will choose fishing, canoeing, or sailing, or all of the above. The Great Calusa Blueway Paddling Trail is a truly remarkable newly charted route for beginning or advanced paddlers—well worth a half day's exploration for even the most timid boater.

The end of each October and beginning of November, the **Calusa Blueway Paddling Festival** (www.calusabluewaypaddlingfestival.com) is another event around which to plan an outdoors-oriented trip. Lee County has been recognized as one of the best U.S. kayaking destinations by both *Paddler* and *Canoe & Kayak* magazines. Paddlers, competitors, families, and outdoors enthusiasts enjoy nine days of festivities including competitive canoe/kayak races, a pro-am kayak fishing tournament, paddling clinics and demonstrations, seminars, family activities, archaeological and environmental events, guided tours, a speakers' series, and more celebrations along the Great Calusa Blueway.

Fall is beautiful here, while summers are fairly soporific with heat and humidity. If your aim is winter, it's cheaper to visit in the first two weeks of December. Rates generally increase for high season during the third week of December, and the large crowds arrive in February and March. In early December, you'll find lots of accommodations and nominal traffic (which can be frustrating on Sanibel and Captiva in March).

Fort Myers

A hurricane in the 1840s drove the soldiers out of Seminole War Fort Dulaney at the mouth of the Caloosahatchee. The evacuation had an upside. First Lt. John Harvie found a safer, more sheltered place for a fort, which he named Fort Myers in honor of that war's Col. Abraham C. Myers. Retired soldiers came back to the area after the war, making use of the picturesque Caloosahatchee to ship cattle to Cuba. Fort Myers was a sleepy cowpoke town, not even on the beach, when Thomas Alva Edison visited and fell in love with it in 1885.

Fort Myers was incorporated that same year, and the banks of the Caloosahatchee Intercoastal Waterway started to be settled by intrepid northerners. Edison talked his buddy Henry Ford into exploring the area, and Ford promptly bought the house next door on McGregor Boulevard. Because of Edison's gift to the city of hundreds of royal palms, its nickname is "City of Palms," which I suppose has a catchier ring to it than "Gladiolus Capital of the World" (some of the area's original settlers were zealous gladiola growers from Belgium, The Netherlands, and Luxembourg).

These days, Fort Myers is Lee County's working center, the biggest urban center in southwest Florida (well, nearby Cape Coral has greater land mass). There are attractions, restaurants, and hotels centered around the bustling downtown historic district and along the riverfront, and a recent downtown city renovation designed by famous New Urbanist architect Andres Duany is underway, promising a major renaissance in the near future.

Its easy access to nearby barrier islands (Sanibel, Captiva, Pine Island, Gasparilla, etc.), combined with its wealth of family-friendly attractions, makes it an obvious home base for the dynamic traveler. There are full-service marinas connected to several of the hotels along the river, so boaters can pull right up.

While the city of Fort Myers is beachless, head down to Fort Myers Beach on Estero Island for fun in the sun and sand—its gentle slope and lack of steep drop-offs make it a safe beach for young swimmers or waders. At the north end of the island a casual beach village offers a cluster of restaurants and shops, and at Estero's southern end Lovers Key State Park is a huge draw, with a number of nearby resort hotels.

SPORTS AND RECREATION
Spring Training
The Boston Red Sox have certainly made New England swell with pride in recent years. If you're a fan and you want to do some extra gloating, take in a **Boston Red Sox Spring Training** (City of Palms Park, 2201 Edison Ave., Fort Myers, 239/334-4700, www.mlb.com, $10–46) game. It's a great little ballpark into which Lee County has poured tons of money—a good place to see a Grapefruit League home season game, and to get a preview of what the Sox are capable of this season. Spring training games are the whole month of March at 1:05 P.M.

Minnesota Twins Spring Training (Hammond Stadium, 14400 Six Mile Cypress Pkwy., Fort Myers, 239/768-4210, www.miraclebaseball.com, $16–18) also takes place locally at the Lee County Sports Complex, recognized widely as one of baseball's top five spring training facilities. Games are at 1:05 P.M. all of the month of March, and after that, in April, fans can watch the Miracle League, a minor-league affiliate of the Minnesota Twins and member of the Florida State League.

Beaches
Fort Myers Beach is actually on the island of Estero, connected to Fort Myers by a causeway. There are several worthwhile beaches here. **Bowditch Point Regional Park** (50 Estero Blvd., 239/765-6794) is a 17-acre park that fronts both the Gulf and the bay at the northern tip of Estero Island, with a boardwalk over to a beach with beautiful views of nearby barrier islands. Parking is available

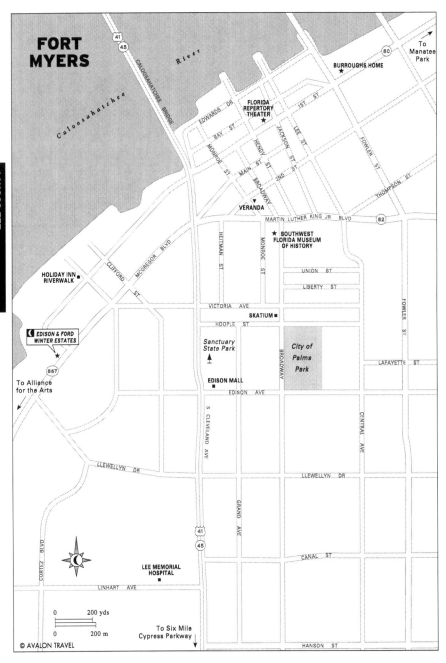

LEE COUNTY

FORT MYERS

LEE COUNTY

COURTESY OF LEE COUNTY VCB

Like its New York counterpart, Times Square on Fort Myers Beach is a hub of activity.

behind the bathhouse (nice showers and changing rooms), and there's a 25-cent trolley from the Main Street parking lot. Just a bit to the south and on the Gulf side, **Lynn Hall Memorial Park** (950 Estero Blvd., 239/765-6794, parking $1/hour) is a great family beach and a teen hangout. There's also a fishing pier here, heavily frequented by opportunistic pelicans. (If you happen to hook a pelican or other bird while fishing, reel the bird in slowly; cover its head with a towel to calm it; cut the line close to the hook and remove all monofilament from wings and body; then call **Clinic for the Rehabilitation of Wildlife,** C.R.O.W., 239/472-3644, a local nonprofit bird rescue organization.)

◖ Lovers Key State Park

Lovers Key State Park (8700 Estero Blvd., Fort Myers Beach, 239/463-4588, 8 A.M.–sundown, $5/car up to eight people, single occupancy car $3, pedestrians and bicyclists $1) is the newest of Florida's state parks and actually occupies four small barrier islands (Black Island, Long Key, Inner Key, and Lovers Key) between Fort Myers Beach and Bonita Beach to the south. The park contains a 2.5-mile stretch of beautiful beach and 5 miles of bike trails (bike, canoe, and kayak rentals available on-site), including the Black Island Trail through a maritime hammock. There are brand-new picnic facilities at the New Lovers Key Bayside area on Estero Boulevard. There's free tram service to the beach (9 A.M.–5 P.M. daily).

In addition to roseate spoonbills, snowy egrets, and American kestrels, birders will see active osprey nests and a couple of bald eagle nests. The park offers one-hour sunset ecotours (239/594-0213, $25 adults, $15 children ages 3–12) Tuesday, Thursday, and Saturday at 5 P.M., and there is a dolphin cruise and shelling excursion every Sunday, 8:15–9:15 A.M.

Parks

Six Mile Cypress Slough (7751 Penzance Crossing, Ft. Myers, 239/432-2004, www.lee

parks.org, 8 A.M.–sunset daily, parking $1/ hour) is a fabulous wild spot in south Fort Myers, easily accessible to those on the way to or from the airport. You'd never know you were in a county of a half-million people. There are ongoing free guided nature walks (twice daily during high season at 9:30 A.M. and 1:30 P.M.) along a 1.5-mile fully accessible boardwalk trail through a wooded wetland; monthly nature programs in which children and adults learn to identify animal tracks; evening moonwalks; and summer camps for kids and wilderness exploration camps for teens. In 2008, an interpretive center opens on-site, Lee County's first LEED-certified green building.

Manatee-Watching

Spend a little time on the Orange and Caloosahatchee Rivers, and chances are you'll see a West Indian manatee. Take a two-hour boat tour with **Manatee World** (16991 State Road 31, Fort Myers, 239/693-1434, www.manateeworld.com, 11 A.M. daily, $20 adults, $10 children 12 and under) and the odds are better you'll see a few of these mammals, related biologically to the elephant and, unlikely though it may seem, the aardvark. The narrated ecotour provides insight into the life of the area's most famous species, as well as information about their continued plight (outboard motors, habitat destruction, etc.). Manatees seem to congregate in the Orange River in the winter, basking in the waters warmed by the outflow of the nearby power plant. This is a good family adventure, and if you are smitten by these gentle sea cows, you can trudge over to **Manatee Park** (10901 Hwy. 80, 1.5 miles east of I-75, North Fort Myers, 239/690-5030, 9 A.M.–4 P.M. daily, parking $1/hour, kayak rentals $10/hour). There are three observation decks for viewing and hydrophones so you can listen in (I don't speak manatee, but the cool thing is, even scientists are unsure how they make these chirps, whistles, and squeaks). A cow and her calf are especially talkative, vocalizing back and forth. The park rents kayaks in winter and on summer weekends, with kayak clinics the second Saturday of the month and

free guided walks through the native plants habitats at 9 A.M. every Saturday.

Discovery Day at Manatee Park is always the last Saturday in January and draws 3,000 people to ecotourism activities, butterfly gardening, manatee-viewing, and kayaking on the Orange River.

Golf

The greater Fort Myers area has around 100 public and semiprivate golf courses, the egalitarian nature of which makes the city duly proud. The city of Fort Myers itself maintains two professionally designed golf courses. **Fort Myers Country Club** (3591 McGregor Blvd., 239/936-3126, public, 18 holes, 6,414 yards, course rating 70.5, slope 118, greens fee $25–55, depending on season and time of day par 71,) was designed by the great Donald Ross in 1916 and opened in 1917—one of the oldest courses on the Gulf Coast. It hosts the pro-am Coor's Open every year in January and is only a mile from downtown. **Eastwood Golf Course** (4600 Bruce Herd Lane, 239/275-4848, public, 18 holes, 6,772 yards, par 72, course rating 73.3, slope 130, greens fee $25–60) reopened in December 2007 after a $1.5 million renovation that included 84 new bunkers, 54 new tee grounds, new irrigation, resurfaced cart paths and a new driving range. Golfers will also enjoy the new $2 million clubhouse.

Tracker School

North and east of Fort Myers is a little town called Alva. Not much to do there amongst the dense Florida live oak, slash pine, and palmetto, unless you want to learn to be a tracker. New Jersey–based **Tom Brown, Jr.'s Tracker School** (Caloosahatchee Regional Park, 18500 North River Road, Fort Myers, www.tracker-school.com, 908/619-3809, about $950 for one week) relocates part of the year to this lush stretch of Florida wilderness. Students spend a week learning how to observe nature, track animals, and survive in the wilderness. Brown started his tracking school in 1978, on the heels of a number of successful books like his first, *The Tracker, Tom Brown's Field Guide* to *Wilderness Survival,* and *Grandfather.* The Florida school site has swimming holes, trails, and camping areas, all dense with local flora and fauna. If you need a hair dryer and a dry pair of socks, this may not be for you.

SIGHTS
◖ Edison & Ford Winter Estates

Thomas Edison arrived in Fort Myers on March 20, 1885. Not one to be indecisive, evidently, he purchased 13-plus acres along the Caloosahatchee River within 24 hours, with the aim of building his winter home.

Seminole Lodge was duly built in pieces in Maine from his designs and then sailed to Florida and assembled. The home served as the winter retreat and workplace for the prolific inventor until his death in 1931. It's encircled with large overhanging porches, and grand French doors encourage a cross breeze. There are electric chandeliers—"electroliers"—designed by Edison. It's a fascinating house, donated to the city for $1 by Edison's widow, Mina.

Edison's close buddy Henry Ford was obviously smitten, too, upon his visit to Fort Myers in 1915. He bought the house next door. The Mangoes became another mecca for the country's elite—Harvey Firestone, naturalist John Burroughs, Nobel Laureate Alexis Carrel, and Charles Lindbergh all made their way to this Florida paradise. For ages it was essentially Fort Myers's biggest tourist destination, not as big league as Disney World but more glamorous than, say, Gatorland.

Edison & Ford Winter Estates (2350 McGregor Blvd., Fort Myers, 239/334-3614, www.efwefla.org) raised $10 million in the past few years through a laudable public-private partnership, restoring the houses and grounds and repositioning the attraction as a community and cultural center.

The two estates encompass 14 acres of botanical landscaping, the two titans' historic homes and guest cottages, Edison's laboratory, a museum containing his famous inventions and exhibits, a museum store, a garden shop, and an outdoor café. It's worth at least a couple hours of wandering through the gorgeous

A native of India, the Edison banyan tree was the first banyan introduced to Florida.

LEE COUNTY

COURTESY OF LEE COUNTY VCB

LEE COUNTY

Thomas Edison, Harvey Firestone (both pictured), Henry Ford, and John Burroughs went off on a series of motor camping caravans in 1914 and 1915, said to be the first link between the automobile and outdoors "road tripping."

environs, but the real draw is peeking into the lives of these fascinating men.

Poke your head into the laboratory and the museum of Edison's inventions and artifacts, spend a little time in Ford's garage, then walk through the tropical botanical garden. Edison planted it as an experimental garden with more than 1,000 species, focusing on the byproducts of plants (rubber for his buddy Firestone's tires, for instance). Later, Mina Edison prettied it up by adding roses, orchids, and bromeliads.

In the painstakingly restored houses (Edison's lab is slated to be restored next), the year 1929 was chosen as the "period of interpretation," the interiors accurately reflecting the decor and accoutrements of that time. It's fun to mosey on your own with the electronic audio tour, but the staff-led tours are a must, giving the place context and depth.

You can dispel Edison myths (alas, the light bulbs burning in the estate are not Edison's originals), hear funny stories (Henry Ford stuffed the seats of his first Model T imprudently with local Spanish moss, which prompted the first automotive recall when little chiggers started crawling out and biting drivers on the butts), or just learn a little about the quirks of these American legends (Edison hated paparazzi, so he disembarked from the train before the station and walked the rest of the way).

The very young may be underwhelmed by all the Edison-Ford-obilia, but everybody feels a sense of awe when navigating the huge banyan tree out front. Its circumference spans more than 400 feet, making it one of the largest in the country, a gift to Thomas Edison from Firestone.

A combined tour of the estates runs 9 A.M.–5:30 P.M. daily, with the last tour leaving promptly at 4 P.M.; cost is $20 adults, $11 children 6–12, free for children 5 and younger. Botanical tours are offered at 9 A.M. Thursday and Saturday; you'll pay $24 adults, $10 children 6–12.

McGregor Boulevard

Fort Myers is sometimes called the City of Palms. Why? Edison and Ford's estates are poised just at the edge of McGregor Boulevard, which is lined on both sides by 60-foot-tall royal palms. The original 200 or so, from Cuba, were gifts from Thomas Edison to the city. The idea caught on, and now more than 2,000 palms flank the roadside of stately McGregor Boulevard. Drive the length of the 15-mile boulevard and the city's nickname seems fairly apt.

Museums

Southwest Florida Museum of History (2300 Peck St., 239/332-5955, www.cityftmyers .com, 10 A.M.–5 P.M. Tues.–Sat., a fairly steep $9.50 adults, $8.50 seniors and children 12 and under) is a quirky mix of stuff, but its wide net gathers a broad catch. The history of the Calusa and Seminole people, as well as that of this area's Spanish explorers, is a major focus of the museum, and more broadly the history of Fort Myers. Set in a restored Atlantic Coastline railroad depot built in 1924, the museum houses photographs and memorabilia; there's an 84-foot-long Pullman rail car built in 1929 and a replica of a late 1800s Cracker house.

A changing exhibit lends a different flavor to the museum every few months (UFOs in Roswell, King Tut, Treasures of Eden)—a recent one, called "Art Expressions of Latin America," brought vibrant oils, pastels, acrylics, and sculptures representing the fastest-

LEE COUNTY

GET OUT OF TOWN

Something to think about: If you have an extra day and nothing on the docket, why not pop off to Key West? Explore the country's southernmost city just for the day. There are high-speed shuttles from Fort Myers, a welcome alternative to driving (about seven hours) or flying (usually several hundred clams).

Key West Express (239/394-9700, $128 adults, $118 seniors, $68 children 6-12, $3 children 5 and under, but prices fluctuate by season and there are sometimes coupons in local papers) has a couple of boats that head out of Fort Myers.

Before I get too much further, I must tell you a cautionary tale. My family and another family elected to go together to Key West this way. Twenty minutes into our sea voyage Other Family Child One began to feel queasy, turning eventually toward his mother, plaintively wailing, "Mommy," and vomiting directly onto her front. She, then, began to feel ill and vomited repeatedly over the side of the ship, Child One joining her. We sat with Child Two until he, also, began projectile vomiting. Upon arrival in Key West, the entire family invested in new clothes, undergarments to sneakers. When confronted with the idea of the return ferry, the family elected to fly instead.

The company currently operates four vessels, the 130-foot *Whale Watcher*, the 140-foot *Atlanticat* catamaran, the 155-foot *Big Cat* catamaran, and the brand new 170-foot *Key West Express* catamaran. The catamaran ferry zips over to Key West in 3.5 hours.

Most seating on the boat is contoured, airplane-like chairs, but there are also plush couches with tables. The floor-to-ceiling windows provide plenty of entertainment (and there's a full outdoor deck upstairs), but there are still six plasma screen TVs showing movies, sports, whatever. The one from Salty Sam's Marina (2500 Main St., Fort Myers) features two enclosed cabins, a sun deck, satellite TV, slot machines, and full galley and bar. The ships depart Fort Myers Beach 9 A.M., arrive Key West 12:30 A.M.; depart Key West 6 P.M., arrive Fort Myers Beach 9:30 P.M. That gives you five hours or so to noodle around town. Alternatively, you can find a hotel or inn, stay overnight, and come back on the next day's ferry for no additional ferry fee. This tiny three- by five-mile island, 100 miles from the coast, has the only living coral reef in the U.S. in addition to great restaurants and nightlife. And for 10 days in October, Fantasy Fest makes Key West the biggest party around.

growing segment of the southwest Florida population.

The museum also runs 90-minute architectural and historic downtown walking tours in Fort Myers on Wednesdays and Saturdays at 10 A.M. ($5 adults, $3 children, reservation required).

Koreshan State Historical Site

Hands-down winner of Weirdest Attraction in the Area prize is the Koreshan State Historical Site (U.S. 41 at Corkscrew Rd., Estero, 239/992-0311, 8 A.M.–sundown, $4/car, $1 for walkers or bicycles, $22 camping, $5.30/hour canoe rentals). It commemorates an eccentric religious sect begun by Dr. Cyrus Teed in 1894 after he had a spiritual "great illumination." It seems he and his followers believed the world is a hollow globe, with mankind residing on the inner surface, gazing into the universe below. Whoa. This Koresh, by the way, is no relation to the other wacky Waco Koresh of 1990s vintage. The Koreshan followers (at its peak there were 250 of these) gave their commune to the state if it would be maintained as a historic site in perpetuity. Now the site is a compound of buildings and a theater, but visitors also avail themselves of the park's fishing, camping, nature study, and picnicking. There's a boat ramp and canoes for rent, and guided walks and campfire programs are offered seasonally.

ENTERTAINMENT AND EVENTS
Wine-Tasting

About 10 miles east of Fort Myers you'll run across the southernmost bonded winery in the continental United States. **Eden Vineyards** (19709 Little Ln., at Exit 141 off I-75, Alva, 239/728-9463, www.edenwinery.com, 11 A.M.–4 P.M. daily, free) makes six wines (all around $12), none of them identified by varietal. They're made of hybrid grapes that have proven themselves capable of withstanding the Florida sun and heat. It's fun to do a little tasting in an area not known for its wine—and these fruity, low-alcohol wines somehow suit the climate.

Music and Theater

The **Barbara B. Mann Performing Arts Hall** (on the campus of Edison College, 8099 College Pkwy., 239/481-4849, www.bbmannpah.com) is the center of arts activity for Fort Myers. The full-sized and fully equipped stage hosts traveling Broadway musicals, popular music, and **Southwest Florida Symphony** (4560 Via Royale, 239/418-1500, www.swflso.org) concerts. The professional symphony orchestra offers classical and pops series annually (its chamber orchestra series takes place in Schein Hall at BIG Arts on Sanibel Island).

For theater, the **Florida Repertory Theatre** (Arcade Theater, 2267 Bay St., 239/332-4488) is a 10-year-old ensemble-based company with a year-round season. Split between musicals, comedies, and serious dramas, the professional repertory's season features nine productions, staged in a great, restored 1908 Victorian movie house.

Broadway musicals and family-friendly comedies are the mainstay at **Broadway Palm Dinner Theatre** (1380 Colonial Blvd., 239/278-4422, www.broadwaypalm.com), which has a main stage as well as a more intimate black-box theater (in which Off Broadway Palm stages smaller-scale comedies and musical revues as well as children's theater). Some of the performers are local, and they occasionally bring in talent from farther afield. Performances are accompanied by cocktails, salad bar, and a buffet.

Visual Arts

Lee County isn't the visual arts smorgasbord of Naples to the south. Still, there are several nice galleries and the local arts center. The Lee County **Alliance for the Arts** (10091 McGregor Blvd., 239/939-2787, www.artinlee.org, 9 A.M.–5 P.M. Mon.–Fri., 10 A.M.–3 P.M. Sat., free admission) is a multipronged arts organization founded in 1975. On a 10-acre campus, the organization contains the Frizzell Cultural Center of galleries, classrooms, a 175-seat indoor theater, and an outdoor amphitheater. The adjacent Charles Edwards Building houses local artists and arts groups. Local, regional, and national art and crafts are displayed in the public galleries, and the theaters host live theatrical performances and festivals throughout the year. Locals use the facility for adult and youth art classes of all kinds, from glass fusing to acrylics.

The densest concentration of crafts and fine arts in the area is to be found on the main drag of Matlacha on Pine Island. Many of the galleries are housed in little houses painted in a riot of sunset colors. Leoma Lovegrove's work is on display at **Matlacha Art Gallery** (4637 Pine Island Rd., 239/283-6453), you'll find the metal sculptures of Peggy McTeague next door at **Wild Child Art Gallery** (4625 Pine Island Rd., 239/283-6006), with a dozen or so other whimsical galleries within walking distance of the Matlacha drawbridge. So visitors can tour a number of these small galleries, Art Nights are held the second Friday of each month November–April, with the artists on hand to discuss their work.

Family-Friendly Attractions

Cape Coral, north of Fort Myers, isn't among the area's biggest draws for adults. As soon as children get a say, however, you may find yourself driving north with regularity. On a hot day, the kids will help navigate you to **Sun Splash Family Waterpark** (400 Santa Barbara Blvd., 239/574-0557, www.sunsplash waterpark.com, open March 12–Sept. 25, mostly 10 A.M.–6 P.M., Thurs. and Sat. until 9 P.M. in the summer, $14.95 adults, $12.95 children under 48 inches tall, $8.95 seniors, $4.95 age two and under), on the shore of Lake Kennedy. It's not huge, but there are two new tall water flume rides, a big family pool, a tot playground, a "river" tube ride, a café, and a super-fast ride called the Electric Slide, which is an enclosed tube in which you twist and turn at high speed. Not far away is **Mike Greenwell's Family Fun Park** (35 Pine Island Rd., Cape Coral, 239/574-4386, 10 A.M.–10 P.M. Sun.–Thurs., Fri. and Sat. until 11 P.M., $2.50–5.50 for miniature golf, 24 pitches/$2 in batting cages, plus equipment rental $1, $4–6.50 for go-carts). It fills in the gaps, with miniature

golf, batting cages, four go-cart tracks, a maze, an arcade, a sweet fish-feeding dock, and that abomination called paintball.

Located in downtown Fort Myers, another bad-weather delight for little kids comes at the **Imaginarium Hands-On Museum** (2000 Cranford Ave., 239/337-3332, www.cityft myers.com, 10 A.M.–5 P.M. Mon.–Sat., noon–5 P.M. Sun., $8 adults, $7 seniors, $5 children 3–12, under 3 free). It's a calm hands-on museum in which kids can fly and be free. A hurricane simulator, fossil dig, a miniature TV weatherman studio—it's hard not to get engrossed. There's also a fairly decent aquarium here, with scary moray eels and a lively coral reef tank.

Bigger kids have a couple of similar options in Fort Myers, science and nature centers more suited to school-age kids and adults. The **Calusa Nature Center & Planetarium** (3450 Ortiz Ave., Fort Myers, 239/275-3435, www.calusanature.com, museum and trail 9 A.M.–5 P.M. Mon.–Sat., 11 A.M.–5 P.M. Sun., $8 adults, $5 children 3–12) enables people to learn about southwest Florida's natural history in a number of ways. There are nature trails on boardwalks through pine flatwoods and cypress wetlands, on which you'll pass a Seminole village replica, a live bobcat, and a native birds-of-prey aviary for permanently injured birds. Dogs are welcome on the trails the first Sunday of the month. Inside the nature center, there are live animals and exhibits about their habitats. The best parts of the center are the regularly scheduled guided walks and animal lectures (cool stuff about snakes, gators, and Florida's endangered species). The center also has a planetarium, in which you can learn about the Hubble telescope and the night sky or just chill out while watching a laser light show.

The kind of Old Florida tourist draw people get nostalgic for, the **Shell Factory & Nature Park** (2787 Tamiami Trail N., North Fort Myers, 239/995-2141, www.shellfactory.com, free admission, miniature golf and boat rides $5) adopts a something-for-everyone approach (and has been doing so more or less successfully since the 1950s). There's a lot of kitschy shell-themed merchandise (inlaid shell toilet seats) to peruse while littler kids get wrapped up in the miniature golf, bumper boats, pitching cages, and a video arcade. Supposedly it has the world's largest collection of rare shells and coral, but the glass-blowing artisans are more entertaining to watch (there's also a funny little History of Glass Museum on-site). Outdoors you'll have to visit the nature park with a petting zoo (camels, llamas, donkeys, potbellied pigs, goats), trails, and a botanical garden. Sounds like a lot under one roof, huh? This is the kind of place where you simply have to give in and consume a batter-dipped hot dog followed by a pound of fudge.

After the fudge, you may need to get the blood flowing at Fort Myers's **Skatium** (2250 Broadway, Fort Myers, 239/461-3145, www.fm-skatium.com, public skating 1–2:45 P.M. and 5:30–7:30 P.M. Sat., 1–3 P.M. Sun.), a 72,000-square-foot facility with an ice-skating rink, an inline rink, laser tag arena, and video arcade. Most of the time, the rink is given over to local youth hockey and figure skating. If your kids are more into outdoor in-line skating or skateboarding, the **Fort Myers Skate Park** (2277 Grand Ave., downtown Fort Myers, 239/461-4445, 3–9 P.M. weekdays, 11 A.M.–9 P.M. weekends, $3/day, helmets mandatory) is right next door, the area's premier street-style course with wood and galvanized steel ramps surfaced with Skatelite Pro sitting on a 15,000-square-foot base.

SHOPPING

Downtown Fort Myers is the city's entertainment district, but east of **Centennial Park** there is a strip of cute shops, galleries, and cafés perfect for exploring on a walk. Strictly a driving route, the **Tamiami Trail,** or U.S. 41, is lined with the basic businesses that cater to locals. You'll also find chain restaurants of all stripes along the busy road.

Serious shoppers will head to **Tanger Outlets** (20350 Summerlin Rd., 239/454-1974), which has more than 60 shops stocking deeply discounted clothing, housewares, and gifts. It's

nothing you haven't seen before: Polo Ralph Lauren, Liz Claiborne, Mikasa, Jones New York, Gap, Dana Buchman, Ellen Tracy, Nine West, Easy Spirit, Greg Norman, Bass, Coach, Van Heusen, Izod, Koret, Swim Mart, Zales, etc.

A more pleasant shopping experience, capitalizing on the area's glorious weather, is the **Bell Tower Shops** (13499 U.S. 41 SE, 239/489-1221). It's an outdoor mall anchored by Saks Fifth Avenue with the usual upscale chains (Banana Republic, Ann Taylor, Williams-Sonoma) and a 20-screen movie theater.

Edison Mall (4125 Cleveland Ave., 239/939-5464) is more of a workhorse mall serving the local community, with Macy's, Dillard's, JCPenney, Sears, and lots of little mall stores. It's the biggest mall in southwest Florida.

Fleamaster's (4135 Dr. Martin Luther King Blvd., 239/334-7001, www.fleamall.com, 8 A.M.–4 P.M. Fri., Sat., and Sun.) is a serious hoot. It's a vast, 400,000-square-foot indoor flea market with something like 900 vendors—perfect for a rainy day exploration. From hardware to bath soap, this place sells some of everything.

The **International Design Center** (10800 Corkscrew Road, Estero, 239/390-5111, www.idcfl.com) opened in 2007 as an interior design resource for fine furniture, accessories, fabrics, wall coverings, lighting, kitchen and bath products, flooring, and antiques. More than 80 internationally known showrooms (Agostino's, Ann Sacks Tile & Stone, Clive Christian, Gallery on Fifth, Paris Ceramics, Stickley) anchor the 250,000-square-foot first phase, with more on the horizon.

Another newcomer in Estero, **Coconut Point** (23106 Fashion Dr., Intersection of U.S. 41 and Coconut Rd., 239/992-9966, www.simon.com) is an open, Main Street–style shopping destination with Mediterranean Revival architecture. The property includes 90,000 square feet of office condominiums, residential units, and 1.2 million square feet of retail space (not all of it yet occupied). There you'll find Dillards, West Coast Surf Shop, Coldwater Creek, Z Galleries, Old Navy, Muvico Theatres, and restaurants like Bice Grand Café, Ruth's Chris Steakhouse, California Pizza Kitchen, and Blue Water Bistro.

And the **Gulf Coast Town Center** (9903 Gulf Coast Main St., Fort Myers, 239/267-0783, www.gulfcoasttowncenter.com) is another new shopping center with some of the usual suspects, but its real calling card is the hugely buff **Bass Pro Shops Outdoor World** (www.basspro.com), a 75,000-square-foot retail center that includes Islamorada Fish Company Restaurant and a boat showroom along with outdoor gear, clothing, and accessories for hiking, backpacking, wildlife-viewing, camping, outdoor cooking, and hooking those bass. Kids will be entertained by the indoor aquariums and water features stocked with native fish species.

ACCOMMODATIONS
Under $100

For not a lot of money, you can get just about everything at **Rock Lake Resort** (2930 Palm Beach Blvd., 239/332-4080, www.bestlodgingswflorida.com, $63–105). The nine little cottages (18 units) encircling a small lake were built in 1946. Canoeing, lighted tennis courts, a nature trail, barbecue facilities, and comfortable porches overlooking the water—it all sits on Billy Creek, which allows direct access for small boats to the Caloosahatchee River. Rock Lake isn't fancy, but it's just a short drive to the beach and half a mile from downtown. Rooms are wheelchair accessible, and they also have rooms for the hearing impaired. Pets welcome.

$100–$150

At Matlacha Pass right near the drawbridge on Pine Island, we bedded down one night at the funky **Bridge Water Inn** (4331 Pine Island Rd., Matlacha, 800/378-7666, $109–175). Some multitasking enthusiasts have been known to throw a line right out their motel window into the water off the west deck below—fishing and catching the football game simultaneously. We contented ourselves watching the late-night

Enjoy nightly live music at the outdoor tiki bar at the Outrigger Beach Resort on Fort Myers Beach.

snook anglers battling catfish for their bait right out our window.

On Fort Myers Beach, a natural family destination, there are lots of midprice hotels and motels that fit the bill. **Sandpiper Gulf Resort** (5550 Estero Blvd., 239/463-5721, $90–245) is a fairly big, fairly low-rise hotel set in a few buildings. Opened in 1969, the resort has 63 large guest suites, some of them recently remodeled. There's a big pool surrounded by tropical gardens and the beach just beyond.

Over $150

Not far away from the Sandpiper, the **Outrigger Beach Resort** (6200 Estero Blvd., Fort Myers Beach, 239/463-3131, www.outriggerfmb.com, $160–270) is a comfortable highrise hotel with its own built-in entertainment that obviated the need for television one night: We watched through our big windows as a violent evening thunderstorm buffeted the beach directly below.

Significantly more money, but probably still a fairly good deal for what you get, **Gull Wing Beach Resort** (6620 Estero Blvd., 239/765-4300, $165–649) is another high-rise hotel on the quiet south end of Estero Island. There are 66 fairly upscale luxurious one-, two-, and three-bedroom family suites, with a lovely Gulf-side swimming pool, tennis courts, outdoor spa, barbecues, and gazebo area. Its parent company, SunStream Hotels & Resorts (800/625-4111, www.sunstream.com), is headquartered in Fort Myers Beach and has a number of other luxury properties locally, from the **Diamond Head Beach Resort** (2000 Estero Blvd., Fort Myers Beach, $200–420) to the **Pointe Estero Beach Resort** (6640 Estero Blvd., Fort Myers Beach, $151–529) to the **Santa Maria Harbour Resort** (7317 Estero Blvd., Fort Myers Beach, $155–355). These properties all share the full-service **Esterra Spa & Salon** (6231 Esterro Blvd., Fort Myers Beach, 239/765-4772, www.esterraspa.com) opened at the end of 2007.

Sanibel Harbour Resort & Spa (17260 Harbour Pointe Dr., Fort Myers, 239/466-4000, www.sanibel-resort.com,

$150–600) had a huge renovation and reopened in 2005 with swanky new guest rooms, lobby, meeting space, and restaurants (including a good Chicago-style steakhouse). This is a big place, with 240 hotel rooms, 107 more elite and "I-vant-to-be-alone" private concierge-style accommodations at Grande Bay, and waterfront condominiums as well. It's just about the most luxurious resort-style spot in Fort Myers, with two gorgeous pools, restaurants and lounges to suit all needs, and a spa.

Bonita Springs is a growing residential area of Florida's Gulf Coast, and one of the allures for the visitor is ◖ **Hyatt Regency Coconut Point Resort & Spa** (5001 Coconut Rd., Bonita Springs, 239/444-1234, $255–600), halfway between Fort Myers and Naples in Bonita Springs. It's a deluxe destination-style hotel with 454 elegantly appointed guest rooms and lots of stuff on-site, including a Raymond Floyd–designed championship golf course, a day spa, and views of pretty Estero Bay (beach not far away). Golf packages ($225–425 for a standard room) include accommodations, one round of golf at 18-hole Raptor Bay per night stay, a golf cart, unlimited range balls, a yardage book, and a golf club bag tag.

FOOD

Fort Myers is awash in chains, from Carrabba's to Olive Garden to T.G.I. Friday's. You have to look a little to find the quirky, independent gems.

Breakfast

For rib-sticking Am-UR-ican breakfasts, **Mel's Diner** (4820 S. Cleveland Ave., 239/275-7850, 6:30 A.M.–9:30 P.M. Sun.–Thurs., until 10 P.M. Fri. and Sat., $4–8) gives you competent diner staples. Mel's biscuits and sausage gravy will give you the get-up-and-go for a day at the beach, and kids love it here. It's a regional chain.

A delicious short stack of banana nut pancakes can be had for a song at **The Island's Pancake House** (Seagrapes Plaza off Estero Blvd., Fort Myers Beach, 239/463-0033, $1.50–7.50), along with a sturdy array of essential pre-kayaking breakfast foods.

We were assured that **Ristorante Adria** (4597 Pine Island Rd., Matlacha, 239/283-5151, 6:30A.M.–9P.M. daily, $10–25), formerly known as Mulletville, was the best place in Matlacha for breakfast. I can't disagree in light of my scrambled eggs, pork chop and grits, not to mention a little friendly banter with owner Luciano Moretti.

Fort Myers residents swear by the hangover special at **Oasis Restaurant** (2222 McGregor Blvd., 239/334-1566, 7 A.M.–3 P.M. Mon.–Fri., 8 A.M.–2 P.M. Sat. and Sun., $5–9), not that I'd ever need to know about that kind of thing— three fluffy eggs enfolding cheese, sausage, and sautéed veggies, instrumental in the post-booze, saturated-fat-induced flushing, topped off by 26 ounces of Gatorade in the car on the way back to the hotel to take a nap. Anyway, it serves breakfast all day, very unfussy, near the Edison & Ford estates.

Casual

With live piano and jazz singers nightly, **Biddle's Restaurant & Piano Bar** (Sanibel Beach Plaza, 20351 Summerlin Rd., 239/433-4449, 11 A.M.–10 P.M. Sun.–Thurs., until 11 P.M. Fri. and Sat., $19–36) is a fairly chic hangout: faux-painted walls, richly upholstered booths, and a Pacific Rim fusion menu at dinner (macadamia-crusted grouper). The weekend brunch is lovely and à la carte, with excellent shrimp and grits and nice outdoor seating.

If you find yourself at the Bell Tower shopping center, you can't go too far wrong with a stop at **Blue Pointe Oyster Bar & Seafood Grill** (13499 S. Cleveland Ave., 239/433-0924, www.bluepointerestaurant .com, 11:30 A.M.–10 P.M. Mon.–Thurs., until 11 P.M. Fri. and Sat., noon–9 P.M. Sun., $17–33). It's a slick New England–style fish restaurant with exemplary broiled swordfish and Florida black grouper, a pleasant crab cake, and good but slightly pricey oysters on the half shell.

Also at the Bell Tower, **Bistro 41** (13499 S. Cleveland Ave., 239/466-4141, 11:30 A.M.–10 P.M. Mon.–Thurs., until 11 P.M. Sat. and Sun., noon–9 P.M. Sun., $15–35) seems to be a local business favorite,

sophisticated with an American seafood-and-steaks menu. Beware the daily specials' prices, which can run close to $40. Otherwise, it's a pleasant, something-for-everyone kind of place with a nice outdoor patio.

On Fort Myers Beach on Estero Island, lots of casual beachfront restaurants make great use of the location and purvey mostly seafood-centric cuisine. **Matanzas Inn Restaurant** (416 Crescent St., 239/463-3838, 11 A.M.–10 P.M. daily, $15–23) has a great deck and a nice fried grouper plate. **Chloe's on the Beach** (2000 Estero Blvd., 239/765-0595, 7:30–11 A.M. and 5–9 P.M. Mon.–Sat., 7:30 A.M.–1 P.M. Sun., $16–32) is in the DiamondHead Beach Resort, with more upscale continental cuisine and gorgeous water views. Watch for Bonnie Lancaster on piano and check out the daily frozen drink special. And **Beach Pierside Grill** (1000 Estero Blvd., next to the pier, 239/765-7800, 11 A.M.–11 P.M. daily, $12–20) is more family friendly, featuring ribs, fried seafood platters, and the fat beach burger.

Fine Dining

My favorite fancy restaurant in Fort Myers is **◖ Veranda** (2122 2nd St., 239/332-2065, 11 A.M.–2:30 P.M. Mon.–Fri., 5:30–10 P.M. Mon.–Sat., $25–37), partly because it's set in two stately 100-year-old homes joined by publishing heir Peter Pulitzer in the 1970s for his buddy Fingers O'Bannon, who ran the restaurant then. So, it's the history, but the Veranda also seems like a happening place. The day I was there it was overrun by dozens of women in the Red Hat Society. (If you don't know about this, it's a huge international society of fun-loving older women who were galvanized by Jenny Joseph's poem "Warning," which reads: "When I am an old woman I shall wear purple/ With a red hat which doesn't go and doesn't suit me./And I shall spend my pension on brandy and summer gloves/And satin sandals, and say we've no money for butter." It goes on, but what you need to know is: older women in purple dresses and crazy red hats with plumes, whooping it up.) The menu at Veranda is traditional but with contemporary touches, meaning pan-seared local grouper crowned with wilted spinach, New York steak swathed in gorgonzola, and artichoke fritters stuffed with blue crab.

The new Coconut Point Mall, Estero has introduced a number of upscale eateries to the local gastronomic scene, the best of which are probably the hip **Blue Water Bistro** (239/949-2583, www.bluewaterbistro.net, 5:30–9:30P.M. Mon.–Thurs., 5:30–10P.M. Fri. and Sat., 4:30–8:30P.M. Sun.), the **Grillroom** (239/390-9081, 11:30A.M.–10P.M. Mon.–Thurs., 11:30A.M.–11P.M. Fri. and Sat., noon–

9P.M. Sun.), or the ubiquitous **Ruth's Chris Steakhouse** (239/948-8888, 4:30–10P.M. Mon.–Sat., until 9P.M. Sun.)—but only if you're planning on being at the mall anyway. Otherwise, settle in for a glass of something good and a nibble at the new **H2 Tapas and Wine Bar** (221 Bay St., Fort Myers, 239/226-1687, 4-11P.M. Mon.–Sat.), or a selection from the huge salad bar and then the slow-roasted prime rib at **Charley's Boat House Grill** (6241 Estero Blvd., Fort Myers Beach, 239/765-4700, 4:45–10P.M. daily).

Sanibel Island

There are more than 100 tiny, squiggly barrier islands that flank the coastline of the greater Fort Myers area. Of these, Sanibel stands out. Literally because it bucks the system and lies east–west in a gentle, shrimp-shaped curve, and figuratively because it is so well known and widely trafficked. The single biggest draw is nothing the chamber of commerce had any control over. The island's orientation, coupled with the fact that there are no offshore reefs, means that Sanibel is the recipient of the Gulf of Mexico's beneficence: more than 400 varieties of shells have been found along the 16 miles of white-sand beaches. The gently sloping sea floor, the patterns of tides and water circulation—it means that crown conch, lion's paw, angel wings, alphabet cones, and sand dollars wash up whole at your feet.

Birders would take issue with the smug shellers, though, on top draw. The birding on Sanibel is impressive for breadth as well as sheer numbers. More than half the island is taken up with the J. N. "Ding" Darling National Wildlife Refuge, 6,354 acres of preserved subtropical barrier island habitat for Florida's native wetland, part of the largest undeveloped mangrove ecosystem in the country. Either on foot, biking, canoeing, or with a narrated tram ride—but invariably with reverence and binoculars—naturalists and sightseers observe wading birds, wetland birds, and the array of other Sanibel wildlife.

Connected to the mainland by a three-mile-long scenic drive across a causeway from the mainland, Sanibel is a comfortable island. It welcomes families and traveling couples with an affable, easy charm and fairly reasonable prices. It isn't the kind of island on which you'll find gigantic resort hotels. Most accommodations are low-rise; in fact, buildings on the island can be only as tall as the tallest palm. There are no traffic lights, no street lamps, no motorized water sports (Jet Skis, Ski-Doos).

Sanibel's main street is Periwinkle Way, a picturesque thoroughfare that, pre-Hurricane Charley, was canopied by a tall stand of Australian pines (not native) and palms. A massive replanting effort in recent years has made it lushly leafed once again (but no pines). Shops, small inns, and casual restaurants punctuate the road from the Sanibel Lighthouse to Tarpon Bay Road, the air along the way alternately scented with fragrant blooming joewood and buckthorn and then a whiff of fat shrimp tossed in the deep fryer. Fort Myers is where to have your home base if you want museums, spectator sports, attractions; Captiva is where to go for blissful inaction. Sanibel is like the middle child who likes to mix it up a little—there are things to do beyond beach walking, with friendly restaurants and a great shell museum, but there's an inexorable pull toward sloth. It can't be a mortal sin if it's a vacation, right? Then it's just a venal one?

SPORTS AND RECREATION
Beaches

Sanibel is unusual among barrier islands due to its east–west orientation. Because of this, the surf is gentle and the shells arrive whole and pristine. The beaches along East, Middle, and West Gulf Drive slope gradually, making the shallows vast and safe for young waders and beachcombers. There are some beach rules to follow: Pets must be on leashes and cleaned up after (no pets at all on Captiva beaches); no alcoholic beverages on the beaches November–May; no open fires; and no collecting live shells. All public beach accesses on the island have restrooms, some with concessions and picnic tables. Beach parking is $2 per hour.

If you have to pick two beaches to visit from among the 14 miles of sand, start with **Lighthouse Beach & Fishing Pier** (turn left on Periwinkle Way, the first stop sign as you enter island, and follow Periwinkle Way, which terminates at the parking lot for the boardwalk) and **Bowman's Beach** (off Sanibel-

Captiva Rd.; turn left on Bowman's Beach Rd.). The heart of the former is the **Sanibel Lighthouse Boardwalk** (1 Periwinkle Way, Sanibel, 239/472-6397, www.ci.sanibel.fl.us), the most frequently photographed landmark on the island. It's been here since 1884 on the eastern tip of the island, near the bay side. The beach has a lovely T-dock fishing pier and a boardwalk nature trail through native wetlands. Bowman's Beach is more remote and quiet. Park in the lot and walk over a bridge to secluded white beach. It also offers showers and barbecue grills.

Beyond these, **Gulfside City Park** (mid-island on Algiers Ln. off Casa Ybel Rd.), **Tarpon Bay Beach** (also mid-island at the south end of Tarpon Bay Rd. at W. Gulf Dr.) and the **Causeway Beaches** (adjacent to the causeway on both sides) are inviting.

Shelling

Beaches are the most magnetic draw on Sanibel, with wide lengths of white-sand beaches and

The fruits of family togetherness can be washed away by the incoming tides. No matter, as there's always the beach again tomorrow.

SEA TURTLES

From the beginning of May to the end of October, the beaches of Sanibel play host to a different kind of visitor. Loggerheads, the most common sea turtles in Florida, make their way out of the Gulf and up the beaches to lay their eggs. An estimated 14,000 females nest in the southeastern U.S. each year, many of them from the northern tip of Fort Myers Beach to the Lee-Collier border of Bonita Beach. Called loggerheads because of their big heads, they can reach 200-350 pounds and measure about three feet long.

Female loggerheads return to the beaches on which they were born to lay their own eggs. They painstakingly dig nest cavities with their rear flippers, deposit about 100 golfball-sized eggs, cover them up, and head back out to sea. And two months later the two-inch hatchlings bust out and flap their way toward the moonlit sea. Sanibel has a lights-out policy on beaches so the little turtles aren't confused in their mission, stumbling toward a brightly lit condo instead.

According to the National Oceanic and Atmospheric Administration, the number of known nesting loggerheads has decreased 40 percent between the years 1998 and 2007. Habitat destruction, drought, hurricanes – all of these contribute to the dismal numbers. While currently listed as threatened, petitions have been drawn up to suggest their status should be changed to the more dire endangered.

What you can do to help:

- Pack up your beach trash, monofilament fishing line, and especially plastic bags and those plastic six-pack holders (they should have a name – I will henceforth refer to them as "flanisters"). Turtles mistake this stuff for tasty sea creatures undulating in the water, and they often get snarled in fishing line.

- Observe nesting turtles only from a distance. That goes for your curious pets, too. Dogs must be leashed on Sanibel, but do so even at night when no one's around to bug you. Last year a dog on one of the local beaches wiped out 67 hatchlings with one exuberant gambol.

- Stack up beach chairs or other items that might impede the baby loggerheads' progress toward the water.

- If you're staying in a beach house, close your drapes or blinds after dark and make sure if you use exterior lights that they are 25-watt yellow bug lights. Don't use flashlights, fishing lanterns, or flash photography on the beach.

- Leave nest identification markers in place. To report a wandering hatchling or a dead or injured turtle, call the Florida Fish & Wildlife Conservation Commission (800/DIAL-FMP) or the volunteer organization Turtle Time (239/481-5566).

some of the best shelling in the world. Some say 400 species of seashells dot the beaches here, from polka-dotted junonia to lacy apple murex and fat lightning whelks.

The most fruitful time to shell is early morning, at low tide, and after a storm, especially after the big-wave coastal storms in January and February. Other experts say the peak season for shelling is May–September. Walk slowly and look for seashells hidden just beneath the surface of the sand where the surf breaks, about where the water comes up to your knee. Wear polarized sunglasses so you can see

into the water, bring a bag or fanny pack for your treasure, and don't take any shell that's inhabited.

The south side of Sanibel has a wide shallow beach that seems to attract shells without battering them—they stay whole and perfect. You're more likely to find good ones where the competition isn't too fierce—the less populated stretch of beach, the better. (The beaches of North Captiva and Cayo Costa islands are known, among aficionados, for their lack of people and wealth of starfish, conchs, and sand dollars.) Generally, smaller shells are found closer to the Lighthouse Beach end, with larger shells the closer you get to Captiva. Common shells include: lightning whelk, cockle and scallop, murex, tulip, olive, little coquina, and conch. If you find a junonia, hang on to it for the bragging rights.

If you're coming up empty-handed, turn it over to the professionals, with one of the local shelling charters. **Duke Shells** ('Tween Waters Marina, Captiva, 239/472-5462) customizes three- and four-hour trips to include nature tours and shelling. **Captain Mike Fuery's Shelling Charters** (Captiva Island, 239/466-3649, private charter for up to four passengers is $225 for a three-hour trip) is another famous shelling outfit, its tours featured in *National Geographic, Southern Living, Martha Stewart,* and other magazines. Shelling trips for romantic couples seem to be a specialty.

But as Anne Morrow Lindbergh exhorted in *Gift from the Sea,* a book the aviator's wife penned in these parts:

The sea does not reward those who are too anxious, too greedy, or too impatient. To dig for treasures shows not only impatience and greed, but lack of faith. Patience, patience, patience, is what the sea teaches. Patience and faith. One should lie empty, open, choiceless as a beach—waiting for a gift from the sea.

Kayaking

The **Great Calusa Blueway Paddling Trail** is a 100-mile mapped-and-markered route for paddlers of all skill levels to explore. Following the trail of the area's early fishermen, the Calusa people, it runs along Lee County's coastal waters from Cayo Costa and Charlotte Harbor south through Pine Island Sound and Matlacha Pass to Estero Bay and the Imperial River in Bonita Springs.

Now, I'm not one of those outdoorsy types whose idea of fun is an Eskimo roll in fierce white water. I wanted a couple days of nice, easy kayaking, with stops for lunch and bird-watching, and a comfy bed at the end of each day.

The website (www.greatcalusablueway.com) gives details on the routes, what you'll see along the way, where to launch or stop, maps, GPS coordinates and more, but you still need to pick up a kayak or canoe somewhere. Outfitters offer guided trips (some even moonlight excursions) and there are numerous rentals and launch areas if you want to head out on your own.

We started the first day on the Pine Island Sound–Matlacha Pass section of the paddling trail. Crunching over the gravel at the Fish House Marina, we found our way to **Gulf Coast Kayak** (4530 Pine Island Rd., Matlacha, 239/283-1125, single kayak $30 half day, $40 full day). A shack, really, it had been graffitied with all the relevant information, from Watch Your Head to rental prices. We got paddles, life jackets, trail maps, and kayaks and put in just at the drawbridge at Matlacha Pass.

The second segment to be mapped, the Pine Island Sound trail is gentle and sheltered. We stopped to watch tiny black crabs scuttling along red mangrove trunks, great blue herons poised stoically in their shade. The odd bloop of leaping mullet kept things exciting as we meandered through backwaters and mangrove tunnels from marker 84 to marker 89. A few hours later, a couple of things became clear: The osprey population has rebounded in spades and paddling makes you hungry.

We headed back down through the deliciously named Buzzard Bay until we reemerged at the Old Fish House. Lunch was local shrimp quesadillas, local smoked mullet and a novelty food: fried mullet gizzard (it seems that the mullet, mostly vegetarian, is like a chicken in that it has no stomach but a crop and a gizzard). Order at the counter, eat at picnic tables, and watch the snook and needlenose gar churn the water down below.

Day two we put in at Fort Myers Beach, which is actually on the island of Estero, connected to Fort Myers by a causeway. There are several worthwhile beaches here (Bowditch Point Regional Park, Lynn Hall Memorial Park), but we set our sights on **Lovers Key State Park** (8700 Estero Blvd., Fort Myers

Lovers Key State Park on Estero Island contains a snack bar and bicycle, canoe, and kayak rentals.

Beach, 239/463-4588, 8 A.M.–sundown, $5/ car up to eight people, single occupancy car $3, pedestrians and bicyclists $1), another key embarkation point on the Great Calusa Blueway.

We headed to the **Nature Recreation Management** concessioneer (239/314-0110, www.naturerecreationmanagement.com, single kayak $20 for half day), picked up paddles and gear, then headed to the launch spot to put in our kayaks. Using our Blueway map, we made our way from marker 8 to markers 13 and 22, a bit of a headwind making progress slow. In parts the water was shallow, maybe a foot deep, and we quietly made our way out to congregations of ibis, egrets, and herons. Our ambition was to keep paddling to **Mound Key** (Estero Bay, 239/992-0311, daylight hours, free), a complex of Calusa mounds made of shells, fish bones, and pottery. Thought to be a sacred ceremonial center for the native people, in 1566 it was settled by the Spanish and became the site of the first Jesuit mission in the Spanish New World. That didn't last long as the Calusa weren't thrilled with the interlopers.

The shell construction contains mounded platforms, ceremonial mounds, ridges, substantial carved-out canals, and open water courts—evidence of a fairly elaborate community some 2,000 years ago. There are not a lot of interpretive markers or signs here, but it's a nice place for a picnic.

The wind thwarted our plans and we contented ourselves with a shorter paddle, peering up at osprey and American kestrels, then abruptly down as bottlenose dolphins kicked up a wake as they fed in the water near us.

Adventure Sea Kayak ('Tween Waters Inn Marina, 14000 Captiva Dr., Captiva, 239/437-5161, www.geocities.com/adventureseakayak, $40/person) conducts kayak tours, its specialty being interactive trips that focus on the wildlife, ecology, and history of the barrier islands. Also based in Captiva, **Captiva Kayak Company & Wildside Adventures** (11401 Andy Rosse Ln. at bayside McCarthy's Marina, Captiva, 239/395-2925, www.captivakayak.com) offers rentals, instruction, and sunrise, sunset, and starlight tours. On

Sanibel, **Tarpon Bay Explorers** (900 Tarpon Bay Rd., Sanibel, 239/472-8900, www.tarpon-bayexplorers.com, $15–180) has a range of services, from canoe, kayak, and bike rentals to guided tours. And if you just want to rent a kayak or canoe, try **Gulf Coast Kayak** (4530 Pine Island Rd., Matlacha, 239/283-1125, www.gulfcoastkayak.com, single kayak or canoe $30 half day, $40 full day) or farther south with **Estero River Canoe & Tackle Outfitters** (20991 S. Tamiami Trail, Estero, 239/992-4050, www.all-florida.com/swestero. htm), which offers 300 canoes and kayaks, all different kinds.

Sea School

The newly opened **Sanibel Sea School** (414 Lagoon Dr., 239/472-8585, www.sanibelseaschool.org) is dedicated to teaching children and adults about marine ecosystems using the setting of the barrier island habitats of Sanibel and Captiva as an opportunity to touch, feel, and understand. Adult classes may focus on bivalves, gastropods, local history, and natural history, say, with field trips to study mollusk distribution, fish seining, investigating the mangroves at Blind Pass and exploring the island on Indigo Trail and the Bailey Tract hikes. Call for a schedule of classes and drop-in events.

Biking

It's an island pastime partly because it's relatively safe (there are 25 miles of wide, paved biking path) and partly because you can cover serious ground on these pancake-flat islands. I biked blissfully from the eastern tip of Sanibel to the northern tip of Captiva, stopping occasionally to dip my toe in the Gulf. You can bike on the main drags, Sanibel-Captiva Road and Periwinkle Way, or swing through a stretch of the J. N. "Ding" Darling Wildlife Refuge, or skirt the water's edge along Gulf Drive. The **Sanibel-Captiva Islands Chamber of Commerce** (1159 Causeway Rd., Sanibel, 239/472-1080) has a free bike path map.

Many inns on Sanibel and Captiva offer complimentary bikes to their guests—ask

before you set up a rental elsewhere. The oldest bike shop on Sanibel is **Billy's Rentals** (1470 Periwinkle Way, 239/472-5248, www.billys rentals.com, 8:30A.M.–5P.M. daily, two-hour bike rentals range $5–10, also daily and weekly rentals). Billy's offers regular hybrids, but a range of kooky stuff as well, from adult trikes to recumbent bikes, Segways, and these multiperson surreys (that, given their width, make them somewhat of a liability on the bike paths). You can also rent jog strollers and cool motor scooters at Billy's. **Finnimores Bikes & Skates** (2353 Periwinkle Way, 239/472-5577, www.finnimores.com, 9 A.M.–5 P.M. daily, four-hour rentals $8–15) is another wonderful shop, with no charge for delivery and pickup for a multiday rental. It also has inline skates (they come with free helmet and pad rentals), umbrellas, fishing equipment, boogie boards, and most other fun-in-the-sun paraphernalia.

Birding

Birds just like it here. Some live here year-round, other migrating species choose this island as a stopover or a convenient flyway terminus. J. N. "Ding" Darling National Wildlife Refuge is a wealth of avian splendor, but the rest of the island is a birder's paradise, too. Sanibel boasts so many habitats—freshwater wetlands, brackish mangrove estuaries, beaches, woodland—that 240 different species feel at home here.

The ornithologically inclined have websites and chat groups devoted entirely to bird trails and spots on Sanibel. One of the local papers even has a regular bird column, and traffic stops fairly regularly for the recalcitrant crossing heron or egret.

Part of the thrill is the chase, tramping around with your binoculars trained on the treetops or water's edge at low tide. Here's where to look for them: rare white pelicans hang out in Pine Island Sound; ospreys and eagles nest on telephone poles above the bike paths and along Sanibel-Captiva Road; wood storks troll for snacks in roadside ditches in the winter; burrowing owls dig tunnels in shopping center parking lots; sandhill cranes walk gracefully across expanses of lawn in groups of three. The list goes on. The lighthouse area of Sanibel is a good place to see birds, as are the mangrove islands off Pine Island Sound, as is Tarpon Bay on Sanibel. The little clumps of island off the causeway area attract lots of species as well. For an absolute sure thing, you'll hit pay dirt in Periwinkle Park, which has an aviary for lovebirds, toucans, flamingos, and talking birds.

J. N. "Ding" Darling National Wildlife Refuge

J. N. "Ding" Darling National Wildlife Refuge (1 Wildlife Dr., Sanibel, 239/472-1100, www.fws.gov/dingdarling, 7:30 A.M.–sunset, $5/vehicle, $1 walker/biker, $10 tram ride) takes up more than half of Sanibel Island. The refuge was named for Pulitzer Prize–winning cartoonist Jay Norwood Darling, the first environmentalist to hold a presidential cabinet post (during FDR's administration), and is an absolute marvel. It contains a visitors center, a five-mile driving tour route, hiking trails, tram service, canoe and kayak rentals, and guided interpretive programs.

The 6,354-acre refuge is made up of a variety of estuarine and freshwater habitats. You'll see mudflats and mangrove islands, wide swaths of seagrass and open water, West Indian hardwood hammocks and ridges, places poetically described as spartina swales, etc. But the real draw is birds.

Ordinarily I'd advise walking or biking through a refuge like this, 2,825 acres of it designated as wilderness area—you know, go at your own pace, get a close-up look at things. But then you'd miss out on the naturalist-narrated tram ride full of competitive birders. Equipped with binoculars, one yells out, "There's a tricolored heron." Someone else, dripping disdain, counters, "No, it's a little blue."

An up-close look at birders is half the fun of a day at "Ding" Darling. On the tram ride, listening to these birders, I learned to recognize black-crowned night herons and immature ibis, and I saw wood storks, peregrine falcons, and a wealth of the 238 bird species that hang out in the refuge. The best birding time is early morning, about an hour before or after low tide, when you'll see birders equipped with cameras set up on tripods. Watch what they're watching, and ask questions. You'll see things rare and magnificent. The wildlife observation tower is a glorious place to hang out any time of the day, and the education center (open 9 A.M.–5 P.M. daily Nov.–Apr., until 4 P.M. the rest of the year) provides a little guidance to the rookie.

Tarpon Bay Explorers (900 Tarpon Bay Rd., Sanibel, 239/472-8900), which runs the tram tour, also offers a 90-minute kayak trail tour ($30 adults, $20 children) along the Commodore Creek water trail and a sunset paddle ($40 adults, $25 children) out to the rookery islands in the refuge. You'll see hundreds upon hundreds of egrets, herons, anhingas, ibis, etc., all bedded down in the treetops for the night, the lush green dense with brilliant puffs of white feathers.

SIGHTS
Bailey-Matthews Shell Museum

Slippersnail. White baby ear. Ponderous ark. So poetic, these names for shells. The Bailey–Matthews Shell Museum (3075 Sanibel-Captiva Rd., Sanibel, 239/395-2233, www.shellmuseum.org, 10 A.M.–5 P.M. daily, $7 adults, $4 children 5–16, children 4 and under free) will make a shell collector out of most people. It's not a vast museum, a pleasant 90 minutes or so, but it equips you to go out there and get yourself some of Neptune's treasures. Shells are arranged in thematic groupings from around the world, with an emphasis on the local offerings, and there are anthropological exhibits on humanity's relationship to shells (did you know that Native Americans' use of conch shells as weapons was the origin of the expression, "conk on the head"?). There's also a video called *Mollusks in Action* (oxymoron? you be the judge) shown five times each day. Children, upon entering the museum, are given a maddeningly difficult scavenger hunt sheet, in which they need to locate certain

COURTESY OF LEE COUNTY VCB

Exhibits display shells from local waters and around the world at the Bailey-Matthews Shell Museum.

kinds of shells around the museum. I'm going to find them all next time.

Sanibel Historical Village and Museum

A work in progress, Sanibel Historical Village and Museum (950 Dunlop Rd., Sanibel, 239/472-4648, 10 A.M.–4 P.M. Tues.–Sat., until 1 P.M. in the summer, $3 suggested donation) is the kind of loving effort feasible only by a truly smitten group of local boosters. Longtime residents of Sanibel are zealots, and as such they celebrate the local history with a vengeance. This little cluster of historic buildings dragged from all over the island includes pioneer Clarence Rutland's original island home from the early 1900s, the Burnap Cottage built in 1898, Miss Charlotta's Tea Room restored to its 1930s look, Bailey's General Store, the original Sanibel post office, an old schoolhouse, an antique Model T, a Sanibel Lighthouse display, archived newspaper articles, and photos. The on-site town historian is a wealth of information and a wonderful storyteller.

Old Town

For more historical sightseeing, the East End village of Old Town was originally a fish camp built by Cuban fishermen in the 1860s, prior to construction of the lighthouse in 1884. The Sanibel Historical Society has a walking and biking tour map of 19 historic sites along a stretch of about 2.5 miles. You can pick up a copy of the map at the chamber of commerce (1159 Causeway Rd.) or at the Sanibel Historical Village and Museum.

ENTERTAINMENT AND EVENTS
Theater

The **Schoolhouse Theater** (2200 Periwinkle Way, Sanibel, 239/472-6862, www.theschoolhousetheater.com, 8 P.M. Mon.–Sat., $25), an institution in town, moved in 2004 to a larger, 160-seat theater. The little community group puts on crowd-pleasing musical reviews. With a grand piano on stage, the theater does all-music performances. The restored 1896 one-room schoolhouse that used to house the theater has been hauled over to the Sanibel Historical Village and Museum to add another element to the little cluster of historic sites.

If you're just itching to be entertained, catch a flick at the **Island Cinema** (535 Tarpon Bay Rd., in Bailey's shopping center, 239/472-1701). It shows first-run mainstream films.

Festivals

The biggest festival in the area takes place peak season, in March, but it's still worth considering. Sanibel hosts an annual **Shell Fair** (usually held at the Sanibel Community House, 2173 Periwinkle Way) which draws serious shell collectors from around the world. It's the largest and longest-running shell festival in the country.

SHOPPING

Sanibel's shopping is as low-key as the island itself. **Periwinkle Place** (2075 Periwinkle Way, www.periwinkleplace.com) boasts 28 cute shops, a tropical bistro called Gully's, and the pleasant Sanibel Day Spa, all connected by covered walkways and shaded by banyan trees. Its clothing shops are mostly geared to beach-and sportswear; there are nice toy and swimsuit shops. **Olde Sanibel Shoppes** (630 Tarpon Bay Rd., 239/939-3900) is another cluster of gift shops, clothing, and jewelry, with a couple of casual restaurants thrown into the mix. The **Village Shops** (2340 Periwinkle Way) has roughly a similar lineup, and the 15 shops arrayed in the low pink buildings of **Tahitian Gardens** (1975–2019 Periwinkle Way) sell artisan candles, bright cotton clothing, jewelry, bathing suits, T-shirts, giftware, etc. This center also contains one of the island's best breakfast spots, the Sanibel Café.

None of this will rock your world—for a real one-of-a-kind island shopping experience, browse a while in **She Sells Sea Shells** (1157 Periwinkle Way, 239/472-8080). The funky shop contains shells from all over the place, but many are the same species you'll see stooped enthusiasts mining for (some even have lighted miner's hats in the early mornings) along Sanibel beaches.

And if you need a regular old grocery store, **Bailey's** (2477 Periwinkle Way, 239/472-1516, 7 A.M.–9 P.M. daily) is the biggest local market.

Galleries

Now, Sanibel has got some galleries worth investigating. It seems to attract residents of artistic temperament, many of them opening shops that feature their work. **Tower Gallery** (751 Tarpon Bay Rd., 239/472-4557, www.tower-gallery-sanibel.com) is a good place to start, and it's hard to miss in an electric blue and green building. It's a cooperative of 23 local artists. Representing all media and a real mix of styles, the work in the gallery is all juried. Right nearby you'll find another small cooperative called the **Hirdie Girdie Gallery** (2490 Library Way, 239/395-0027), and next door to it the **Tin Can Art Gallery** (2480 Library Way, 239/472-9002), with the whimsical work of artist Bryce McNamara.

Sanibel's **BIG Arts** (Barrier Island Group for the Arts, 900 Dunlop Rd., 239/395-0900) is a community cultural arts organization that has a center for island arts. It has two galleries open to the public (1–4 P.M. Mon.–Fri.), a sculpture garden, and performance space. Exhibits change monthly, and there are frequent workshops, lectures, films, and concerts.

Periwinkle Way is home to several small galleries. One of the more notable is the **Seaweed Gallery** (2055 Periwinkle Way, 239/472-2585, www.seaweedgallery.com), an explosion of color, showing local artists' work from whimsical painted furniture to tropical paintings, jewelry, pottery, and mermaids.

ACCOMMODATIONS

There's very little on Sanibel Island that's dirt cheap. On the other hand, nothing is particularly glamorous and über-swanky. It's the kind of place where you get a sweet apartment, hotel, or motel rental a few steps from the beach, and you don't worry about whether there are luxurious Aveda products in the bathroom because you are lulled to sleep by the sound of gentle, rhythmic surf.

If you're thinking about staying for a whole

week it makes sense to rent a condo or cottage. **Cottages to Castles of Sanibel & Captiva** (2427 Periwinkle Way, 239/472-6385, www.cottages-to-castles.com) has a number of intimate and affordable one-week rentals (okay, they also offer this gigundo seven-bedroom pink house called Sandhurst that was featured as the 2004 MTV Summer Beach House). The rates on the condos are very reasonable off-season ($600–1,750 weekly).

Under $150

My two favorites on the island have a subtle patina of Old Florida nostalgia to them. Both are well appointed and with contemporary touches (Wi-Fi, yada, yada), but they have a historic feel, the kinds of places you could imagine visiting unswervingly for decades until you're putting your teeth in a glass before you turn the bedside light off. The **(Island Inn on Sanibel Island** (3111 W. Gulf Dr., 239/472-1561, www.island-innsanibel.com, $150–660) in fact opened in 1895. Look at the scrapbook of clippings to get a sense for who has roamed this compound of lovely little cottages and larger lodges on 10 acres with 550 feet of unobstructed beachfront. Allures include shuffleboard, table tennis, and bike rentals, but it's the warmth of the staff and other guests that seems anachronistic. The same can be said of **(West Wind Inn** (3345 W. Gulf Dr., 239/472-1541, www.westwind-inn.com, $174–303), a casual beachfront place in the quiet part of the island. Rooms have kitchenettes, but don't skip breakfast at its Normandie Seaside Restaurant, which seems to be a locals' morning hangout. West Wind's stretch of beach is a marvel for stargazing.

Shalimar Resort (2823 W. Gulf Dr., 239/472-1353, www.shalimar.com, $165–385 per night, $2,095–2,625 per week) is another beloved getaway, with 33 one- and two-bedroom cottages, apartments, and motel efficiencies spread around a huge property right on the Gulf. All units have full kitchens and the pool is lovely.

Over $150

Sundial Beach Resort (1451 Middle Gulf Dr., Sanibel, 239/472-4151, www.sundialresort.com, $179–749) has 270 one- and two-bedroom suites that all have a condo vibe, complete with full kitchens. It sits in 33 acres of tropical lushness right along the beach and has a tremendous weekday camp for children 4–11. **Sanibel Inn** (937 E. Gulf Dr., Sanibel, 239/472-3181, www.sanibelinn.com, $189–589) is smaller, with 68 hotel rooms and one-bedroom suites. Outside, the inn sits in the shade of more than 600 palms, with the gentle flutter of butterfly gardens all around. Inside, Zen-like bamboo flooring and a warm palette of grass green, sea blue, and golden wheat imbue rooms with a quiet grace. The Sanibel Inn also offers a wonderful children's educational/entertainment program. For adults, the nearby Dunes Golf & Tennis Club awaits.

FOOD

There's something funny about the restaurants of Sanibel. Mostly spread out across Periwinkle Way, there's a tremendous homogeneity to them: fun, a little raucous, lots of fried seafood, a stunning dearth of green vegetables. (Iceberg lettuce doesn't count as a green vegetable. It's a cellulose doorstop.) Prices are steep but not alarmingly so at most Sanibel restaurants. You're paying for the view, but you can defray the cost by doing the, gulp, early-bird special before 6 P.M. offered at many restaurants.

Breakfast

Lighthouse Cafe (362 Periwinkle Way, 239/472-0303, breakfast served 7 A.M.–3 P.M. daily, open 5–9 P.M. in the winter months, $5–9 for breakfast) usually beats the early-morning competition, hands down, whether you're a fan of the seafood Benedict or the blueberry whole-wheat hotcakes.

Lunch

Novelist Randy Wayne White is about the biggest booster this area has. Although I know when he was young he was a light tackle fishing guide right in this neighborhood, I'm not quite sure how often he's in residence at the restaurant named for the main character of many of his books set in these parts. Wayne White is actually purported to be a good cook, with a seafood cookbook to his name. Regardless of who's cooking, **Doc Ford's Sanibel Rum Bar & Grille** (975 Rabbit Rd., 239/472-8311, 11 A.M.–1 A.M. daily, $11–30) is a hoot, with lots of TVs blaring the game, good sandwiches, great drinks. The food—panko-crumb fried shrimp, Cuban sandwich, pulled pork—is better than it needs to be for such a laid-back setting.

Sanibel Café (2007 Periwinkle Way, 239/472-5323, 7 A.M.–3 P.M. daily, $8–17) seems like a locals' hangout, unpretentious and friendly. Go for the fat hamburgers peeking from under a mantle of molten blue cheese.

Dinner

The menus at the following three places seem cut from the same mold. At **McT's Shrimp House & Tavern** (1523 Periwinkle Way, 239/472-3161, 4–10 P.M. daily, $12–22) the draw is the Sanibel Steamer, a huge tray of steamed seafood, or the all-you-can-eat shrimp and crab platters. It's lively, it's casual. The same can be said of **Island Cow** (2163 Periwinkle Way, 239/472-0606, 7 A.M.–10 P.M. daily, $8–16), which occasionally has a mooing contest among the guests, the winner of which

gets a T-shirt in addition to deep and abiding respect. There's also live music, a wonderful outdoor patio, and generous heart-stopping seafood baskets with fries. And **Jacaranda** (1223 Periwinkle Way, 239/472-1771, 5–10 P.M. daily, $16–32) has a funky bar and a screened patio (good for when the bugs are biting). The Jac has music nightly (reggae on the weekends), sweet briny treats from the patio raw bar, and a fairly extensive late-night menu.

For Italian cuisine, Sanibel has a couple of options. **Dolce Vita** (1244 Periwinkle Way, 239/472-5555, 5:30–10:30 P.M. nightly, $17–30), glamorous by island standards, is organized around a central bar with live music on a baby grand. The menu is really only nominally Italian (there's veal piccata), but other items, like rotisserie chicken with corn tortillas or Moroccan chicken tagine, are nicely done, so why be a stickler. **Matzaluna** (1200 Periwinkle Way, 239/472-1998, 4:30–9:30 P.M. daily, $11–17) is more traditional. The wood-fired pizzas get top honors, with sturdy baked pasta dishes (lasagna, stuffed shells) placing a close second. Like many island spots, it offers two-for-one drink specials during happy hour, and $0.99 pizza slices at the bar.

Captiva Island

Sanibel's northern neighbor, Captiva Island, is tinier, only about a half-mile wide and five miles long. It is at once more laid-back and more exclusive, perfect for meditative solipsism or romantic cocooning. Captiva has less commerce, fewer hotels and inns, fewer people in general. A fair percentage of the island's houses, all recessed demurely behind dense pines and brambly foliage, are the beach retreats of affluent and often absentee owners.

It's quieter than Sanibel, Captiva Drive running its length. Captiva has a relaxed downtown area of beach bars, restaurants, and gift shops that draw their inspiration from the beaches of Key West and the winsome lyrics

of Jimmy Buffet tunes. Captiva Village uses loud pastels with reckless abandon, the colors of orange sherbet and plastic pink flamingos, and some of the restaurants adopt a flotsam-and-kitschy-jetsam approach to decorating (see the Bubble Room), but there's still an underlying sophistication. Things are casual without being slipshod—which allows for much more upscale accommodations on Captiva without them seeming out of place. South Seas Island Resort dominates a whole section at the northern tip of Captiva, where it breaks before the island of North Captiva (once attached). Its sprawling grace and glorious beach set a tone for the island.

There are few attractions on the island, although much to do. Walk, run, fish, canoe, sit and read, or just sit. Anne Morrow Lindbergh was so inspired by Captiva's tranquility that it's where she wrote her best-selling book, *A Gift from the Sea,* parts of which serve as testament to this small island's salubrious effect on people's psyches:

> I want first of all . . . to be at peace with myself. I want a singleness of eye, a purity of intention, a central core to my life that will enable me to carry out these obligations and activities as well as I can. I want, in fact–to borrow from the language of the saints–to live "in grace" as much of the time as possible.

SPORTS AND RECREATION
Beaches
Captiva's beaches are less populated than those on Sanibel, for a couple of reasons. First, there are more private homes on Captiva, visited sporadically by their affluent owners. Thus, there are just fewer feet to churn the sand and rustle the packs of waterbirds. Second, the shelling is better on Sanibel. But Captiva's waters are clearer, the swimming slightly better. **Captiva Beach** (at the end of Captiva Dr., free but limited parking) is a case in point—beautiful sand, lovely clear water, and only a few people in sight. It's a great place from which to watch the sunset. Because of fairly swift currents, don't count on swimming at **Turner Beach** (Sanibel-Captiva Rd. at Blind Pass Bridge), but it's still a favorite among fisherfolk and shellers.

Gulf-side beach erosion has been a problem in recent years, exacerbated by recent storms. Private and public funds have been raised to restore beaches by pumping in sand from offshore.

Fishing
Usually at the beginning of July, anglers start convening in Boca Grande Pass for the annual **World's Richest Tarpon Fishing Tournament,** but the Board of Directors of the Boca Grande Area Chamber of Commerce voted to take a couple years off since 2007 to allow the fish population to rebound. The South Seas Island Resort hosts the annual **Caloosa Catch & Release Tournament** on Captiva each June. This one is known as the largest single-site public flats tournament in Florida, with more than $120,000 in cash and prizes in 2007. People here are serious about fishing, and not just about the seasonal giant tarpon.

What are you likely to catch? Redfish is a pretty steady catch in these parts, some over 10 pounds. The species has rebounded since the New Orleans blackening craze made them a hot commodity. They can be fished on the flats. Snook is best in the springtime (season is closed Dec. 15–Jan. 31 and June, July, and Aug.), and you'll catch lots of speckled trout in the winter when they're especially large. They tend to hang out in 3–5 feet of water near the edges of the grass flats and sand holes. Tarpon are the area's biggest draw, huge fish that range 100–150 pounds with lots of fight in them. (Some say the very first tarpon ever taken on rod and reel was in southwest Florida, near Punta Rassa across San Carlos Bay from Sanibel in 1885—but how would anyone know that?) Tarpon season runs from the latter part of April through August. Then there are cobia (here Feb.–July, but best in Apr. and May), tripletail, and jacks for much of the year on the flats, and black grouper far out in the Gulf. Commercial catches of grouper have been limited recently, so sportfishers might benefit from increased numbers.

Fishing charters start at around for $200 for a half-day trip, and the charter captain provides the boat, fishing license, fishing gear, equipment, and bait. Sometimes the client pays an additional fee for gas—ask about this. As a matter of etiquette, a tip of $20–50 is customary, as is buying your captain and crew a meal or drinks at the end of your fishing trip. Many guides will clean and fillet your edible catch—if you don't want all the fish, give it to whomever seems interested dockside. As for mounting and taxidermy: Big fish are largely catch and release, so have a picture taken of yourself with your catch before you release it.

Then, one of the new breed of high-tech taxidermists will create a lifelike plastic model of your prize.

Figure out whether you want to do deepwater fishing, cast in the flats, or maybe take a fly-fishing lesson, then visit the marinas to ask around about charter captains, prices, what people are catching, and where. **Capt. Jim's Charters** ('Tween Waters Marina, 15951 Captiva Dr., 239/472-1779, $225–350) does back-bay fishing; **Capt. Joe's Charters** (Castaways Marina, Sanibel-Captiva Rd., Sanibel, 239/472-8658, www.captjoescharters.com, $250–400) does back-bay and fly-fishing; **Captain Van Hubbard/Let's Go Fishin'** (239/697-6944, www.capt-van.com, $350–600) does sight casting for giant tarpon and snook seasonally; **Soulmate Charters** (17544 Lebanon Rd., Fort Myers, 239/851-1242, www.soulmatecharters.com, $350–550) offers backcountry fishing with light spin tackle and fly-fishing. The list goes on, with more than 50 charter captains willing to help you wet a line.

Sailing

I have a little book that looks like a passport. I keep it in a safe place and flip it open occasionally to impress people. It says I'm U.S. Sailing certified for basic keelboat, which means I am henceforth only to be addressed with, "Hey, sailor." I took the three-day certification program with **Offshore Sailing School** (16731 McGregor Blvd., Fort Myers, 800/221-4326, www.offshore-sailing.com, courses for beginners, racers, and cruisers, basic keelboating class tuition $895). It's a tremendous amount of fun, three days on the water with an instructor and three other students, plus hours of classroom time learning all the sailing jargon (who you calling a "jibe ho"?), parts of the boat, points of sail, etc. At the end of the class you take a fairly difficult 80-question test, and you get out and show your sailing chops to your teacher, complete with man-overboard demonstrations and doing a quick stop by "shooting" into the wind (I stank at that).

If you're a goal-oriented person, it's a great

activity to build a vacation around. You learn on a midsize daysailer, a Colgate 26, designed specifically for training and chosen by the U.S. Naval Academy to replace their training fleet. From here, you can take any number of other courses designed for more advanced sailors—performance sailing, live-aboard cruising, a camp for racing sailors—or just occasionally wave your little blue U.S. Sailing book around like I do, and as a party trick tie nautical knots.

Classes are held at the Pink Shell Beach Resort & Spa in Fort Myers Beach and the South Seas Island Resort on Captiva. Call for information.

SHOPPING

Hand-painted gewgaws and shell trinkets, you'll find this stuff along Sanibel-Captiva Road and in the Captiva Village area along Andy Rosse Lane, at the only four-way stop on Captiva. The most compelling of the shops here is **Jungle Drums** (11532 Andy Rosse Ln., 239/395-2266), a collection of wildlife, island, and environmental art in an array of media. **HO2 Island Outfitters** (Celebration Center, Andy Rosse Ln., 239/472-7507) nearby purveys funky sandals, sunglasses, and beach-appropriate attire.

ACCOMMODATIONS
Under $150

If you want to be where the action is, **C** **Captiva Island Inn** (11508 Andy Rosse Ln., 239/395-0882, www.captivaislandinn.com, $99–300) is a darling bed-and-breakfast right in the middle of teeny Captiva Village. There are traditional B&B rooms, one- and two-bedroom cottages, a loft, and a suite. The owners also have a four-bedroom, four-and-one-half-bath house for big gatherings.

Jensen's has two options, one more fishing-focused, the other beachier. **Jensen's on the Gulf** (15300 Captiva Dr., 239/472-5800, motel suites $150–300, apartments $175–400, houses $300–600) has nine units directly on the Gulf. **Jensen's Twin Palm Cottages** (15107 Captiva Dr., 239/472-5800, one-bedroom $110–180, two-bedroom $125–190), on the other hand, are spread out along the bay-side marina and fishing action. You can rent a boat right here, grab some bait, and be out on the water before your pajamas have had time to miss you. The 14 cheerful tin-roofed cottages have kitchens and screened porches.

Over $150

The biggest game in recent years in town has been **(** **South Seas Resort** (5400 Plantation Rd., Captiva, 239/472-5111, www.south-seas-resort.com, $229–1259) at the northern tip of the island, which closed after Hurricane Charley in 2004 for a massive $140 million renovation. Set in 330 acres of lush mangroves, the resort, which has an ownership time-share complex too, is casual but stunning, with lovely rooms (Euro Top bedding, granite countertops, and flat panel televisions) and added draws such as a much-lauded children's program, world-renowned sailing, pools, kayaking, a fishing pier, and 2,100 feet of dockage for boats up to 130 feet in length, and Gulf-edged golf.

The main pool area at the resort offers posh cabanas for rent with a private butler and spa services. The Point restaurant overlooking the pool offers casual Caribbean fare and an up-scale bar upstairs provides sweeping views of Pine Island Sound. The renovation includes 24,000 square feet of enhanced meeting space complete with high-speed Internet access, video and data projectors, and new sound and lighting systems. Captiva Golf Club was redesigned by Chip Powell as one of the Top Five Short Courses in the world.

'Tween Waters Inn Beach Resort (15951 Captiva Dr., Captiva, 239/472-5161, www .tween-waters.com, $155–650) is another heavy-hitter on the island, with a huge resort complex that stretches from the bay side to the Gulf side. The inn dates back to 1926, when the collection of cottages hosted Teddy Roosevelt, Charles and Anne Lindbergh, Roger Tory Peterson, and J. N. "Ding" Darling. There are 137 water-view rooms, suites, and cottages; Olympic-sized and children's pools; tennis courts (free to guests); a day spa; four restaurants; and a full-service marina. The rooms are perfectly lovely, and there's a nice complimentary breakfast for guests, but it's all the cool amenities that make this a great experience. Rent a canoe or kayak and head out for the day.

FOOD

How to break this into categories? There are few discernible cuisines in restaurants here, and most all of them are casual and reasonably priced, set in pastel-colored cottages with sprawling outdoor seating. There's a pervasive beachy aesthetic and a funky charm.

A case in point is the ridiculous **(** **Bubble Room** (15001 Captiva Dr., 239/472-5558, 11:30 A.M.–2:30 P.M. and 5–10 P.M. daily, $15–28). First off, the waiters and bartenders are all in scouting uniforms, with patches of their own devising meticulously sewn on. They wear neckerchiefs, deep tans, weird hats, and mischievous grins. No explanation. Then there's the decor—like Santa's workshop, with toy trains and elves and hobbyhorses, but then add in 2,000 movie stills and glossies, lots of Betty Boop stuff, oh, and a list of other stuff too long to enumerate. It's a "more is more" motif. The food is fairly good, from fried shrimp to grilled fish brushed with a pineapple/ginger marinade, but beware the mammoth cakes in the dessert case—when taken internally, they are known to cause side effects such as bloating, night sweats, and, in very rare cases, total paralysis.

Andy Rosse Lane, the area often called Captiva Village, has a cluster of fun places. The **Keylime Bistro** (in the Captiva Island Inn, 11509 Andy Rosse Ln., 239/395-4000, 8 A.M.–10 P.M. daily, lounge until 1 A.M., live entertainment daily) has a robust purple and lime green color scheme, hard to miss, and a guy on the patio playing Jimmy Buffet covers or things that sound like Jimmy Buffet covers. The kitchen serves a great grouper sandwich as well as a delicious but dangerously drippy sausage sandwich with onions and peppers; at dinner, head for shrimp scampi or grouper piccata. Good margaritas, and they have a Bloody Mary bar for Sunday brunch.

TROPICAL FRUIT

Jackfruit, carambola, mamey sapote, sapodilla, lychee, longans, pineapple, papaya. These are the kinds of fruits you imagine eating on a far-flung tropical island. Fling a little closer, and you've got Pine Island. Just west of Cape Coral, it is the largest island along the southwest coast of Florida and the producer of some of the state's most exotic fruits. Not the humdrum Florida orange, Pine Island's king of fruits is the mango. Its reign is so celebrated that there is an annual two-day festival, the **Pine Island Mango-Mania Tropical Fruit Fair** (239/283-0888) in July with mango-inspired foods, entertainment, and lots of fragrant fruits and plants for sale.

From late May to about Labor Day, enthusiasts can also stop into the tent-covered **Pine Island Tropical Fruit Market** in Bokeelia (10 A.M.-4 P.M. Fri.-Sun.) for a wide array of tropical fruits. The **Fort Myers Downtown Farmers' Market** in Centennial Park offers a fair sampling of the local exotic fruits (7 A.M.-2 P.M. Thurs.). Even the local **Eden Vineyards** applauds the local fruits with one of its wines, made from carambola.

But what is a carambola, exactly, you say? Maybe you need a few pointers:

Carambola is another word for starfruit, that light yellow, ribbed, ovoid fruit that, when sliced, has star-shaped cross-sections. The flesh is yellow, crisp, juicy, and not fibrous, ranging from very sour to mildly sweet.

Mamey sapote is a large, football-shaped fruit that grows on an ornamental evergreen. The brown skin has a rough texture like a kiwi, only rougher. The flesh is either creamy pink or salmon color, and it has a big avocado-like pit. The flavor is described as a combination of honey, avocado, and sweet potato. Closely related, the **sapodilla** has soft brown flesh that tastes a little like very sweet root beer. The sapodilla tree is also the source of chicle, a chewing gum component.

Lychee are those beautiful, nubby red fruits you see in Chinese painting. The inside is pearly white, the texture of a grape. The flesh is sweet but tart, and highly perfumed. Experienced lychee eaters bite lightly through the skin of the top and then squeeze the fruit out (if you bite off a chunk, the black seed with the white fruit around it looks disconcertingly like an eyeball). The **longan** is known as the little brother of the lychee. They look alike, only the longan is smaller. The flesh is whitish and translucent like the lychee, but less perfumey and a little muskier.

Jackfruit is the fruit for the intrepid. The largest tree-borne fruit in the world, up to 80 pounds, the unopened fruit has a strong, disagreeable smell. The exterior is spiky and green, and the inside has these large edible bulbs that taste like a cross between banana and papaya. Sound creepy? Fine, you don't need to know jack about jackfruit, but check out the rest of Lee County's tropical bounty.

RC Otter's Island Eats (11506 Andy Rosse Ln., 239/395-1142, 7:30 A.M.-10 P.M. daily, $8-20) is right across the street, with a vast menu of accessible American staples, with care put into vegetarian options. The wine list is fairly decent, and they have housemade beer. Depending on the weather, you can sit indoors, on the covered veranda, or out on the patio where there's usually live island music. **Mucky Duck** (11546 Andy Rosse Ln., 239/472-3434, 11:30 A.M.-2:30 P.M. and 5-9:30 P.M. daily, $18-28) is more of an English pub vibe, only set right on the beach. The only thing on the menu that might be construed as English is

fish and chips, but no matter when the seafood platter and its accompanying creamy dill sauce are so good. Every night at sunset, revelers convene on the beachside patio to watch the colorful show.

The **'Tween Waters Inn** (15951 Captiva Rd., 239/472-5161) is something of an institution around here, going from the bay side to the Gulf side across the island, and with a couple of restaurants on-site. For my money, I'd skip the fine-dining **Old Captiva House** (7:30-11 A.M. and 5:30-10 P.M. daily, $18-34) and head for the ◖ **Crow's Nest Island Pub** (5:30-10 P.M. daily, cocktails until late, $8-15).

Not that the former isn't good—it often wins Florida's Golden Spoon Award, with elegant swordfish saltimbocca, jerked grouper, seafood jambalaya, and the archetypal key lime pie served in an intimate special occasion kind of space (sit in the Sunset Room). It's more because the latter is so fun. Good drink specials, fine bar staples, a band Tuesday–Sunday. But it's Monday you need to go. It's the NASCrab races, 6 P.M. for families, 9 P.M. for adults. Pick your hermit crab, the one who looks most like Dale Earnhardt Jr. or Jeff Gordon, and line him up. Who wins is ESPN-worthy drama. For lunch at 'Tween Waters, opt for the **Canoe and Kayak Waterfront Restaurant** (11 A.M.–6 P.M. daily, $7–10) on-site, where you can eat a fat deli sandwich while watching the marina's commotion.

For when you're looking for a cocktail and a place to watch the sun go down, the **Green Flash Bayside Bar & Grill** (15183 Captiva Dr., 239/472-3337, 11:30 A.M.–3:30 P.M. and 5:30–9:30 P.M. daily, $13–20) is the place. At the site of the longtime island favorite called The Nook, the two-story restaurant is situated on Roosevelt Channel and overlooks Buck Key and Pine Island. What you need to know about the menu is what is written at the top:

A green flash occurs because sunlight spreads out in air of increasing density, just like water vapor creates a rainbow. The atmosphere refracts the light into a spectrum with the longest (red-orange) wavelengths at one end and the shortest (violet-blue-green) at the other. The dispersion is greatest at sunset and sunrise because that's when sunlight takes a long, low path through the atmosphere. The blue-green light is bent toward the top of the sun, but usually it is scattered by air molecules. But sometimes only the blue is scattered, leaving the root of the bent light—the green part—visible once the sun sets. The chances of seeing the green flash are better in tropical or desert areas since an observer has more opportunities to view a horizon free from clouds and haze. Experts recommend watching a sunset from the beach on a calm day with a horizon free of clouds. A yellow sun, rather than a red one, will have the best potential for a green flash.

Charlotte Harbor and the Barrier Islands

From Charlotte Harbor south past Fort Myers, a stew of wonderful little islands thickens the waters of the Lee County and Charlotte County coastlines. A long line of curves, squiggles, and dots on the map between the Gulf waters and the Intracoastal Waterway, some of these islands are accessible by causeway, others just by boat. What unifies them is robust natural beauty and romantic, often pirate-related histories. Sailboating outfits, fishing charters, regularly scheduled ferries, and water taxis head out to these barrier islands. One of the area's first tourists was Spanish explorer Ponce de Leon, who ended up taking a Calusa arrow and dying in these waters. The natives are friendlier now.

CHARLOTTE HARBOR

Most people hadn't heard of Florida's Charlotte Harbor and Punta Gorda until Hurricane Charley blew through and over them on August 13, 2004. Punta Gorda took one of the category IV storm's worst beatings, with loads of people months later still trying to decide whether to renovate or rebuild.

In spite of the destruction, the community united to care for each other and the environs in such a way that so reflected the character of its people. That spirit—along with an estimated 500 new hotel rooms, the $5.5 million new Bailey Airport Terminal at Charlotte County Airport, opened in 2007, several "live, work, play" projects, and new attractions (like the $46 million rebuilt and expanded sports arena that will purportedly host the Tampa Bay Rays for spring training beginning 2009)—defines the renaissance of Charlotte Harbor and the Gulf Islands. In what could be considered a deus ex machina situation, the area is now finding its stride and strength as a destination that revels in all things nature. A $19 million waterfront Charlotte Harbor Event & Conference Center, located in downtown Punta Gorda, is scheduled to open in January 2009, as the capstone of the post-hurricane renaissance.

The whole area is worth exploring, especially for the ecotraveler. Charlotte Harbor is the second-largest estuary in the state, encompassing 270 square miles. It has 365 miles of canals, 190 miles of them saltwater, 175 miles freshwater. Most of the area bordering the harbor is preserved land, with parks, 53 blueway trails, and the largest undisturbed pine flatwoods in southwest Florida.

The area has been featured on *Sail* magazine's list of the "10 Greatest Places to Sail in the United States," ranked by *Golf Digest* as the "Third Best Place to Live and Play Golf in America," and annually hosts the Oh Boy! Oberto Redfish Cup broadcast by ESPN. It's the nation's premier saltwater fishing championship with a field of anglers limited to 40 professional two-man teams representing the best of the Redfish Cup.

If you're visiting Lee County, don't skip **Punta Gorda.** It's worth the drive north from Fort Myers to visit **Babcock Wilderness Adventure** (8000 Hwy. 31, Punta Gorda, 800/500-5583, tours by reservation 9 A.M.–3 P.M., $17.95 adults, $10.95 children 3–12, also special group and seasonal prices) for a swamp buggy ride in which you are bumped and jostled on an open vehicle through an exhilarating 90-minute tour through the Babcock Ranch, Telegraph Cypress Swamp, and the 90,000-acre Crescent B Ranch. Guides offer narration on birds, animals, plants, and the cattle and horses that are raised on the ranch. You'll see Florida panthers (okay, not wild exactly), big gators, white-tailed deer, wild turkeys, and ornery-looking Florida Cracker cattle

that are raised on the ranch. It's thrilling, but especially so for kids.

Out of Fisherman's Village in Punta Gorda, **King Fisher Fleet** (1200 W. Retta Esplanade, 941/639-0969, cruises roughly $21.95 adults, half price for kids 3–11, free under 3, back bay fishing $400/day, deepwater $650/day) pays equal attention to sightseers and anglers. It offers sightseeing cruises to the out islands, ecotours, full- and half-day cruises, sunset cruises, and harbor tours. We opted for a quickie. It's a narrated cruise around the waterfront on which a suspiciously chipper pod of dolphins tags along. What do they get out of it, we wonder, as we snap the 20th leaping-dolphin photo? At Christmastime, all of the houses and boats along the canals in Punta Gorda are decorated lavishly for the holidays. King Fisher offers a lovely evening cruise along the canals to gawk.

If you want to learn to sail or cruise in the sheltered waters of Charlotte Harbor, **Florida Sailing & Cruising School** (Burnt Store Marina on Charlotte Harbor, 800/262-7939, www.flsailandcruiseschool.com) offers liveaboard sailing beginning at $395 for a two-day basics class.

And the little town of Englewood, west of Charlotte Harbor and north of Cape Haze, is definitely worth the drive. I spent a whole evening hanging out with the hippies and perennially bronzed beach folk for an impromptu barbecue and sing-along in the covered pavilion of downtown beachfront **Chadwick Park.**

There's also the newly opened 135-acre **Oyster Creek Regional Park** in Englewood, located on the greenway waterway corridor known as the Oyster Creek, Lemon Bay Aquatic Preserve, Ainger Creek waterway.

Lemon Bay is at the north end of Cape Haze peninsula, where evidence suggests early Floridians lived swimmingly from about 1000 B.C. to A.D. 1350. You can see their faint evidence at **Paulson's Point** (Orange St., 941/474-3065, dawn–dusk, free), also known as the Sarasota County mound. The tall, shell mound park features helpful interpretive markers and a lovely gentle walkway around and through the Native American mound.

Food

The area has a number of worthwhile restaurants. There's **Amimoto Japanese Restaurant** (2705 Tamiami Trail, Punta Gorda, 941/505-1515, 11 A.M.–2:30 P.M. and 5:30–9:30 P.M. Mon.–Sat., $15–22), with clean, bright sushi flavors presented artistically. A great lunch spot. Also worthwhile in Punta Gorda is **Mamma Nunzia Ristorante** (1975 Tamiami Trail, 941/575-7575, 11:30 A.M.–10 P.M. Mon.–Fri., 4–10 P.M. Sat. and Sun.) for solid Italian; **Zen Asian Bistro** (127 W. Marion Ave., 941/639-9080, 5–9 P.M. Tues.–Sat.) for more contemporary Italian; and the restaurants of **Fisherman's Village** (1200 W. Retta Esplanade, www.fishville.com), including **Village Oyster Bar** (941/637-1212, 11:30 A.M.–8 P.M. Sun.–Thurs., until 9 P.M. Fri. and Sat.) and **Bella Luna** (941/637-1212, 11:30 A.M.–8 P.M. Sun.–Thurs., until 9 P.M. Fri. and Sat.).

Then in the sweet town of Englewood, sophisticated water-view dining can be had at **Gulfview Grill** (2095 N. Beach Rd., 941/475-3500, 3–9 P.M. Sun.–Thurs., until 10 P.M. Fri. and Sat., Sun. brunch 10 A.M.–2 P.M.). Get the stone crab claws if they're in season.

Undoubtedly the best restaurant in the area is **The Perfect Caper** (121 East Marion Ave., Punta Gorda, 941/505-9009, 11:30 A.M.–9 P.M. Tues.–Thurs., until 10 P.M. Fri. and Sat., $20–40), which recently changed locations in this unpretentious waterside town. While "gourmet" is a fairly bankrupt word these days, it's the only thing in Punta Gorda that really fits that description. James and Jeanie Roland's approach to California-Asian fusion is cerebral and stunning. Jeanie, a CIA grad, presides in the kitchen, an absolute stickler about ingredients. Her passion for season's best is obvious from starters like jumbo prawns wrapped in shredded phyllo, fried crisp and served with avocado relish and blood orange vinaigrette, to an entrée of grilled venison tenderloin with roasted purple Peruvian potatoes, berry-fig glace and haricots verts.

The nearby **Swiss Chocolate** (403 Sullivan St., 941/639-9484) is a stunning shop filled with utterly tempting chocolates and European pastries. Also nearby, hearty breakfasts are to be had at **Pies & Plates** (2310 Tamiami Trail, Suite 3117, 941/505-7434). The little café also does cooking classes—a perfect girls' getaway endeavor, but so is a naturalist-led kayak trip with **Grande Tours** (12575 Placida Rd., Placida, 941/697-8825, www.grandetours.com) or a visit to one Punta Gorda's two excellent day spas (**Spago Day Spa,** 941/205-3030, 115 Taylor Rd.; and **Bisous at the Spa,** 941/575-6363, 321 Taylor St.).

◖ PALM ISLAND

Almost everything on Palm Island revolves around **Palm Island Resort** (7092 Placida Rd., Cape Haze, 941/697-4800, www.palmisland.com, $300–1,200), and it's practically my favorite place to stay on the entire Gulf Coast. You drive to Cape Haze, the directions are a little tricky. Take I-75 29 miles north from Sanibel. Take the County Road 768 W exit (Exit 161) toward Punta Gorda. Almost immediately, turn right onto Taylor Road (County Road 765A), which then runs into the Tamiami Trial (U.S. 41 N). Follow this nine miles, then turn left onto El Jobean Road (Hwy. 776 W). Follow this eight miles, turn left onto Gasparilla Road (County Road 771) and drive another eight miles. Turn right onto Placida Road (County Road 775), go two miles and you're there. Then you wait in line in your car for the car ferry. It comes, you drive on, and about 60 seconds later the ferry lands on Palm Island (but not before the salty-seadog ferry captain has had a chance to be crabby with a few ferry passengers). Then you're in paradise. Nice young men in shorts greet you, take all your stuff, and tell you where to ditch your car; you get your own golf cart, and you motor over to your unit along gravel roads. (Careful: My 12-year-old once drove the cart recklessly, fatally wounding a frog, first-degree frogslaughter.)

The island is really due north of Boca Grande, with about 200 private homes, plus 15 more private homes within the resort. Resort guests stay in 154 one-, two- or three-bedroom villas right on the Gulf. In clusters of low-rise

LEE COUNTY

LEE COUNTY

Stress is not an option at the secluded barrier island Palm Island Resort, where time stands still and crowds give way to solitude.

buildings, spacious units reflect a real range of tastes, from beachy casual to swanky contemporary—be specific about your tastes and needs when you call. There are several pools, tennis courts, a comfy restaurant called the Rum Bay, childrens' programs, kayak rentals (a good first-kayak experience in the protected inner-island waterways, with the mullet jumping enough to add some excitement). My only caveat is this: Bring your own groceries from the mainland, as the prices at the little on-island market are mercenary.

Luscious beaches, clear green-blue waters, gorgeous sunsets, gently undulating sea oats— it's all worth the price of admission, and makes a perfect multigenerational getaway that everyone will appreciate, except for that one frog.

GASPARILLA ISLAND

Named for the infamous pirate José Gaspar, who may or may not have hidden out (and buried his treasure, never to be found) on this island in the 1700s with his band of bloodthirsty men, Gasparilla Island has had a much more posh and refined recent history. Connected to the mainland by a short causeway near Punta Gorda, the island was founded as a vacation retreat and fishing spot by the DuPont family in the late 1800s. Its town of **Boca Grande**, at the mouth of Charlotte Harbor, is besieged May through mid-July by tarpon fishers; the opening between Cayo Costa and Gasparilla Island was once considered by some to be the "Tarpon Fishing Capital of the World." Tarpon are sparser in the pass and the estuarine waters of Pine Island Sound these days, but during peak season the dense cluster of fishing boats makes a picturesque scene. There is driving access to the island via the Boca Grande Causeway, the causeway at County Road 775, and at Placida.

Boca Grande is on the southern tip of Gasparilla Island and retains its quaint fishing village aura, but with enough swanky shops and restaurants to lure affluent anglers (President Bush has been a regular guest). While there, walk around **Boca Grande Lighthouse Park** (Gasparilla Island State Park, 880 Belcher Rd., Boca Grande, 941/964-0375, 8 A.M.–sunset, $2/car). The wooden Boca Grande Lighthouse was built in 1890 and is a maritime landmark. The lighthouse is open to the public 10 A.M.–4 P.M. the last Saturday of the month, and there's a little lighthouse museum ($2), gift shop, and the Armory Chapel. The waters in these parts have strong currents, not great for swimming, but you'll see people sailboarding.

The **Gasparilla Inn and Club, Boca Grande** (500 Palm Ave., 800/996-1913, www.gasparillainn.com, $173–748) completed renovations in 2007 and received designation as a Historic Hotel of America. Built in 1912 and opening to guests in 1913, the historic pale yellow wooden frame, white pillar entrance, and Victorian-style gable roofs define this grand resort, its main hotel surrounded by cute cottages. With a major Old Florida feel, it sits on 156 acres of well-manicured grounds with great views of the Gulf of Mexico and Charlotte Harbor. A Pete Dye–designed golf course, croquet lawn, two pools, fishing, spa, and 200-slip marina are some of the reasons it's been a Bush family favorite over the years. It's also pet friendly.

USEPPA ISLAND

Across from Cabbage Key is **Useppa Island,** which pirate José Gaspar supposedly named for one of his more favored captives, a Mexican princess named Joseffa. Calusas may have lived here as far back as 5000 B.C., discarding their oyster and clam shells so as to create a greater swath of dry land. Barron Collier, for whom Collier County is named, bought the 100-acre island in 1912 and built a resort there in his own name that lured wealthy and famous fishing enthusiasts from all over. The island is really a chichi private residential club called the Useppa Island Club, with a couple of places on-island for visitors to stay. The **Collier Inn** (239/283-1061) offers seven lavishly decorated suites, but there are also a number of cottages for rent. The **Useppa Marina** accommodates visitors' boats and the **Tarpon Restaurant** is basically the only place to eat. The Useppa Island Historical Society's little **Useppa Museum** (239/283-9600, noon–2 P.M. Tues.–Fri., 1–2 P.M. weekends, $2.50 suggested donation) is a very worthwhile museum, full of an odd assortment of things. There are uniforms, from when Cuban leaders of the Bay of Pigs were chosen on Useppa in secrecy by the CIA as part of the preparations for the doomed Bay of Pigs invasion. And there's a forensic restoration of the "Useppa Man" taken from a skeleton unearthed during an archaeological dig in 1989. Other finds delve into the Paleo nomadic hunter-gatherer people who must have hung out here 10,000 years ago when the island was part of the mainland.

If you'd like to visit the island, **Captiva Cruises** (239/472-5300, 10 A.M.–3:30 P.M. Tues.–Sun., $30 adults, $15 children) has a luncheon cruise to Useppa that includes a visit to the museum.

CABBAGE KEY

The **Cabbage Key Inn** (Intracoastal Waterway, marker 60, Pineland, 239/283-2278, www.cabbagekey.com, $99 rooms at the inn, transient dockage available), built by writer Mary Roberts Rinehart and her son in 1938, has two very tempting allures for the visitor. Ostensibly it was here that Jimmy Buffet drew his inspiration for "Cheeseburger in Paradise." And indeed, the inn serves a fairly laudable burger, cheese optional. The second reason is the **Dollar Bill Bar,** located in the inn, which rides atop a 38-foot Calusa shell mound. The pub is lined with dollar bills, a custom that began in 1941 when a fisherman autographed and taped his last dollar to the wall for safekeeping (assuring a beer on his return). Since then, people sign and date a buck, and tack them up—more than 30,000 $1 bills are taped to the walls, ceilings, and woodwork, providing a historical collage. (It's illegal to deface currency, but no one in this live-and-let-live bar will tell on you.)

Cabbage Key is accessible only by boat, helicopter, or seaplane, located directly across from mile marker 60 on the Intracoastal Waterway. It doesn't really have sandy beaches or many amenities, but it's a great day trip or overnight. **Captiva Cruises** (239/472-5300, 10 A.M.–3:30 P.M. Tues.–Sun., $30 adults, $15 children) also offers a narrated cruise to Cabbage Key, and there are regularly scheduled water taxis every day from Pine Island, Captiva Island, and Punta Gorda.

CAYO COSTA

It's one of the quietest, unbridged barrier islands in the chain, but one of the largest. Immediately to the west of Cabbage Key, stretching from Boca Grande Pass to Captiva Pass, it offers eight miles of pristine beach and unspoiled beauty. **Cayo Costa State Park** (P.O. Box 1150, Boca Grande, 941/964-0375, 8 A.M.–sunset, $1 honor system) is the least-visited state park in Florida, but it's because there are no cars, no electricity, and no hot water, not because it's not worthy. It is where Hurricane Charley made landfall in October 2004, but it has bounced back entirely with the time-lapse foliage growth that is Florida's subtropical birthright.

Calusas occupied the island for hundreds of

It's the cheeseburger that launched a thousand ships – or at least provided Jimmy Buffet his lyrical inspiration.

years, then in the early 1800s Cuban fishermen landed here, and in 1848 the U.S. government started managing the land. There are 20 private homes on the island, only a couple of them lived in year-round. Really, it's a place to tent camp ($18/night) or overnight in one of 12 rustic cabins ($30), all on the northern end of the island. There's a small pioneer cemetery and a fair number of wild pigs—other than that it's sea creatures, birds, and swaths of sun-warmed sand.

Cayo Costa is accessible only by passenger ferry or private boat. Call **Tropic Star of Pine Island** (239/283-0015) to make reservations.

NORTH CAPTIVA ISLAND

Once a part of Captiva Island, this island was severed during the hurricane of 1926. And darned if it didn't just happen again. The right eyewall of Hurricane Charley in October 2004 passed over North Captiva Island and severed it into two parts (not surprisingly, folks call it

Charley Pass). But all has been basically set to right in the past few years—lost rooftops, demolished docks, and uprooted trees are merely a memory.

The island has maintained a reputation as a remote retreat for the super wealthy. There are four miles of state-owned beaches—the state bought 350 acres, almost half of the island, in 1975. At the turn of the 20th century the island contained a vast tomato plantation; after that it was the processing plant for the Punta Gorda Fish Company. In recent years there have been about 50 year-round residents on the island, most of them on the northern part in an enclave known as the Island Club, with the rest of the island given over to affluent vacationers driving golf carts and strolling the sparsely populated beaches.

PINE ISLAND

Pine Island is one of the largest islands off the Gulf Coast of Florida and consists of **Matlacha** (mat-la-SHAY), **Pine Island Center, Bokeelia** (bo-KEEL-ya), **Pineland,** and **St. James City.** It's a great fishing retreat (the tarpon fishing craze started here in the 1880s) and a lovely place from which to observe wildlife, such as the bald eagle nesting sites.

Matlacha is a funky fishing village, with a drawbridge over Matlacha Pass that has seen a lot of fishing action in its day. If you want to wet a line, there are plenty of bait and tackle shops and boat rentals at the **Olde Fish House Marina** and **Viking Marina.** Pine Island Center is the island's commercial district, where you'll go for shopping, with the school, fire station, ball fields, and community pool.

Bokeelia is the home port for many of the island's commercial fishing boats and the agricultural part of the island (you'll see mangoes and a whole bunch of only vaguely familiar-looking tropical fruits: carambola, longan, loquat). This part of the island contains a few historic buildings, including the **Museum of the Islands** (5728 Sesame Dr., Bokeelia, 239/283-1525, www.museumoftheislands.com, 11 A.M.–3 P.M. Tues.–Sat., 1–4 P.M. Sun., in the winter only Tues.–Thurs., $2 adults, $1 children 12 and under), with exhibitions on Pine Island pioneers.

Pineland is home to the **Randell Research Center** (13810 Waterfront Dr., Pineland, 239/283-2062, www.flmnh.ufl.edu/RRC, $7 adults, $4 children), one of the main historical sites of Calusa mounds. After spending a day paddling the Calusa route, the Randell seemed a topical field trip. We wandered the Calusa Heritage Trail opened at the end of 2004, a series of artistic signs interpreting the Calusa way of life and religious beliefs, quite serendipitously running into Dr. Karen Walker, a South Florida archaeologist and ethnographer who studies the Pineland Site Complex. She stopped to talk about the Calusa's response to climate change over centuries, the changing coastal water levels causing them to move repeatedly—chilling in light of current concerns about climate change and the Gulf Coast's shoreline.

There are also guided tours Wednesday at 10 A.M. Also in Pineland you'll find one of the country's smallest **post offices** and boat rentals and fishing charters out of **Pineland Marina.**

Within a stone's throw of celebrated Florida author Randy Wayne White's house, the Randell Research Center is also just across the street from the **Tarpon Lodge** (13771 Waterfront Dr., Pineland, 239/283-3999) where we stopped for dinner. Blue crab and roasted corn chowder, followed by fat Gulf shrimp scampi over linguini, all served graciously in a historic house (for a spell it was an alcohol rehab center, many of the patients eventually returning to its Sportsman's Lounge for old time's sake, preferably for a Diet Pepsi).

St. James City is Pine Island's residential community, with about two-thirds of the island's population living here. Most homes are located on canals with easy access to Pine Island Sound, San Carlos Bay, and the Gulf of Mexico.

LEE COUNTY

Information and Services

Lee County is located within the **Eastern time zone.** The area code is **239,** but it used to be 941, an area code now used farther north.

Tourist Information

For visitor information, the **Lee County Visitor & Convention Bureau** (12800 University Dr., Ste. 550, Fort Myers, 239/338-3500 or 800/237-6444, www.FortMyersSanibel.com) has an absolutely tremendous website, with well-written text, good graphics—an easy resource for planning a trip. Its office is less convenient for walk-ins. The **Sanibel & Captiva Islands Chamber of Commerce** (1159 Causeway Rd., Sanibel, 239/472-1080, www.sanibel-captiva.org) maintains a visitors center on Causeway Road as you drive onto Sanibel from Fort Myers. The chamber gives away an island guide and sells a detailed street map for $3.

This area has a fair number of small papers that serve Lee County, but no big metro paper. The **Fort Myers News-Press** (239/335-0233) is the daily in these parts. In Fort Myers Beach, look for the **Fort Myers Beach Observer** (239/765-0400), which is the weekly newspaper distributed every Wednesday. The **Island Reporter** (239/472-1587) is the newspaper of record for Sanibel and Captiva Islands, and there's also a magazine covering Sanibel called **Times of the Islands Magazine.** On Boca Grande, look for the weekly **Boca Beacon.**

Police and Emergencies

As always, if you find yourself in a real emergency, pick up a phone and dial 911 or the local **Emergency Management Office** (239/477-3600). For a nonemergency police need, call the **Sheriff's Office** (239/332-3456), **Florida Highway Patrol** (239/278-7100), **U.S. Coast Guard** (239/463-5754), or **Florida Poison Information Center** (800/222-1222).

Sanibel and Captiva medical facilities serve the local community during business hours. For emergency medical needs, **HealthPark Medical Center** (16131 Roserush Ct., Fort Myers, 239/433-4647) and **Lee Memorial Hospital** (2776 Cleveland Ave., Fort Myers, 239/332-1111) are full-service hospitals on the mainland with 24-hour emergency service. For your pharmacy needs on the islands, **CVS** (2331 Palm Ridge Rd., Sanibel, 239/472-0085) is convenient, and if your pet has a medical problem, there's **Coral Veterinary Clinic** (1530 Periwinkle Way, Sanibel, 239/472-8387).

Radio and Television

If you're looking for NPR radio, turn to **WGCU 90.1 FM.** For local music programming, **WARO 94.5 FM** is classic rock; **WCKT 107.1 FM** is country music; **WDRR 98.5 FM** has smooth jazz; **WINK 96.9 FM** offers adult contemporary programming; **WJBX 99.3 FM** is alternative rock; **WOLZ 95.3 FM** is, of course, oldies; **WRXK 96.1 FM** gives you classic rock; and **WXKB 103.9 FM** is Top 40 radio.

And on the television, **WBBH Channel 2** is the NBC affiliate, **WINK Channel 11** is the CBS affiliate, **WZVN Channel 7** is the ABC affiliate, **WGCU Channel 30** is the PBS affiliate, and **WFTX Channel 4** is the FOX affiliate out of Cape Coral.

Laundry Services

Large hotels and beach rentals often have laundry services of one sort or another. If you need to throw in a load of wash, launderettes are limited on the islands. Try an RV park along the route. In Fort Myers the laundry options are much broader. **60 Minute Cleaners** has three locations (12842 S. Cleveland Ave., 239/936-3616; Cypress Trace Shopping Center, 239/481-1900; and 16970 San Carlos Blvd., 239/466-5115). In Fort Myers Beach, there's **Beach & Bubbles Coin Laundry & Dry**

If you want to see what's biting, grab a fishing license, sold at many bait-and-tackle shops.

Cleaners (7205 Estero Blvd., 239/765-1771), a garden-variety coin-op laundry.

Fishing Licenses

Fishing licenses are sold at all county tax collectors' offices and at many bait-and-tackle shops, or by phone (888/347-4356). On Sanibel, you can buy a license at the **Bait Box** on Periwinkle Way; at **Bailey's** at the corner of Tarpon Bay Road and Periwinkle Way; at **Tarpon Bay Explorers;** and at all the marinas. Also pick up the Florida Marine Fisheries Commission's publication about size and bag limits. You do not need a license if you are fishing from a boat that has a valid recreational vessel saltwater fishing license, if you are under 16, or if you are Florida resident fishing from a pier or bridge.

Getting There and Around

BY CAR

Lee County is along southwest Florida's Gulf Coast between Naples and Sarasota. The biggest north–south driving routes are I-75 and U.S. 41. East–west major arteries include Alligator Alley (I-75) and U.S. 41 (where it jogs east at around Naples).

To get to Fort Myers, you can take either I-75 or U.S. 41. In town, McGregor Boulevard runs alongside the Caloosahatchee River and is also called Highway 867. Highway 865 (also known as Hickory Boulevard, Estero Boulevard, and San Carlos Boulevard, depending on where you are) is the route south to Fort Myers Beach on Estero Island.

To get to Sanibel from I-75, take New Exit 131 or Old Exit 21 (Daniels Parkway) west to Summerlin Road, approximately seven miles. Turn left on Summerlin Road and drive approximately 15 miles to the Sanibel Causeway (a $6 toll). Drive across and onto Sanibel Island. At the four-way stop at Periwinkle Way, either a right or a left turn will lead you to beaches, shops, and accommodations. Sanibel Island has a couple of main roads that parallel each other: Periwinkle Way, the main business route, and Gulf Drive, segmented into East, Middle, and West Gulf Drive. Tarpon Bay Road connects Sanibel-Captiva Road with Periwinkle Way at its west end. And Sanibel-Captiva Road—most folks call it San-Cap—goes by most of Sanibel's attractions before crossing over a short bridge at Blind Pass, where it becomes Captiva Drive on Captiva Island.

So, to reach Captiva, turn right on Periwinkle Way, drive two miles, turn right onto Tarpon Bay Road, and at the next left turn onto Sanibel-Captiva Road. Drive for approximately eight miles, cross Blind Pass Bridge, and you're there.

Driving into Florida from the north via Jacksonville, take I-95 south to I-4 to I-75, and then follow the directions above.

BY AIR

By air, the area is served by **Southwest Florida International Airport** (16000 Chamberlin Parkway, Fort Myers, 239/768-1000, www.fly lcpa.com), which has just opened the new Midfield Terminal Complex designed to expand to 65 gates and five concourses. The terminal is one of the first in the U.S. to be built with new security equipment and procedures incorporated into the design. The $438 million project focused on passenger convenience with a lovely subtropical look and permanent photography collection of the work of Florida photographer Alan Maltz.

Most major domestic airlines serve the airport, and there are international flights from Germany and Canada. The airport, opened in 1983, currently serves: Air Canada, AirTran, American, Continental, Delta, Jet Blue, Northwest, Southwest, United, US Airways, and many smaller carriers, as well as German airlines Condor and LTU International.

Alamo (800/327-9633), **Avis** (800/230-4898), **Budget** (800/227-5945), **Dollar** (800/800-3665), **Enterprise** (800/736-8222), **Hertz** (800/654-3131), **National** (800/227-7368), and **Thrifty** (800/847-4389) provide rental cars from Southwest Florida International Airport. Enterprise and Thrifty offices are directly across the street from baggage claim.

BY BUS AND TRAIN

LeeTran (239/275-8726, www.rideleetran .com) has hourly service 6 A.M.–10 P.M. to a transfer point at Daniels Parkway and U.S. 41 with connections to other routes.

Greyhound Bus Line (239/774-5660) offers bus service to the Fort Myers station, but from here you really need to rent a car. Public transportation to and between the islands is limited to taxis and limousines.

THE PARADISE COAST

Many people describe this part of Florida as the Paradise Coast. Unhelpful, it seems to me, as one person's paradise is another's episode of *Survivor*. And really, the three cities that make up the paradise in question couldn't be more different. Like three wildly disparate siblings stifling under the umbrella of a common surname, Naples is all glamorous sophistication and effete charm; Marco Island is the uncomplicated, sunny, outdoors "jock" of the family; and Everglades City is the sinister, infinitely more interesting ne'er-do-well of the kids, the one mama worries about.

Take a luxury boat tour through the canals that make up the backyards of the multimillion-dollar homes of Naples's Port Royal, then pilot your own kayak quietly through the mangrove jungle of the Ten Thousand Islands and you'll see: Paradise is in the eye of the beholder.

The Calusa people were the first to recognize paradise, settling in southwest Florida centuries before Spanish explorers found their way here. But even after the Spanish had evicted and killed off these first residents, the land lay virtually empty until the late 1800s. Survey teams brought back news of the beauty of the wilds of southwest Florida, sparking the imagination of General John S. Williams, a senator from Louisville, and Walter N. Haldeman, owner of the *Louisville Courier-Journal*. The men chartered a boat and came to look, mesmerized by the miles of white-sand beaches. Not long after, in 1886, the Naples Town Improvement Company was formed, purchasing 3,712 acres

HIGHLIGHTS

◖ Naples Municipal Beach and Fishing Pier: Some of the area's top beaches here are a little more urban than in other parts of the Gulf Coast. Naples Municipal Beach features a 1,000-foot fishing pier considered the heart of the city, flanked on either side by a wide swath of beach and the long length of fancy houses known as "Millionaires' Row" (page 98).

◖ Corkscrew Swamp Sanctuary: Head north out of Naples to this wildlife sanctuary. You'll see wood storks with faces only a mother could love and a strange wizened plant called a Resurrection Fern that comes back from the botanically deceased (page 100).

◖ Naples Museum of Art: A recent addition to the Philharmonic Center for the Arts complex, the museum packs quite a bit, from modern Mexican masters to a smart little show of works from the Olga Hirshhorn collection, exhibits are mesmerizing and expertly curated (page 107).

◖ Naples Zoo: Families visiting Naples usually find their way here, with good reason. Little ones enjoy the gator-feeding show, the Panther Glade, the big cats show, and the boat ride out to see the antic monkeys on their little islands. Parents, on the other hand, will appreciate the park's incredible native and exotic plants, as well as the adult humor of the animal handlers (page 108).

◖ Third Street South: Some of Florida's most sophisticated boutiques, antiques shops, and galleries line both sides of Naples's main drag. There's even a street concierge to help get you oriented (page 110).

◖ Tigertail Beach: Against the backdrop of Marco Island's tall skyline of resort hotels, Tigertail Beach draws a fun-seeking crowd. For some, fun is Jet Ski rentals and water sports, for others a cutthroat game of beach volleyball, and still others linger equipped only with a pail and shovel (page 118).

◖ Calusa Shell Mounds: Take a boat tour through the deep backwater with Florida Saltwater Adventures. You'll motor out through the tiny mangrove islands near Marco Island, stopping to gingerly walk around, peering to find remnants of this extinct Native American culture (page 120).

◖ Everglades Eco Adventures: Paddle through the Ten Thousand Islands and part of Everglades National Park with the Everglades Rentals and Eco Adventures Company. A guide glides with you through mangrove tunnels, drifting by wading birds, rare orchids, and gators of all sizes (page 128).

◖ Totch's Island Tours: There are other ways to get out and explore the area's exotic "walking trees." Don a pair of protective headphones and hop aboard a backcountry or open-water airboat tour of mangrove islands with Totch's Island Tours (page 129).

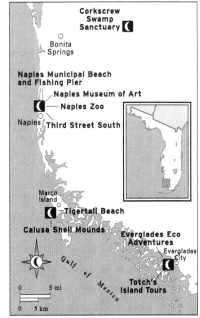

LOOK FOR ◖ TO FIND RECOMMENDED SIGHTS, ACTIVITIES, DINING, AND LODGING.

THE PARADISE COAST

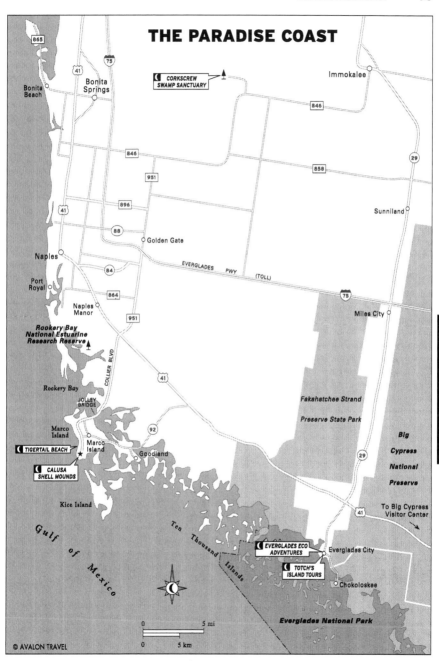

THE PARADISE COAST

between the Gulf of Mexico and what is now known as Naples Bay.

They had big plans. The name alone says quite a bit: These founders were modeling the new Naples on the cultured and thriving Italian seaport city (heck, if you squint, the Florida peninsula looks a little like the Italian peninsula, right?). They built a pier, blocked out plans for a city, built their own homes on the beach—and then the Naples Town Improvement Company ran out of money. It was sold at a public auction in 1890 to the only bidder, Walter Haldeman, who now owned 8,600 acres of land, the swanky Naples Hotel, the pier, and a steamship that brought guests to and from Naples. Instead of making him rich beyond his wildest dreams, Naples was more of an avocational interest, a financially draining hobby for Haldeman. In fact, in the early 1900s, the area that is now Collier County was mostly populated by feisty herds of scrub cattle that grazed the open prairies.

The city chugged on with minimal growth until rail service came to Naples in 1927 and Memphis-born millionaire Barron Collier's Tamiami Trail was completed the next year. Poised at the verge of vigorous expansion, the city's growth was quashed by the Great Depression followed swiftly by World War II. A direct hit by Hurricane Donna in 1960 devastated Everglades City but served to bolster growth in Naples—not long after the storm, the county seat was transferred from Everglades City to East Naples.

Since then, Naples has experienced an enormous population boom, mostly amongst midwestern retirees (it's funny, but every other person you meet here used to live in Chicago, Milwaukee, and so forth), such that it was deemed the fastest-growing community in the country in the 1980s. It's got the look of many monied, sunny American cities (Santa Barbara, Palm Springs): lawns that seem maintained round the clock with tweezers and nail scissors, women of a certain age in Lilly Pulitzer pink-and-green cardigans, and everywhere fancy new Mercedes badly parked, their gleaming bumpers shellacked with "I'd rather be golfing" stickers. (People here are Republican, but not way to the right; often county and state offices are filled with pro-choice, anti-school-voucher candidates.)

As for Marco Island and Everglades City, differences go deeper than a lack of Lilly Pulitzers and a dearth of Mercedes. It's not a story of the haves (Naples) and the have-nots (Marco and E.C.). Much of Marco Island is a real place to live—year-rounders' houses are modest, ranch-style homes built a couple of decades ago before the Deltona Corporation began building and the island heated up as a vacation destination. The heat is focused on the beach, where tall resort hotels and condos stretch for two miles along the strand on Collier Boulevard. Vacationers (often families) may never see much of the island, their eyes focused assiduously on the gorgeous warm water of the Gulf, the maze of mangrove islands just to the south, and whether their tans are even.

Everglades City and the little town to the south called Chokoloskee (chuck-uh-LUSK-ee, not chock-oh-losk-ee) are the end of civilization before you run into Everglades National Park. Some of the mystery and wildness of that park has rubbed off on these little towns, or maybe it's just that the residents, over generations, have self-selected an iconoclastic, entrepreneurial-unto-illegality, free-spirited bunch. Hang out at the Rod and Gun Club, or paddle a kayak through the quiet tunnels of mangroves, and you'll feel like you've entered the Wild West, only with gators.

PLANNING YOUR TIME

How much you do during a visit here depends on the size of your luggage. You need three utterly distinct sets of duds to blend in in Naples, Marco Island, and Everglades City. For urban, sophisticated Naples, you need clothing that could be described as millennial-preppy (Lacoste shirts, navy blue blazers sans brass buttons, maybe a pair of those weird red golfing pants); on Marco you need beachwear (no thongs, please), and lots of it, and maybe a Hawaiian shirt; in Everglades City you need your oldest sneakers (what my dad calls "manure spreaders"), comfy T-shirts, and a constant sheen of bug spray.

Obviously, where you stay depends on what your primary objectives are. Naples's accommodations are generally fairly expensive, as are those on Marco Island. Everglades City is more budget-minded and a little lean on luxury. For romantic travel à deux—dinner at a fine restaurant, then a moonlit walk on the beach—you'll find plenty in Naples. A couple of fishing poles, a double kayak, and your sweetie paddling in sync with you—this is Everglades City. Family travelers are courted most diligently on Marco Island, with most of the large hotels offering programs for kids.

Peak season in and around Naples is roughly December 23–April 16. Rates for hotels reflect this, and you may save a bundle visiting instead in the late spring or early fall (when the weather in Naples and on Marco Island is divine). Everglades City, on the other hand, can be a little trickier as things heat up. The thick heat, the wet blanket of humidity, and dense fog of mosquitoes act as a real enthusiasm damper as you tramp around outdoors in the Everglades.

Naples

Naples has been dubbed "the Palm Beach" of Florida's Gulf Coast. With nearly 90 golf courses, Naples has one of the highest ratios of greens to golfers in the United States. Beyond the links, Naples is known for world-class shopping, dining, and a preponderance of beautiful people. Although a stroll of trendy 5th Avenue is certainly reminiscent of the posh Atlantic Coast resort, the analogy breaks down as soon as one sees Naples's tranquil beauty, which begins just five miles out of town: the Rookery Bay National Estuarine Research Reserve (with sprawling mangroves and a rainbow of rare birds), Big Cypress National Preserve to the east, and the untamed mystery of Everglades National Park.

And then there are the nine miles of sun-soaked, white-sand beaches. A locus of sun-worshipping these days, the Naples shorefront was once populated by the Calusa people. In the late 1860s, Roger Gordon and Joe Wiggins were the area's first white settlers, drawn to the abundant fish and mild climate—a climate that was often compared to the bay in Naples, Italy. (Thus the name.) In 1887, a group of wealthy Kentuckians, led by Walter N. Haldeman, owner of the *Louisville Courier-Journal,* purchased enormous parcels of land in the town of Naples. Quickly gaining a reputation as a winter resort, Naples boasted a glamorous social life that revolved around the exclusive Naples Hotel, a magnet for celebrities at the turn of the 20th century.

As their first civic act, Haldeman and the Naples Town Improvement Company set to work building a 600-foot-long wooden pier in a T shape to allow large ships to dock easily. Completed in 1888, the pier was destroyed and rebuilt three times (most recently demolished by Hurricane Donna in 1960) and remains the center of the town's fishing activity.

At the western end of 12th Avenue South, locals and visitors alike congregate at the pier, but the city has a number of draws that are broadly distributed around town. The shopping district on the nearby Gordon River is called Old Marine Market Place or, alternately, Tin City. For more upscale commerce, walk along 5th Avenue, between 3rd and 9th Streets South, chockablock with stylish shops, restaurants, and cafés. Not far from there, in the center of town, the 13 acres of the **Conservancy of Southwest Florida** (9 A.M.–4:30 P.M. Mon.–Sat., noon–4 P.M. Sun., $9 adults, $4 kids 3–12) provide opportunities for canoe tours and nature hikes, as well as aviaries and a serpentarium (that's a snake house). Its Discovery Center has just undergone extensive renovations, replacing the aquatic touch tank and constructing a brand new Florida panther exhibit, which shows the endangered Florida panther in its natural environment.

Boosters often describe Naples as the crown jewel of southwest Florida. The jewel that sparkles brightest may just be the downtown beach, arguably the finest city beach in Florida. Accessed at the Gulf end of each avenue—the downtown is a grid, streets run north and south, avenues run east and west—the beach has ample metered parking (bring quarters). There you may find a loggerhead sea turtle nest, a swirl of prehistoric-looking pelicans, or any of the other allures that have made Naples a vacation spot among the cognoscenti for the past 150 years.

SPORTS AND RECREATION
◖ Naples Municipal Beach and Fishing Pier

Stop someone on the street in Naples and put them on the spot: Quick, what's the greatest thing about this town? Some of them will immediately point to the cultural amenities (museums, theater, cosmopolitan restaurants, incredible shopping), others will unswervingly steer you to the beaches. Who's right depends on your own predilections. There are 11 miles of stunning beach and nature preserve bordering the Gulf of Mexico in Naples that exert their magnetic pull on millions of would-be beach bums from around the globe.

For an urban beach experience, stroll along **Naples Municipal Beach & Fishing Pier** (access the pier at 12th St. and Gulf Shore Blvd., just south of downtown, 239/434-4696, open 24 hours, no fee, metered parking near entrance). Known locally as The Pier, the 1,000-foot structure that juts into the Gulf attracts anglers, new and old (best fishing months: May–July and Sept.–Oct.). There's a bait house, fish cleaning tables, chickee shelter, restrooms, and concessions on the pier, which was originally built in 1888 as a freight and passenger dock. The pier is a symbol of the locals' tenacity and civic pride, having been damaged by fire and hurricanes and rebuilt repeatedly in 1910, 1926, and 1960. It's perhaps the most photographed spot in Naples,

Fishing opportunities abound from area shorelines, piers, and bridges.

© NAPLES, MARCO ISLAND, EVERGLADES CVB

the emerald green Gulf water and wide swath of beach flanking it on either side. The beach's proximity to downtown (and the stretch of fancy houses known as Millionaires' Row) makes it ideal for a moonlit stroll after dinner or even a bit of sandy respite from an afternoon of serious shopping.

Clam Pass Beach Park

At the south end of Naples, you'll find Clam Pass Beach Park (at the end of Seagate Dr., 239/353-0404, 8 A.M.–sunset, $6 parking). Clam Pass consists of 35 acres of mangrove forest, rolling dunes, and 3,200 feet of white-sand beach. There's a three-quarter-mile boardwalk from a high-rise development through the mangroves and out to the beach. It's easily walkable (and you're likely to see eagles, ospreys, and waddling, pillbug-like armadillos along the way), but you can also take a fun, free tram that runs continuously throughout the day. Once at the beach, there are kayak, canoe, sailboard, and catamaran rentals. The water is shallow and the surf mild, a perfect

THE PARADISE COAST

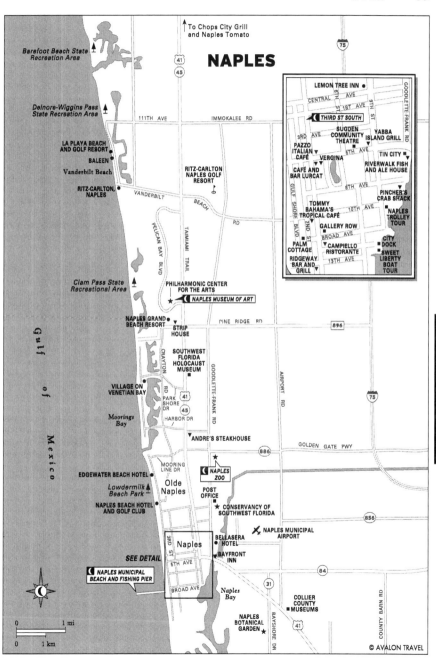

NAPLES

To Chops City Grill
and Naples Tomato

Barefoot Beach State
Recreation Area

Delnore-Wiggins Pass
State Recreation Area

111TH AVE
IMMOKALEE RD

LA PLAYA BEACH
AND GOLF RESORT
BALEEN
Vanderbilt Beach

RITZ-CARLTON
NAPLES GOLF
RESORT

RITZ-CARLTON,
NAPLES
VANDERBILT

BEACH

RD

PELICAN BAY BLVD

TAMIAMI TRAIL

Clam Pass State
Recreational Area

PHILHARMONIC CENTER
FOR THE ARTS
NAPLES MUSEUM OF ART

NAPLES GRAND
BEACH RESORT
STRIP
HOUSE

PINE RIDGE RD
896

SOUTHWEST
FLORIDA
HOLOCAUST
MUSEUM

CRAYTON

GOODLETTE-FRANK RD

AIRPORT RD

75

VILLAGE ON
VENETIAN BAY

RD
PARK
SHORE
DR
HARBOR DR

Moorings
Bay

Gulf

of

Mexico

ANDRE'S STEAKHOUSE

886

GOLDEN GATE PWY

MOORING
LINE DR

NAPLES
ZOO

EDGEWATER BEACH HOTEL

Lowdermilk
Beach Park

Olde
Naples

POST
OFFICE

NAPLES BEACH HOTEL
AND GOLF CLUB

CONSERVANCY OF
SOUTHWEST FLORIDA

856

3RD
ST

Naples

NAPLES MUNICIPAL
AIRPORT

BELLASERA
HOTEL

SEE DETAIL

6TH AVE

BAYFRONT
INN

84

NAPLES MUNICIPAL
BEACH AND FISHING PIER

BROAD AVE

Naples
Bay

31

COLLIER
COUNTY
MUSEUMS

NAPLES
BOTANICAL
GARDEN

BAYSHORE DR

41

COUNTY BARN RD

0   1 mi

0   1 km

© AVALON TRAVEL

Detail inset:

LEMON TREE INN

CENTRAL   AVE

1ST AVE

9TH ST

GOODLETTE-FRANK RD

THIRD ST SOUTH

3RD   AVE

SUGDEN
COMMUNITY
THEATRE

YABBA
ISLAND GRILL

PAZZO
ITALIAN
CAFÉ

6TH   AVE

VERGINA

TIN CITY

CAFÉ AND
BAR LURCAT

RIVERWALK FISH
AND ALE HOUSE

8TH AVE

GULF SHORE BLVD

PINCHER'S
CRAB SHACK

TOMMY
BAHAMA'S
TROPICAL CAFÉ

10TH AVE

NAPLES
TROLLEY
TOUR

GALLERY ROW

2ND ST

BROAD AVE

CITY
DOCK

PALM
COTTAGE

CAMPIELLO
RISTORANTE

SWEET
LIBERTY
BOAT
TOUR

RIDGEWAY
BAR AND
GRILL

13TH AVE

THE PARADISE COAST

combination for a family day at the beach. Clam Pass also contains a concession area and picnic pavilions.

Delnor-Wiggins Pass State Park

To the north end of the city, Delnor-Wiggins Pass State Park (11100 Gulfshore Dr., five miles west of I-75, Exit 17, 239/597-6196, 8 A.M.–sunset, $5 parking, five parking areas) regularly makes Dr. Beach's (a.k.a. Dr. Stephen Leatherman of the University of Maryland) top 20 list of America's best beaches. On Delnor-Wiggins you'll find the white-sand swath framed by picturesque sea oats, sea grapes (Seminoles and early settlers ate their ripe berries, but it's a seriously acquired taste), and cabbage palms. Delnor-Wiggins is on a narrow barrier island separated by a maze of mangrove swamp and tidal creek, and boasts a nature trail and observation tower from which to spy on the abundant wildlife. It's a superior shelling beach, and Wiggins Pass generates much enthusiasm amongst anglers. Again, the water is shallow, with a gentle slope and calm surf suitable for swimming. There are picnic facilities, a lifeguard on duty, and a boat ramp. (Caution: Stay out of the dunes and don't pick the sea grass, which is protected due to its important role as a sand stabilizer.)

Other Beaches

Other beaches in the area would be star attractions anywhere but here, but the wealth of possibilities make **Lowdermilk Beach Park** (Gulf Shore Blvd. S., 239/263-6078), **Vanderbilt Beach** (near the Ritz-Carlton at the end of Vanderbilt Dr., 239/353-0404), and **Barefoot Beach Preserve,** also known as **Lely Barefoot Beach** (take U.S. 41 to Bonita Beach Road and head west, 239/353-0404) also-rans here in Naples. All of them have restrooms and picnic facilities, are open sunrise–sunset, and charge $6 for parking. In addition, Lowdermilk has lively sand volleyball courts (all the guidebooks say the play is "world class," but I certainly didn't see any Olympic hopefuls, or even particularly impressive play); Vanderbilt offers exceptional

bird-watching; and Barefoot boasts a learning center with exhibits on sea turtles and shorebirds as well as a nature trail. It was ranked No. 10 among American beaches by Dr. Beach in 2006.

(Corkscrew Swamp Sanctuary

For all of Naples's effete indoor cultural enticements, nature exerts its own draw on visitors. The greater Naples area offers several outstanding—and easily accessible to those with disabilities, seniors, or the stroller-bound—opportunities to commune with nature.

In Collier County, huge swaths of bald cypress forest stood until right around World War II. Logging quickly decimated most of it, with just one virgin stand of cypress left in southwest Florida—the Corkscrew Swamp near Immokalee, now Corkscrew Swamp Sanctuary (take I-75 to Exit 111, go approximately 15 miles, turn left on Sanctuary Rd.,

A ghost orchid with multiple blossoms created a sensation during the summer of 2007 at the Corkscrew Swamp Sanctuary.

375 Sanctuary Rd. W., Naples, 239/348-9151) The sanctuary is open 7 A.M.–7:30 P.M. daily April 12–September 30, 7 A.M.–5:30 P.M. daily October 1–April 11; the entrance fee is $10 adults, $6 college students, $5 Audubon Society members, $4 children 6–18, children under 6 free. It offers visitors a 2.25-mile raised boardwalk—also a 1-mile trail if the longer one sounds daunting, and benches and rain shelters along the way—through four distinct local environments: a pine upland, a wet prairie, a cypress forest, and a marsh. Interpretive signs along the boardwalk give you the basics, but the docent-led tours are tremendous (some of the docents seem a little crotchety and dictatorial, but stick with it), and there's a field guide and a kids' activity book that you can pick up at the admissions desk. There's a birders' checklist and a white board for birders to jot down what they've seen for the benefit of those who've just arrived— make no mistake, birders here can be dead serious, and don't get them talking about wood stork nesting. (Wood storks are these magnificent endangered wading birds that often nest here—up close, the ugliest birds ever with nubby, featherless heads, but they have gorgeous white-plumed bodies trimmed elegantly with black.) It's also a great place to see gators and rare orchids.

Rookery Bay National Estuarine Research Reserve

Another worthwhile day trip is to be had at Rookery Bay National Estuarine Research Reserve (about 13 miles south of Naples, 300 Tower Rd., 239/417-6310, 9 A.M.–4 P.M. daily, adults $5, children 6–12 $3, children under 6 free). Rookery Bay and Ten Thousand Islands estuarine ecosystem is one of the few pristine mangrove estuaries in North America, with 110,000 acres of forest, islands, bays, interconnected tidal embayments, lagoons, and tidal streams that are home to bald eagles, cotton-candy-pink roseate spoonbills, and lots of other birdlife. You can explore the estuary on your own by kayak or with a guided kayak excursion through Rookery Bay's mangrove

estuary (offered twice per month). There are also more frequent naturalist-led one-hour historical walks (hourly at 10 A.M., 11 A.M., noon, 1 P.M., and 2 P.M. Tues.–Sat.) on which visitors learn about the mighty Calusas and the pioneering families of the Little Marco Settlement. They opened a new 16,500-square-foot Environmental Learning Center in 2004, with 5,000 square feet of interactive exhibits and a visitors center, four marine research laboratories, a coastal training center, five aquaria, and a brand new authentic Seminole chickee in 2007. (The big fish at the entrance, by the way, is a polka-dot batfish.) The coolest part of the center is the climb-in "bubble" that allows visitors to observe the many creatures that live among the roots of a 14-foot mangrove in the center aquarium.

Big Cypress National Preserve

This part of Florida also boasts the first national preserve in the national park system, the Big Cypress National Preserve (Oasis Visitors Center, midway between Naples and Miami on U.S. 41, 239/695-4111, www.nps.gov/bicy, 9 A.M.–4:30 P.M. daily, free admission), contiguous with Everglades National Park and just about as big. The preserve encompasses 720,000 acres of the Big Cypress Swamp of southwest Florida—terrain is varied, with swamp, freshwater marshes, forests of slash pine and palmetto, and wet prairies containing abundant wildlife. But how best to investigate this vast area?

Hike it. There's a new public boardwalk located at the **Kirby Storter roadside pull off** that allows you to walk into a cypress dome without getting your feet wet. If this sounds too training-wheels, the **Florida Trail** stretches across the state from Gulf Islands National Seashore through the Big Cypress National Preserve. It's wonderful hiking, which the park rangers divide into three logical sections. Part 1, **Loop Road to U.S. 41** (6.5 miles one-way) begins at Loop Road about 13 miles from its east end on U.S. 41. The other end is across from the **Big Cypress Visitors Center** (53 miles east of Naples on U.S. 41). The easy path

TEE TIME

Naples isn't called the golf capital of the world for nothing. Here are the courses available to visitors, plus the driving ranges and pro shops. All of the greens fees quoted fluctuate seasonally and according to the time of day. Call ahead.

THE COURSES

Arrowhead Golf Course
2205 Heritage Greens Drive, 239/596-1000
Semiprivate, 18 holes, 6,832 yards, par 72, course rating 73.4, slope 132
Greens fees: $85 before 10 A.M., $70 10 A.M.-P.M., $40 after 2:30 P.M.

Boyne South Golf Course
18100 Royal Tree Parkway, 239/732-0034
Public, 18 holes, 6,476 yards, par 72, course rating 71.1, slope 122
Greens fees: $70 for 18 holes, $35 for 9 holes

Cedar Hammock Golf & Country Club
8660 Cedar Hammock Boulevard, 239/793-1134
Public May–October, 18 holes, 6,834 yards, par 72, course rating 71.2, slope 128
Greens fees: $36, cart included

Cypress Woods Golf and Country Club
3525 Northbrook Drive, 239/592-7860
Semiprivate, 18 holes, 6,330 yards, par 72, course rating 71.7, slope 136
Greens fees: $87 before noon, $70 after noon, $52 after 3:30 P.M., cart included

Eagle Creek Country Club
11 Cypress View Drive, 239/793-0500
Public, 18 holes, 6,909 yards, par 72, course rating 73.8, slope 138
Greens fees: $50-79

Hibiscus Golf Club
175 Doral Circle, 239/774-3559
Semiprivate, 18 holes, 6,540 yards, par 72, course rating 70.5, slope 125
Greens fees: $75 before noon, $60 afternoon, cart included

Lely Flamingo Island Club
8004 Lely Resort Boulevard, 239/793-2223
Classics Course: private, 18 holes, 6,805 yards, par 72, course rating 72.4, slope 128
Flamingo Course: resort, 18 holes, 7,171 yards, par 72, course rating 73.9, slope 135
Mustang Course: resort, 18 holes, 7,217 yards, par 72, course rating 75.3, slope 141
Greens fees: $45-149 depending on the month for both Flamingo and Mustang courses, cart included

Marco Island Marriott Beach Resort, Golf Club & Spa
400 Collier Boulevard S., Marco Island, 239/389-6600

Greater Naples is world renowned as a golf destination.

Resort, 18 holes, 6,898 yards, par 72, course rating 73.4, slope 137
Greens fees: $149 before noon, $105 after noon, $60 after 3 P.M.

Naples Beach Hotel and Golf Club
851 Gulf Shore Boulevard N., 239/261-2222
Resort, 18 holes, 6,488 yards, par 72, course rating 71.2, slope 129
Greens fees: $120 before noon, $95 after noon, $55 after 3 P.M.

Naples Grande Golf Club
7760 Golden Gate Parkway, 239/659-3700
Resort, 18 holes, 7,102 yards, par 72, course rating 75.1, slope 143
Greens fees: $210, $165 after 1:30 P.M.

Quality Inn and Suites Golf Resort
4100 Golden Gate Parkway, 239/455-9498
Resort, 18 holes, 6,564 yards, par 72, course rating 70.8, slope 125
Greens fees: $70 until 2 P.M., $55 after 2 P.M., $25 after 4 P.M., cart included

Riviera Golf Club of Naples
48 Marseille Drive, 239/774-1081
Public, 18 holes, 4,090 yards, par 62, course rating 60.4, slope 95
Greens fees: $50, $38 after 2 P.M., cart included

(continues on next page)

THE PARADISE COAST

THE PARADISE COAST

TEE TIME (continued)

Tiburon Golf Club
2620 Tiburon Drive, 239/594-2040
North Course: resort, 9 holes, 3,693 yards, par 36, course rating N/A, slope N/A
South Course: resort, 9 holes, 3,477 yards, par 36, course rating N/A, slope N/A
West Course: resort, 9 holes, 3,500 yards, par 36, course rating N/A, slope N/A
Greens fees: $280 before noon, $235 after noon, $170 after 3 P.M.

Valencia Golf Course
725 Double Eagle Trail, 239/352-0777
Public, 18 holes, 7,145 yards, par 72, course rating 74.3, slope 130
Greens fees: $85 before noon, $65 after noon, cart included

DRIVING RANGES
Briarwood Golf & Practice Center 5051 Radio Rd., 239/262-4955
Ferguson Golf Center 9100 Immokalee Rd., 239/353-3699
Naples Golf Center 7700 Davis Blvd., 239/775-3337
North Naples Golf Range 6979 Old 41, 239/566-1303

PRO SHOPS
Coral Isle Golf Center 4748 Championship Dr., 239/732-6900
Different Strokes Golf & Tennis Outlet 6308 Trail Blvd., 239/514-0065
Edwin Watts Golf 3980 Tamiami Trail N., 239/403-0615
Fix Up Stix 1101 Sun Century Rd., 239/591-3743
For the Love of Golf 9765 Tamiami Trail N., 239/566-3395
Golf Balls Galore & More 2181 J&C Blvd., 239/597-6528
Naples Golf Center 7700 Davis Blvd., 239/775-3337
Naples Golf Co. 1029 Industrial Blvd., 239/643-5577
Pro-Am Discount Golf & Tennis 13000 Tamiami Trail N., 239/597-1222
Pro Line Golf And Sportswear 680 Tamiami Trail N., 239/643-1599

meanders through dwarf cypress and prairies and crosses through Robert's Lake Strand (can be very wet during rainy months). Part 2, more for the seasoned backpacker, **U.S. 41 to I-75** (28 miles one-way) has trailheads on U.S. 41 near Big Cypress Visitors Center and on I-75 at the rest area at mile marker 63. A harder hike (for which you'll need to pack in all your own water), it takes you through hardwood hammocks, pinelands, prairies, and cypress. There is high-ground camping at the 13-mile mark. Part 3, **I-75 to Preserve North Boundary** (eight miles one-way) follows an old oil road through hardwood, prairie, and pine forest.

(Part of this trail is restricted to members of the Florida Trail Association.)

Canoe it. The park's main canoe trail begins at U.S. 41 and follows the **Turner River** until it ends in Chokoloskee Bay (about a five-hour paddle). You can also put in at the Everglades National Park Gulf Coast Visitors Center. There's another trail called the **Halfway Creek Canoe Trail,** for which you can put in at Seagrape Drive and paddle south past Plantation Island.

Big Cypress also accommodates camping, hunting, biking, and sightseeing by car. You'll need to go to the visitors center (or visit the

WALKING TREES

This area owes much of its landmass to the mangrove tree. They are often called walking trees because they hover above the water, their arching prop roots resembling so many spindly legs. The mangrove is one of only a handful of tree species on planet Earth that can withstand having its roots sitting in ocean water, immersed daily by rising tides, and that thrives in little soil and high levels of sulfides. The mangrove's hardiness is just one among many of its idiosyncrasies, however.

Mangroves are natural land builders. Seed tubules about the heft and length of an excellent Cuban cigar sprout on the parent tree, drop off, and bob in the brackish water until they lodge on an oyster bar or a snag in the shallows. There, the seed begins to grow into a tree, its leaves dropping and getting trapped along with seaweed and other plant debris. This organic slurry is the bottom of the food chain, supplying food, breeding area, and sanctuary to countless tiny marine creatures. In addition, it is the foundation upon which a little island or "key" begins to take shape, this buildup of sediment and debris creating a thick layer of organic peat upon which other plant species begin to grow. This first tree drops more seed tubules, which get stuck in the soft mud around the base of the parent tree and begin to grow. Soon, it's an impenetrable tangle of trees and roots extravagant enough to support birdlife and other animals.

Three types predominate in the Everglades and Ten Thousand Islands: The red mangrove forms a wide band of trees on the outermost part of each island, facing the open sea. The red mangrove encircles the black mangrove, which in turn encircles the white mangrove at the highest, driest part of each mangrove island (they are the least tolerant of having their roots sitting in saltwater). The mangroves' leathery evergreen leaves fall and stain the water a tobacco-colored tannic brown, but in fact the mangroves and all of the species dependent upon them do much to keep the waters clean and pure.

For all these reasons, mangrove trees are protected by federal, state, and local laws. Do not injure, spindle, mutilate, or even taunt a mangrove or face steep penalties.

National Park Service website at www.nps.gov/bicy) to see an informative 15-minute movie about the preserve, view a small wildlife exhibit, and pick up literature and books about the preserve.

Naples Botanical Garden

If all the Big Cypress National Preserve sounds like too much driving followed by too much walking, the Naples Botanical Garden (4820 Bayshore Dr., Naples, 239/643-7275, 10 A.M.–4 P.M. Wed.–Sat., more limited hours during the summer, $7 adults, $4 children 6–12) won't tax you too much. It's a living botanical museum within minutes of downtown, featuring a 1.5-acre tropical mosaic garden (as in, tile pottery pieces intermingled with cool plants), a butterfly house, and a 30-acre upland preserve where you'll spot gopher tortoises and bald eagles. The garden also hosts history exhibitions and lecture series, and has a nice garden store.

Boat Tours

So many ways to get out on the calm Gulf waters and Naples Bay, wind through the Ten Thousand Islands, and idle along the Gordon, Barron, Marco, or one of the area's many other rivers. Here's just a sampling of the tours to be had. The *Sweet Liberty* (City Dock, 880 12th Ave. S., 239/793-3525) is a 53-foot sailing catamaran available for public tours and private charters. Departing from Boat Haven, the boat offers shelling tours (9:30 A.M.–12:30 P.M., $40 adults, $15 children), sightseeing tours (1:30–3:30 P.M., $29.50 adults, $15 children), and sunset tours (2 hours, $29.50 adults, $15 children). On all of the cruises, the boat is trailed by a playful bevy of dolphins and you'll have an opportunity to see the lovely homes of Port Royal.

THE PARADISE COAST

The **Lady Brett** (departing from Tin City, 1200 5th Ave. S., 239/263-4949, 10 A.M., noon, 2 P.M., 4 P.M., and one hour before sunset, $30 adults, $15 children under 12) offers five one-hour narrated cruises daily out on the lovely waters of Naples Bay, and the double-decker **Double Sunshine** (departing from Tin City, 1200 5th Ave. S., 239/263-4949, 7:45 A.M. and 1 P.M., $70 adults, $55 children under 12) takes folks out on half-day deep-sea fishing trips (grouper, snapper, king fish, mackerel, and cobia) aboard a 45-foot USCG-inspected vessel equipped with bathrooms. Rod, reel, bait, and fishing license are included, but bring your own drinks and lunch. If you want to wet a line in the Ten Thousand Islands (think snook, sheephead, redfish, snapper, and trout), **Captain Paul** (departing from Tin City, 1200 5th Ave. S., 239/263-4949, $55 adults, $45 children under 12) takes people on half-day bay fishing trips on a comfortable pontoon boat.

A fancier experience, the **Naples Princess** (departing from Port-O-Call Marina, 550 Port-O-Call Way, 239/649-2275, $25–45) has narrated breakfast, lunch, and sunset buffet dinner cruises on a 93-foot air-conditioned luxury yacht that can accommodate 149 passengers.

And **Sail Kahuna** (Marco River Marina, 951 Bald Eagle Dr., Marco Island, 239/642-7704) has a range of nice boat trips in and around the Ten Thousand Islands, the most fun of which is the Kahuna Around Marco Daytime Catamaran Sail, which includes a stop at a barrier island beach for shelling, beach walking, and bird-watching; lunch; and plenty of relaxing sail time to get a bead on dolphins and manatees and drink in the sights around Marco Island.

Or make yourself useful. The **Dolphin Explorer** (Marco River Marina, 951 Bald Eagle Dr., Marco Island, 239/642-6899, www.dolphin-explorer.com) is a 30-foot catamaran that takes up to 28 passengers out for a laidback dolphin-watch cruise that is actually part of the Ten Thousand Islands Dolphin Project, an ongoing scientific dolphin research study, the only one in the country that involves the public on a daily basis. Passengers work with a naturalist on board to identify the resident dolphin population and to catalog their activities. Dolphins are identified by their dorsal fins, as unique as human fingerprints, and if a passenger spots a dolphin not already catalogued in the study, he or she gets to name it (mine would be something feisty like Chutney or Garbanzo). Cruises depart at 9 A.M. and 1 P.M. and include a stop at a barrier island for shelling and beach walking.

SIGHTS
Trolley Tours

A good place to start and orient yourself in Naples is with a long ride aboard a **Naples Trolley Tour** (1000 10th Avenue S., 239/263-8687, hourly 8:30 A.M.–5 P.M., $24 adults, $12 children). The open-air trolley has a narrated tour of more than 100 local places of note, including historic Naples Pier and Tin City. The tour itself lasts about two hours, but you can embark and disembark to explore, catching the next trolley when it suits you. Tickets are available at all boarding stops, but to get oriented you might want to begin at the Experience Naples depot, the welcome center for the Naples Trolley, Segway and Everglades van tours offered by Naples Transportation, Tours, and Event Planning.

There are two guided Segway tours available in downtown Naples. One departs from the Charter Club Resort on Naples Bay and the other from the Experience Naples store, which is also the Naples Trolley depot. Both offer insight into the history of downtown Naples and are a fun way to get oriented to the area.

Galleries

Collier County had 134 commercial art galleries at last count, wedged in among the shops of downtown, largely congregated along the length of **3rd Street South,** on what is called "Gallery Row" on Broad Avenue off 3rd Street South, and along **5th Avenue** (many between the 600 and 800 blocks).

Naples was selected as the No. 1 small art town in America by author Robert Villani in his fourth edition of *The 100 Best Art Towns*

NAPLES, MARCO ISLAND, EVERGLADES CVB

Explore Naples on a trolley tour or use the trolley to get to the shopping and dining hot spots.

in America. He cited the area's "amazing range of natural splendor," along with its "sophistication and serious art galleries," its art fairs, community arts centers and theaters, and the Philharmonic Center complex. *American Style Magazine* also named Naples in the top 25 arts destinations in the U.S., with good reason. Whether you're looking for carved African masks, Limoges boxes, or contemporary photography, window-shopping downtown is the way to go. To see the work of many local artists, stop in at the **von Liebig Art Center** (585 Park St., next to Cambier Park, 239/262-6517, 10 A.M.–4 P.M. Mon.–Sat., free admission). It houses the Naples Art Association and features changing exhibitions in five galleries.

(Naples Museum of Art

The Naples Museum of Art is the crown jewel of Naples's cultural attractions, located at the drop-dead-gorgeous $19.5 million Philharmonic Center for the Arts (5833 Pelican Bay Blvd., Naples, 239/597-1900, www.thephil.org). Museum hours are 10 A.M.–4 P.M.

Tuesday–Saturday, noon–4 P.M. Sunday May 2–October 31; it's closed August–Labor Day, and open until 5 P.M. November 2–May 1. General admission is $8 adults, $4 students, but some exhibits require an additional admission ticket. The visual arts center, opened in 2000, is a three-story, 30,000-square-foot museum with 15 galleries. Exhibits are varied and expertly curated, from a small antique walking stick show to the underwater-phantasmagorical blown glasswork of Dale Chihuly, from an Andy Warhol print show to Modern Mexican Masters. Beyond the permanent collection and visiting shows, the space itself is a work of art with a huge glass-domed conservatory, stunning entrance gates by metal artist Albert Paley, and a spectacular Chihuly chandelier.

In my experience, docents here are about as crackerjack as at any museum, able to inform, guide, and cajole you into learning a great deal. There are also film series and lectures held at the museum—many of them sell out, but you can peruse upcoming events and buy tickets via the website.

Collier County Museums

Five minutes east of downtown Naples, history enthusiasts flock to the Naples site of the Collier County Museums (3301 Tamiami Trail E, 239/774-8476, 9 A.M.–5 P.M. Mon.–Fri., until 4 P.M. Sat., free admission). There are three other locations of the museum, the Museum of the Everglades in Everglades City, the Immokalee Pioneer Museum at the home of the Robert Roberts family, and the newly renovated Naples Depot historic train station on Fifth Avenue South, but it's the Naples main museum that's worth the most time. Established in 1978, the museum offers interpretive exhibits that illuminate the history, archaeology, and development of this part of Florida, as well as a five-acre botanical park with a native plant garden, orchid house, two early Naples cottages, a logging locomotive, swamp buggies and, somewhat strangely, a World War II Sherman tank. The museum holds the **Old Florida Festival** every year on the first weekend in March—a hoot for people who like reenactments and historical pageantry.

Palm Cottage

Another walk through Naples history can be had at Palm Cottage (137 12th Ave. S., 239/261-8164, $5 donation suggested). On the National Register of Historic Places, it's the second oldest house in Collier County, built for Henry Watterson, the editor of the *Louisville Courier-Journal*. It reopened recently after a significant facelift that includes new woodwork, a new roof, and improved landscaping. The house is one of the few remaining "tabbie mortar" structures in the area—a mortar goo made from burned seashells mixed with lime and seawater. The Palm Cottage is now home to the Naples Historical Society. Tours of the house are offered 1–3:30 P.M. Monday–Friday. (You may get a broader historical picture by picking up a copy of the pictorial history titled *Naples,* published in early 2005 and compiled by the former Naples Historical Society executive director, Lynne Howard Frazer. It contains fascinating pictures and oral histories and is available at most local bookstores.)

© NAPLES, MARCO ISLAND, EVERGLADES CVB

Broad Avenue South at Third Street South in Naples has so many art galleries it's known as Gallery Row.

Southwest Florida Holocaust Museum

Growing out of an exhibit created by Golden Gate Middle School students in Naples, the Southwest Florida Holocaust Museum (4760 Tamiami Trail N., 239/263-9200, www.swflhm.org, 1–4 P.M. Tues.–Fri. and Sun., $5) is another small history museum. The students collected more than 300 death camp and Holocaust artifacts, which constitute the bulk of the exhibit. Docents lead tours for individuals as well as local school groups. The museum has also embarked on an oral history project with local survivors, liberators, and others, and it installs traveling Holocaust exhibits in local schools as well.

◖ Naples Zoo

Adults will be able to while away days in Naples with the sophisticated pleasures of dining, shopping, the arts, and so forth. But as every

THE PARADISE COAST

parent knows, the kids must be entertained with regularity, or mutiny is assured. The single most mutually agreeable family attraction in Naples is Naples Zoo at Caribbean Gardens (1590 Goodlette-Frank Rd., 239/262-5409, www.napleszoo.com, 9:30 A.M.–5:30 P.M. daily, $18.75 adults, $10.50 children 4–15, children 3 and under free), an "Old Florida" attraction in the best sense. By that I mean that it's slow, sweet, pokey, without any whiff of glitz or Disney slickness.

It began as a botanical garden, founded by botanist Henry Nehrling in 1919. The original garden was expanded in the 1950s by Julius Fleischmann, and the Tetzlaff family introduced the rare animals in 1969. The zoo is now fully accredited by the Association of Zoos and Aquariums and has recently changed to nonprofit status after local taxpayers opted to tax themselves to save the zoo land from being sold to a developer.

In much of the 52-acre garden, the animals are an afterthought, the incredible native and exotic plants taking center stage. There's a cypress hammock, a cactus garden, a dense wall of mondo-huge bamboo, banyan, and other trees ensnared in all directions by strangler fig (in this part of Florida, nights aren't warm enough for the strangler fig to create a tall canopy and kill its host tree, so they live in a certain kind of dramatic symbiosis, the strangler resembling a scary vegetable octopus).

Kids will prefer the baby alligator feeding shows, and be sure to catch the Planet Predator and Meet the Keeper live animal shows. Seeing these animals up close inspires a certain amount of awe, but it's the keepers' wry over-the-heads-of-babes banter that makes the shows so entertaining. There's also a wonderful short boat ride (also with an archly ironic narration) that takes you past a bunch of tiny islands from which various species of primate will grimace at you and sometimes throw unspeakable things.

The zoo has a few new additions worth noting: The Panther Glade and Leopard Rock separate you from the big cats by a thrillingly thin sheet of glass; there are two new rare and beautiful Malayan tigers, the only zoo in Florida where these cats can be viewed. The zoo has also launched a multimedia show called *Serpents: Fangs & Fiction* to shed some light on these slithery stars.

Family-Friendly Attractions

If the weather is nice during your visit, which it doubtless will be, kids enjoy a round of mini golf at **Coral Cay Adventure Golf** (2205 Tamiami Trail E., one mile east of Tin City, 239/793-4999, 10 A.M.–11 P.M. daily, $7 adults, $6 children 5–11, $3 children 4 and under), with its exotic tropical setting featuring caves, reefs, and a waterfall. There's a snack bar with semireal food, slushies, and ice cream, and a game room as well.

North Collier Regional Park (15000 Livingston Rd., 239/254-4000, 6 A.M.–10 P.M. daily, free admission) is a great new addition for families, with eight tournament soccer fields, five tournament softball fields, an interactive playground and Calusa fossil dig play area for children, an exhibit hall with ranger-led tours, and a rec center. For visitors, the more salient part is the **Sun-N-Fun Lagoon Water Park** (239/254-4021, 10 A.M.–7 P.M. daily during the summer, weekends only during the spring and fall, $10 for those taller than 48 inches, $5.50 for children less than 48 inches tall, free children 3 and under), with one million gallons of good times for children and their handlers. Opened in 2006, the center features water-dumping buckets, water pistols, four pools (a family pool, a "tadpole" pool for kids six and under, Turtle Cove for kids seven and up, and a lap/diving pool), and Sunny's River, a lazy river attraction with three waterslides.

Also worth a couple hours of investigation is the Conservancy of Southwest Florida's **Naples Nature Center** (1450 Merrihue Dr., 239/262-0304, 9 A.M.–4:30 P.M. Mon.–Sat., noon–4 P.M. Sun., $9 adults, $4 kids 3–12), just a few blocks from the Naples Zoo. The lovely center has a museum with a sea turtle in an aquarium, a wildlife rescue program with several bird species on display, and guided electric boat tours through the mangrove habitat on the Gordon River.

ENTERTAINMENT AND EVENTS
Music and Theater

The **Philharmonic Center for the Arts** (5833 Pelican Bay Blvd., 239/597-1900, www.thephil.org, ticket prices and times vary, box office hours 10 A.M.–4 P.M. Mon.–Fri.) is an outstanding venue hosting more than 400 events a year including world-class dance, opera, classical, and popular music, and traveling Broadway musicals. The center contains a 1,221-seat main hall and a 200-seat black box theater. The **Naples Philharmonic Orchestra** (239/597-0606) performs here with more than 120 concerts per year including classics, pops, chamber orchestras, and numerous educational performances. The **Miami City Ballet** is in residence performing four programs with the orchestra during the season.

There isn't any resident professional theater company in Naples, although the **Sugden Community Theatre** (701 5th Ave. S., 239/263-7990) is home to the 40-year-old **Naples Players,** a fairly amateurish community theater troupe that stages somewhere around 14 musicals, comedies, dramas, and children's productions (they also host a program called KidzAct with musical theater workshops for kids) annually. The Sugden also screens a "Films on Fifth" series, mostly independent and art house films.

And for mainstream movies, head to the 20-plex **Regal Hollywood 20** (6006 Hollywood Dr., 239/597-4252), the **Towne Centre 6 Theater** (3855 Tamiami Trail E., 239/774-4800), **Pavilion Cinemas** (833 Vanderbilt Beach Rd., 239/596-0008), or **Marco Movies** (599 Collier Blvd., Marco Island, 239/642-1111), where you can dine on Greek salad, beer, or wine with your movie popcorn.

SHOPPING

Of anyplace along the Gulf Coast of Florida, Naples is the reigning queen of retail, no contest. There are often comparisons made to Rodeo Drive and some of the U.S.'s other prime shopping spots, but really Naples may win for sheer diversity.

◖ Third Street South

Third Street South is where to start, with exquisite clothing and giftware shops, chic restaurants, and dozens of galleries. Just a couple of blocks from the beach and Naples Pier, the street was Naples's real core at the turn of the last century. Don't know where to begin? Consult the **street concierge** (239/434-6533, 10 A.M.–6 P.M. Mon.–Sat., noon–5 P.M. Sun.) located just opposite the Fleischmann Fountain at 1203 3rd Street South for help navigating the area's shops and restaurants.

5th Avenue South

Not far from there 5th Avenue South (239/435-3742) is another huge draw. Seminoles once sold their crafts from a stand on 5th, and before that Calusas used this area as a canal connecting Naples Bay with the Gulf. The Ed Frank Garage was the first commercial building—erected in 1923—and growth puttered along organically for decades (maybe a hardware store, then a gas station). Then, as in so many cities around the country, the birth of the mall heralded the death of downtown.

In 1996, savvy civic planners had 5th Avenue South join the Florida Main Street Program, and a master plan was created with the help of Miami urban planner Andres Duany. The upshot was that dilapidated one-story storefronts were razed and replaced with sleek Mediterranean two- and three-story buildings (with room for people to live above). Today, 5th Avenue encompasses 12 blocks and 50 buildings (including the Bayfront and Tin City shopping and dining complexes), with such a crafty mix of shops, dining, and nightlife possibilities (as well as a strange preponderance of brokerages and realties) that the length of it is busy at most hours. There is free street entertainment the second Thursday of the month during Evenings on Fifth, tucked at intervals along the banyan- and flowering poinciana–bedecked avenue.

Village on Venetian Bay

Equally fancy-pants is the Village on Venetian Bay (4200 Gulf Shore Blvd., 239/261-6100),

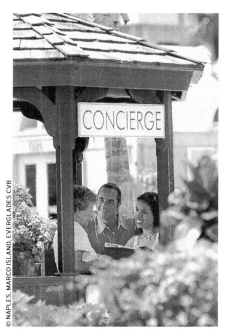

© NAPLES, MARCO ISLAND, EVERGLADES CVB

The concierge booth on Third Street South is also a free Wi-Fi hot spot.

with a kind of Venetian canal-side vibe. You'll find lots of independent clothing boutiques (plus familiar faces like Sunglass Hut, the White House/Black Market, and Chico's), a couple of high-end shoe stores, a handful of restaurants (plus Ben & Jerry's), and some home interior shops.

Tin City

More overtly touristy, but really fun, Tin City (at the eastern end of downtown, U.S. 41 E at Goodlette Rd., 239/434-4693, www.tin-city.com) was built in 1976 on the site of a 1920s clam- and oyster-processing plant. It incorporated the crusty waterfront buildings, with oodles of rustic maritime charm, into a shopping emporium (surf shop, bikini shop, Jimmy Buffet–themed gewgaws) with a few restaurants (Riverwalk Fish & Ale House, Pincher's) worthy of your money. The Naples Trolley drops you right here, and it's an easy walk from 5th Avenue South.

Waterside Shops

The Waterside Shops (5415 Tamiami Trail N., in Pelican Bay, 239/598-1605, www.watersideshops.com) are anchored by huge draws such as Saks Fifth Avenue, Polo Ralph Lauren, MaxMara, Pottery Barn, Banana Republic, and stuff like that. It's a classic, high-end mall with covered walkways and restaurants like the California Pizza Kitchen. Some 30 new retailers were recently added in a major upgrade, led by Tiffany & Co., Gucci, Coach, and Hermes. Nordstrom opens in 2008.

Other Shopping Areas

Before you start getting fatigued by all this shopping, let me put in a word for the boutiques along the **Dockside Boardwalk** (corner of 11th St. and 6th Ave. S) and **Crayton Cove** (at the historic City Dock, off 10th St.), and if you need a good old-fashioned JCPenney or Sears to offset all this glitz, there's the **Coastland Center Mall** (1900 9th St. N., 239/262-2323), with Macy's, Dillard's, and new restaurants including Kona Grill, Ruth's Chris, and Cheesecake Factory.

ACCOMMODATIONS
Under $150

My favorite midpriced hotel in Naples is the **◖ Lemon Tree Inn** (250 9th St. S., 239/262-1414, www.lemontreeinn.com, $85–199). The owner recently remodeled the 35 rooms, adding new carpeting, linens, and bedroom furniture. Some rooms have mahogany four-poster beds. There's a sweet little gazebo and swimming pool, where breakfast is served each morning. But the real draw is the people—the owner is incredibly warm, as are all the people he employs. It has an Old Florida charm married with a sophisticated Naples aesthetic. Oh, and there's free lemonade in the office, very quenching after a long day of beach bumming.

In terms of other decent midpriced chains, **The Holiday Inn Naples** (1100 9th St. N., $85–145) is in a good location with pleasant rooms, a nice pool, and easy access to the beach and shopping; **Bayfront Inn on Fifth** (1221 5th Ave. S., 239/649-5800, $55–200)

THE PARADISE COAST

has spacious rooms, new tropical decor, a very central location, and a full-service marina; and **Hampton Inn** (2630 Northbrooke Plaza Dr., 239/596-1299, $125–175) is off Exit 111, closer to I-75 and Corkscrew Sanctuary Swamp.

Over $150

Where to even begin? Naples is awash in luxury hotels—so much so, in fact, that the Ritz-Carlton boasts not one property, but two in town. Once you enter the luxury accommodation price point, where to stay depends largely on your priorities. If you want an urban experience, so you can roll out of bed and be wandering the downtown shops within minutes, consider ◖ **The Inn on Fifth** (699 5th Ave. S., 239/403-8777, www.naplesinn.com, $310–500), a boutique hotel filled with Mediterranean charm. The 87 rooms are truly elegant, with sliding French doors to a balcony or terrace. The common space features burbling fountains, courtyards, and lavish gardens—all at the center of downtown. The inn opened the Asian-influenced **Spa on Fifth** in 2004, purportedly adhering to feng shui principles.

On a slightly more residential street downtown, the **Trianon Old Naples** (955 7th Ave. S., 239/435-9600, www.trianon.com, $220–500) is another small luxury hotel with a pool, a lounge, off-street parking, and complimentary continental breakfast served in the lobby (although there's no on-site restaurant, so you can't order room service or just go downstairs for dinner). The 55 roomy guest rooms and three large one-bedroom suites have all the usual fine amenities with balconies, multiline phones, computer data ports, and easy access to Tin City and 5th Avenue South.

Relatively new in Naples, **Bellasera Hotel** (221 9th St. S., 239/649-7333, $240–475) was just named one of the "top 10 hidden gems in the U.S." in the Travelers' Choice awards on TripAdvisor. It features 100 luxurious studios, one-, two-, and three-bedroom suites with kitchens and spacious living and dining areas, all with bold Tuscan-style architecture and decor. It's a AAA Four Diamond award-winner just far enough removed from the hub-bub of 5th Avenue to seem restful. A heated outdoor pool, fitness center, Zizi Restaurant & Lounge, meeting space, and business center round out the amenities.

If your favorite time is tee time, there are several golfy wonderlands. The **Naples Beach Hotel & Golf Club** (851 Gulf Shore Blvd. N., 239/261-2222, www.naplesbeachhotel.com, $439–600) is a 125-acre beachfront resort with 318 guest rooms and suites, on-site championship golf, an award-winning tennis center, large beachside swimming pool, fitness center and spa, complimentary kids' program, four restaurants and an open-air beach bar from which to choose, and a handful of lovely boutiques. Opened in 1946, the hotel was renovated a few years ago, with a $5 million lobby and luxurious tropical decor and furnishings.

LaPlaya Beach & Golf Resort (9891 Gulf Shore Blvd. N., 239/597-3123, $325–1,000) was already a stunning property, but then it had its multimillion-dollar makeover in 2002, so it's *da bomb*. The 189 spacious guest rooms and suites are stunningly appointed (I could live here), with goose-down pillows and Frette linens to satisfy even the most persnickety sleeper. There are those cushy waffle-weave bathrobes, marble bathrooms with jetted tubs, a tremendous spa, twice-daily maid service. Oh, and there's golf. You have to drive a little over three miles from the hotel, but enthusiasts say the Bob Cupp–designed course is worth it. It's an 18-hole, par 72, 6,907-yard championship layout with a driving range, practice area, and 12,000-square-foot clubhouse.

Not to be outdone, the **Ritz-Carlton Naples Golf Resort** (2600 Tiburon Dr., 239/593-2000, $450–1,000) has received kudos from *Golf Digest* as one of the best golf resorts in North America. And in fact all of the 295 guest rooms manage to look out on the sweeping vistas of the Greg Norman–designed Tiburon Golf Club. Guests can also enjoy the amenities at the sister Ritz-Carlton in town.

And if your aim is to have sand in your bed, or at least the beach within walking distance, there are several wonderful luxury hotels that fit the bill. The **Edgewater Beach Hotel** (1901 Gulf Shore Blvd. N., 239/262-6511, $200–900) is an intimate, 126-suite boutique hotel right on the beach. All suites, the lobby, and pool deck area had a hip redecoration in 2006. It's another AAA Four Diamond property, with a deliciously edgy lobby restaurant called Coast. Guests also have dining and recreational privileges at the Naples Grande Beach Resort, its sister property.

Speaking of the **Naples Grande Beach Resort** (475 Seagate Dr., 239/597-3232, www.naplesgranderesort.com, $164–869), it was one of the area's most beloved landmarks when it was known as the Registry. This property has undergone a complete transformation in the past few years. A sweeping granite lobby leads to the new Aura restaurant and bar, complete with a South Beach–style, draped Chill Out Lounge. Naples Grande is surrounded by 200 acres of tropical mangrove preserve, with beach access and three swimming pools. The newest additions are the Golden Door Spa, the first Golden Door to open in the Eastern U.S., and a Strip House steakhouse restaurant.

The other **Ritz-Carlton, Naples** (280 Vanderbilt Beach Rd., 239/598-3300, $300–799) is a Mobil Five-Star, AAA Five Diamond resort, all 463 rooms with stunning views of the Gulf of Mexico. There are seven on-site restaurants, tennis courts, a 33-treatment-room spa with fitness center, two pools, championship golf nearby at Tiburon, and white sand as far as the eye can see.

If you want to totally and completely get away from it all, there's **Key Island Estate** (800/770-SAND, www.keyislandestate.com, $2,000/day for up to 14 people). You get your own private island. Located on the eight-mile-long barrier Keewaydin Island between Naples and Marco Island, it's accessible only by boat and overlooks the Rookery Bay Reserve on one side and the Gulf of Mexico on the other. There's a master suite and two separate wings for additional guests, wraparound porches, huge open kitchen, and lovely detailing throughout. It's something to think about

for weddings, corporate retreats, or big family getaways.

FOOD

In Tanzania they say "Jambo." In Papua New Guinea it's "Moning tru." In Australia, "G'day." But in Naples, the greeting goes like, "Have you been to [insert name of red-hot new restaurant here] yet?" It's one of those cities where everyone jostles in line to taste the doings of the latest macaroni maestro, the newest sushi shaman. Dining at the latest big hot spot is a form of social currency, made more delicious in the retelling. Of course, once the cat is out of the bag, he's free to claw your furniture. In high season, this means you need to make a reservation at most of the hip spots.

At the beginning of May, there's the annual **Taste of Collier** in Naples. All the froufrou Naples restaurants showcase their wares in a one-day family-friendly festival.

5th Avenue South

There are a few dense concentrations of wonderful restaurants in downtown Naples; 5th has the greatest embarrassment of riches, assembled between 9th Street and 3rd Street. The gamut is impressive, from trendy to fancy "continental," covering a range of prices and ethnicities. The best ones are listed here from east at 9th (the beginning of downtown) to the west as it reaches the Gulf.

St. George & The Dragon (936 5th Ave. S., 239/262-6546, 11 A.M.–4 P.M. and 4–10 P.M. Mon.–Sat., $14–50) isn't trying to keep up with any of the trendy places nearby. It does what it's been doing best for more than 30 years, with moody lighting, a reason to get dressed up, and nostalgic continental fare like fat escargots redolent of garlic and dripping butter, or creamy Delmonico potatoes. Nearby **Pazzo Italian Café** (853 5th Ave. S., 239/434-8494, 5–10 P.M. weekdays, until 11 P.M. weekends, $15–28) presents diners with an instant conundrum—sit in the lovely modern dining room with its open bar and kitchen, or settle into one of the sidewalk tables through open French doors and watch the world stroll by? Pazzo makes a mean Bellini, those champagne and peach nectar cocktails that are the height of festivity, and lots of elegant spins on familiar Italian dishes. Worth trying are the grouper saltimbocca and the Vincenzo, a molten chocolate cake oozing its way into soft vanilla ice cream and raspberry coulis. Practically right next door is one of downtown's most happening places, **Chops City Grill** (837 5th Ave. S., 239/262-4677, 5–10 P.M. weekdays, until 11 P.M. weekends, $15–34). If I start enumerating the menu possibilities it just sounds schizophrenic, but it all works. I ate the following one night: tuna three ways (citrus seared tuna tataki, shrimp and tuna sushi roll, and tuna summer roll), an order of Mongolian beef satay with an addictive peanut sauce and five-spice apple slices, and a stacked tomato-napoleon salad with a precarious avalanche of Roquefort crumbles. Singles: Dine at the long food bar and you won't be alone long. Everyone's friendly, the dining room has palpable buzz, decor is hip.

A block down you'll find the other hippest, waitlist-for-miles place, **Yabba Island Grill** (711 5th Ave. S., 239/262-5787, 5–10 P.M. weekdays, until 11 P.M. weekends, $20–30). It's no coincidence, really, as Pazzo, Chops, and Yabba are all owned and operated by the same folks. Again, a drama, an excitement that only a very popular restaurant can generate, but in this case the food is a little goofier. It may speak only to my tastes, but it's an island-themed menu in which there's one too many ingredients in everything and a piled-up architectural approach that makes eating hazardous to your outfit. Still, I can recommend the sugarcane-skewered grilled chicken with sweet and spicy barbecue sauce, and the sautéed plantain and macadamia-encrusted black grouper with rum butter sauce and a bunch of other fruity stuff.

From here, take it down a frenzy notch and step into the elegant, breezy world of **Vergina** (700 5th Ave. S., 239/659-7008, 11:30 A.M.–4 P.M. Mon.–Sat., 5–10 P.M. daily, $15–25). I'm sure the word means something beautiful in Italian, but its unfortunate genital sound means that all the ladies-who-lunch in Naples whisper, "Meet me at Vagina" into their cell phones and then cackle. Again, there's wonderful outdoor seating in a sheltered plaza and a soaring indoor space with a long, inviting bar. The food is all familiar Italian, with a punchy Caesar salad and robust seafood pastas. The Italian waiters are simultaneously solicitous and able to poke good-hearted fun at you, an endearing Italian skill.

A fun and rollicking Irish hangout lies just across the street. **McCabe's Irish Pub & Grill** (699 5th Ave. S., 239/403-8777) is in the lobby of the Inn on Fifth, and while the atmosphere is all jovial Irish pub (live, brogue-dripping singers, heavy on the Guinness), the food is fairly sophisticated, from a grilled swordfish napped with a capery lime beurre blanc to an apple-cranberry cobbler with slowly melting vanilla bean ice cream.

A recent addition to the strip, ◖ **Café and Bar Lurcat** (494 5th Ave. S., 239/213-3357, 5–10P.M. Mon.–Thurs., Fri. and Sat. until 11P.M., Sun. until 9P.M., $11–32) has been knocking people's socks off with its New American cuisine and über-stylish atmosphere. It's owned and managed by D'Amico & Partners, which also owns Campiello (see *3rd Street*). The first floor is the bar, with live music and a wonderful small plate approach (the tiny sirloin burgers make a bold case for a carnivorous diet), and the upstairs is the more formal dining room. The wine program is quirky and thoughtful, with keen energy brought to bear on food and wine pairings. And what food it is: pot roast slowly braised in cabernet sauvignon with roasted root veggies; velvety foie gras outfitted with roasted pears; buckwheat crepes with smoked Kentucky ham and figs.

There are plenty of other fine choices along 5th—walk and peer in, reading menus as you go. For a casual sandwich, coffee, or ice cream, try **Cheeburger Cheeburger** (505 5th Ave. S., 239/435-9796), **PJ's Coffee & Tea** (599 5th Ave. S., 239/261-5757), and **Regina's Ice Cream Pavilion** (824 5th Ave. S., 239/434-8181).

Third Street South

3rd Street South was once the central business district of Old Naples, and these days it's fairly overrun with galleries and high-end boutiques and antiques shops. The restaurant choices aren't as myriad as on 5th, but in fact a few of Naples's absolute best restaurants line up along 3rd.

C Campiello Ristorante (1177 3rd St. S., 239/435-1166, 11:30 A.M.–2:30 P.M. Mon.–Sat., noon–2:30 P.M. Sun., 5:30 P.M.–10 P.M. Sun.–Thurs., until 10:30 P.M. Fri. and Sat., $17–38) may be my favorite restaurant around (and a lot of other people's, too, judging from the crowds). It's got a spare, understated elegance achievable only at the best Cal-Ital bistros. Lunch here is an experience that harkens back to the boom-boom '80s power-lunching phenomenon. Biting into a spit-roasted pork sandwich with red onion and smoked mozzarella, or nibbling the point of a housemade chicken sausage and gorgonzola pizza slice, everyone looks like a high-powered executive in the midst of clinching a big deal—wealthy, healthy, and self-satisfied. But maybe it's just because the food is good. At lunch and dinner, presentations are simple and flavors are clean and steady, with a gutsy reliance on great produce and slow-roasted meats.

A totally different vibe, but equally popular is **Tommy Bahama's Tropical Café** (1300 3rd St. S., 239/643-6889, 11 A.M.–2:30 P.M. Mon.–Sat., 5–10 P.M. daily, $11–29). It's the same company as the clothing line or, as they like to say, "purveyor of island lifestyles" (what *does* that mean, exactly?—I'd like to buy me a couple of them there lifestyles), and as one might expect this means an upscale interpretation of island cuisine—smoldering jerk chicken, incredible fruity cocktails—served in a tasteful Polynesian setting with bamboo-blade fans and thatched-roof tikis. Tommy Bahama's also has live music most evenings, making it a wonderful place for a cocktail (Tommy's Bungalow Brew) and some lively conversation.

A longtime Naples institution, **Ridgway Bar & Grill** (1300 3rd St. S., 239/262-5500, 8 A.M.–10:30 P.M. Mon.–Sat., 11:30 A.M.– 10:30 P.M. Sun., $16–30) actually closed up a while back and then was reborn. Owner Tony Ridgway is something of a legend in Naples, having brought one of the first gourmet aesthetics (and wine knowledge) to Naples 30 years ago, when most Americans were woefully in the pre–Julia Child dark ages. He owns a small cooking school as well as **Tony's Off Third** (1300 3rd St. S., 239/262-7999) gourmet deli and wine shop next door, and the restaurant's wine offerings reflect this close proximity, with more than 600 bottlings on the far-reaching list. The food is pretty squarely American, but with a sophisticated French fillip here and there. Live entertainment is provided Thursday through Sunday nights by pianist and comedian Jim Badger.

Tin City

Tin City Waterfront Marketplace is a fairly well done waterside indoor shopping center with about 40 mostly nautical-theme boutiques and a couple of good restaurants. The complex is on U.S. 41 at Goodlette Road. The most casual of the restaurants is **Cafe Europa** (1200 5th Ave S # 19, 239/262-5911, 10A.M.–9P.M. daily, $5–12), where you'll find sandwiches, hamburgers, and subs at decent prices. A little more upscale is the lively **Riverwalk Fish & Ale House** (1200 5th Ave S., 239/263-2734, 11A.M.–10P.M. daily, $13.95–27.95). Stay with the simple here, as the kitchen has a tendency to add just a couple of rogue ingredients to their more "gourmet" items. And then there's the brand new **Pincher's Crab Shack** (1200 5th Ave S # 8, 239/434-6616, 11A.M.–10P.M. weekdays, until 11P.M. weekends, $10–89.99), the newest location in the southwest Florida family of restaurants as famous for their fresh-caught Gulf grouper and snapper as for their cheesy crab dip. Right across from Tin City is a casual joint called **Kelly's** (1302 5th Ave. S., 239/774-0494, 4:30–10 P.M. daily, $15–25) where you'll find the city's best stone crabs. Nothing fancy, but it's one of the oldest restaurants around here.

Downtown and Vicinity

The rest of the area's top restaurants are fairly

spread out, although there's a dense concentration of fine eats north of downtown on the Tamiami Trail (U.S. 41) between about Golden Gate Parkway and Pine Ridge Road. **Andre's Steakhouse** (2800 Tamiami Trail N., 239/263-5851, 5–9 P.M. daily, $24–35) falls squarely in the luxury American steakhouse idiom. Try the porterhouse for four people, like something from the *Flintstones,* paired with an important California cab or first-growth Bordeaux (the list contains 4,000 bottlings) and surrounded by baked potato, creamed spinach, maybe a vat of gilding-the-lily béarnaise sauce.

Chef Claudio Scaduto has serious francophilic followers at his **Cote D'Azur** (11224 Tamiami Trail N., 239/597-8867, 5–9 P.M. daily, $18–28). The menu at the warm, intimate restaurant is pure Provence: *loup de mer Antibois* (Mediterranean sea bass), *noisettes d'agneau peillois* (roasted spring lamb loins), etc.

Back downtown, next to Sugden Theater, **Trulucks** (698 4th Ave. S., 239/530-3131, 4–10 P.M. daily, $15–34) is a fairly new addition to the dining scene, part of a small chain out of Texas, but the seafood is pretty darned good. Especially the crab, and there's lots of it: Northwest Dungeness crab, Florida stone crab, Alaskan Norton Sound Bairdi crab, red king crab.

North of town almost to Bonita Springs is **Naples Tomato** (14700 Tamiami Trail N, 239/598-9800, 11:30 A.M.–11:30 P.M. daily, $8.95–19.95), which opened several years ago with a strong local following. With many serious oenophiles in the Naples area who belong to the restaurant's wine club, this is the first Florida restaurant to install the self-serve, ATM-style Enomatic wine system. Just buy your wine "debit" card and sample either a 2-, 4-, or 6-ounce pour of any number of boutique bottlings. Opt for the classic or low-carb lasagna, several signature seafood dishes, grilled

fish, or selections from the antipasti bar. The restaurant is expanding to provide more dining area and now has a full liquor license.

Hotel Restaurants

These are all pretty fancy, pretty pricey, best for when you can expense it or that wealthy Floridian maiden great-aunt aims to shower you with her beneficence. All of them suggest reservations and slightly fancy dress. Starting at the top, maybe even the over-the-top, **Artisans in the Dining Room** (The Ritz-Carlton, 280 Vanderbilt Beach Rd., 239/598-3300, 6–10 P.M. daily, 10:30 A.M.–2 P.M. Sun. brunch, half portions $20–35, full portions $30–55, jacket suggested) is the only AAA Five Diamond restaurant in southwest Florida. Since reopening as Artisans in the Dining Room, the restaurant features "great regional seafood with style" and a stellar wine list with more than 1,600 selections. Nightly entertainment.

Naples Grande Beach Resort now features the **Strip House** (475 Seagate Dr., 239/598-9600, 5 P.M.–11 P.M. Mon.–Thurs., until midnight Fri. and Sat., 5–10 P.M. Sun., $35–52), created by the Glazier Group of Monkey Bar and Twenty-Four Fifth fame. The well-marbled steaks are paired with decadent sides like potatoes fried with foie gras and black truffle–laced creamed spinach.

Baleen at LaPlaya Beach & Golf Resort (9891 Gulf Shore Dr., 239/597-3123, 7 A.M.–9:30 P.M. daily, $23–37) is also a favorite among visitors and locals livin' large. The dining room has wonderful indoor-outdoor seating that overlooks a perfect swath of beach and Gulf of Mexico. The menu contains some Asian-inspired fare as well as more continental dishes: seared sea scallops with a lo mein noodle cake and charred scallion-miso butter, alongside a roquefort-crusted filet mignon with potato puree and red wine sauce.

Marco Island

The largest and northernmost of the Ten Thousand Islands, Marco is an example of poor civic planning and rapacious builders and developers allowed to run amok. Them's fighting words, I know, but Marco Island might have been the kind of tranquil beach paradise Jimmy Buffet is wont to sing about. Gorgeous sunsets, gentle Gulf breezes, a subtropical lushness—Marco Island has lots going for it, not to mention easy access to the more urbane and sophisticated Naples just to the north and the western gateway to the mysterious Everglades National Park just to the south.

What's my beef, then? It's tall resort hotels and condominiums along the beach that blot out the sun and obscure all beach vistas to those unlucky enough to be staying elsewhere. It's the fact that no overarching development plan established any kind of walking-friendly downtown area that makes use of the four miles of glinting quartz sand beaches and picturesque mangrove islands that dot the blue Gulf waters.

That's off my chest now, so I can afford to be less cranky. Marco Island really is a fairly dreamy family vacation spot. The average annual high temperature is 85 degrees, average low is 65, so most of the year it's a joy to be outside. Beyond the beaches, there are several fine private and semiprivate golf courses; lots of good snook, redfish, and pompano fishing; and access to more tiny, wonderful islands than you can count. People really do live on Marco, many of them in modest, low-rise ranchers on the bridge end of the island, but as I said, the rest of the island is given over to a luxury-resort paradigm, which works nicely when you're in an all-id-all-the-time vacation mode (Marco is one of the few places on the Gulf Coast where a Jet Ski doesn't look out of place).

The island used to be two separate landmasses—one part of it a shell mound raised by generations of shellfish-eating Calusas. Their detritus, along with some more recent swamp dredging and so forth, yielded the current-day

An aerial view shows clusters of red mangrove that together form the stunning Ten Thousand Islands.

6,800-acre island with its rolling sand hills, beaches, and slash pine forests. It's accessed easily from Exit 101 off of I-75, heading south on Collier Boulevard for 20 miles until you cross Jolley Bridge.

The island was named La Isla de San Marco, the Island of St. Mark, by the Spaniards shortly after they landed on these shores in 1513 (around the time the Calusa disappeared). The island's history dates back much further, though—archaeology enthusiasts and history buffs flock to the island's historic markers and wealth of artifacts. A dozen markers around town chart Marco Island history, including one of the most significant excavations in North America—the priceless Key Marco Cat, the

THE PARADISE COAST

first known North American example of a half man-half animal figurine. The cat itself is now at the Smithsonian, but the small sculpture was unearthed here in 1896 and is thought to be more than 3,000 years old (there's a replica in the historical society museum).

Despite all that ancient history, W. T. Collier is credited with founding Marco Island in 1870—the northern end was called Key Marco, the southern end Caxambas. Not too long after that it was incorporated as Collier City. But it wasn't until the 1960s when the Deltona Corporation got big ideas about the island's potential as a resort and leisure destination that Marco became recognizable as the place it is today. A mad scramble of residential and commercial building turned the sleepy town of a few thousand into a beachy retreat for more than 14,000 people in high season.

SPORTS AND RECREATION
C Tigertail Beach
Marco Island boasts a four-mile crescent of white sandy beach. Not too far from the long stand of tall condominiums and resort hotels, Tigertail Beach (entrance at Spinnaker Dr. and Hernando Dr., 8 A.M.–sunset daily, parking $6, showers and restrooms) is pretty much all things to all people. There's a rental stand for water sports and toys, umbrellas, and chairs; volleyball nets that see heavy action; a concession stand; and children's play area. You'll see little Sand Dollar Island out across the lagoon, which was Tigertail's sandbar only 10 years ago, a perfect place for shelling and desultory sand sifting at low tide. The 32-acre beach park is also a birder's favorite for watching shorebirds (but the bird sanctuary nearby is off-limits to visitors).

Marco South Beach
Marco South Beach is a "residents" beach (walkway access from Collier Blvd. north of Cape Marco, 8 A.M.–sunset daily), which has public parking and access. This beach has no facilities, but is a good place to beachcomb for Florida sand dollars, whelks, fighting conchs, lion's paws, calico scallops, and others of the more

than 400 types of seashells found on the island. Be sure to leave all live shells on the beach. Pets are prohibited on Marco Island beaches.

Fishing
Island visitors and locals surf cast for black drum and sheepshead; they take boats out in the backcountry mangrove flats to fish for tarpon, snook, and redfish; or head into deeper water offshore for grouper, amberjack, snapper, and kingfish. A number of species in the area have gamefish status, and are thus the more exotic and often the most sought after. This means redfish, snook, tarpon, bonefish, and sailfish are illegal to buy or sell (that's why you don't ever see them on restaurant menus, although you wouldn't want to eat a tarpon even if you were offered one with a delicate beurre blanc and fancy capers), and many of them have very persnickety catch limits and seasons. For instance, in the Gulf of Mexico and the Everglades, open season for snook, the period of time during which you are allowed to harvest a fish, is now limited to the months of March, April, September, October, and November. Fish must be between 28 and 33 inches to keep, with one snook allowed per person. Closed season is now December–February and May–August. If you catch a snook during those months the fish must be released alive. Don't wet a line until you've studied up on what you can catch, how many, and when.

If you want to head out fishing with an expert, Marco Island, as with much of the Gulf Coast, has many specialists willing to show you the way. Specializing in light tackle and flyfishing, **Captain Gary Eichler** (239/642-9779, www.marcoislandcharters.com, $395–800, depending on the boat and location) has a number of boats from which to choose, lots of experience in the area, and a fun website on which you and your trophy catch can be immortalized. He does individual private charters (no split charters) with six passengers at the most.

Captain Bill Walsh takes visitors out with his company **Dawn Patrol** (Marco River Marina, 951 Bald Eagle Dr., 239/394-0608, $200 for four people for a half day), known for fishing

THE STINGRAY SHUFFLE

It's not a dance, exactly.

It's strictly anecdotal, but Marco Island seems to have more than its share of flat, seafloor-living stingrays. Visitors occasionally step on these creatures, their winglike fins hidden in the sandy shallows. When trod upon, a stingray flips up its tail in self-defense and delivers a nasty stinging puncture with its barb. To avoid this, drag your feet along the sandy bottom (as opposed to stepping up and down). The "shuffle" may not look too swift, but it alerts stingrays to your approach. They are just hanging around the shallows to catch shellfish and crustaceans and they'd rather not waste their time on stinging you.

If you are unlucky enough to be stung, it's important that you clean the wound with freshwater immediately (other bacteria in seawater can infect the area). As soon as you can, soak the wound in the hottest water you can stand for up to 90 minutes to neutralize the venom. The pain can be severe, often accompanied by weakness, vomiting, headache, fainting, shortness of breath, paralysis, and collapse in people who are allergic to the venom. You may want to see a doctor, who might add insult to injury with a tetanus shot.

Always report stingray injuries to the lifeguard on duty.

the nearshore artificial reefs and ledges. Dawn Patrol specializes in family trips and will tailor a fishing trip to include a mix of shelling, fishing, and sightseeing so even nonfishers in your group are entertained.

Specializing in fly-fishing and light tackle angling is **Everglades Angler** (810 12th Ave. S., 239/262-8228 or 800/57-FISHY, $375–950 depending on the length and type of trip) that has a number of boats and captains from which to choose, lots of experience in the area and is ORVIS endorsed.

If you want to go it alone, **Marco River Marina** (951 Bald Eagle Dr., 239/394-2502) rents out the largest array of boats on the island. Boats at **Cedar Bay Yacht Club** (705 E. Elkcam Cir., 239/642-6717) all come equipped with a bimini (sun top), plastic cooler stocked with ice and drinks, VHF radio, USCG equipment, and an easy-to-navigate color chart of the local waters. They're endlessly patient with beginners, too. Prices range deck boat $285 for full day, $210 for half; pontoon boat $260 for full day, $195 for half, center console $260 for full, $195 for half. The Marco River Marina is also the debarkation point for **Sea Key West Express** (239/394-9700), a three-hour cruise to Key West (a very affordable way to explore Key West without having to fly).

Golf

Guidebooks all bandy about the statistic that Naples has more golf courses per capita than anywhere else. Many of these are in East Naples, and many are private. On Marco Island there are several notable private courses—**Hideaway Beach Club** (250 Beach Dr. S., 239/642-6300), **Island Country Club** (500 Nassau Rd., 239/394-3151), and others—but only a couple of public possibilities. The Marco Island Marriott's **Rookery Golf Club** (400 Collier Blvd. S., 239/793-6060), designed by Joe Lee, is an 18-hole, par-72, Scottish links–style course built on 240 acres of rolling terrain and featuring several mounds coming into play around the greens. The signature hole is No. 16, a 165-yard par 3, requiring a tee shot over water to a peninsula green. Swing tune-ups for experienced players as well as beginners' lessons are available at the Marriott's Faldo Institute located at The Rookery at Marco.

Despite its name, the **Marco Shores Country Club** (1450 Mainsail Dr., Naples, 239/394-2581) is in Naples, but very close by. The course has long, wide fairways and well-maintained greens blended seamlessly into the native mangroves and waterways of the Ten Thousand Islands. With four separate tees, Marco Shores accommodates all skill levels.

If you're a golf glutton and want to try out

THE PARADISE COAST

a handful of the legendary local courses, **Golf Vacation Web** (877/767-5445) puts together a five-night stay at the **Hilton Marco Island Beach Resort** with a round of golf at each of the Lely Flamingo Island Club, Lely Mustang Golf Club, Tiburon, Naples Lakes, and Cedar Hammock courses.

◖ Calusa Shell Mounds

The Calusa (kah-LOOS-ah) tribe lived on the coast and along the inner waterways in this area. They were tall and fierce, with a marked inability to play nicely with others. They did not farm, but rather fished and hunted for their sustenance from the bountiful bays, rivers, and Gulf (these were so bountiful, in fact, that as many as 50,000 Calusas may have been living here at a time). They controlled much of the southwest coast of Florida, and many other tribes justifiably feared their aggression. This is all ancient history, though, as the Spanish settlers ran them off or killed them off, either actively or passively with the introduction of smallpox and other diseases, starting close to when the Spanish arrived in the 1500s. By the 1700s the tribe was wiped out, the remaining handful of Calusas purportedly lighting out for Cuba when the Spanish turned Florida over to the British in 1763.

The impact of the Calusas on the area and their unique way of life are still apparent today, however. They built homes on stilts with palmetto leaf roofs and no walls and fashioned nets from palm tree fiber to catch mullet, catfish, and pinfish. But their most ingenious work was with shells. Shellfish provided a staple in the Calusa diet—then once the succulent meat was removed, the shells were used to make jewelry, utensils, spearheads, other tools, and vast heaps upon which other things could be built. Little mangrove keys, uninhabitable on their own, became homes or sacred places with the addition of a few thousand carefully piled shells.

These shell mounds are literally the building blocks for Marco Island and many of the Ten Thousand Islands. If you want to spend a day exploring the remnants of Calusa mounds, **Florida Saltwater Adventures** (239/595-7495,

$270 for a three-hour trip for up to six people, $350 for four hours, $425 for five, reservations necessary) offers wonderful ecotours. Captain Alex Saputo takes small groups out on his 24-foot boat, weaving in and out of the Ten Thousand Islands while pointing out wildlife and spouting horticultural and local history. He's a Calusa and Seminole buff, big time, and his enthusiasm is infectious as you tramp around a shell mound, crouching to see a fat whelk shell once used as a hammerhead or other tool. And on the way back, watch for dolphins that leap in the wake of the boat—they're either playing or "drafting" off the boat's speed (even dolphin experts disagree about why they do it)—but it's about as close as you'll ever get to dolphins outside of Sea World.

SIGHTS
Museums

History enthusiasts have a couple of tiny yet illuminating museums on-island. Marco Island Historical Society operates the **Museum at Olde Marco** (168 Royal Palm Dr., 239/389-6447, 7 A.M.–7 P.M. daily, free admission) next to the oldest building on the island, the Olde Marco Island Inn. The focus is on archaeological finds of the area with an emphasis on Calusa culture. There's even a sweet life-sized diorama of a Calusa household. The second museum, the **Key Marco Museum** (in the lobby of the Board of Realtors office, Waterway Ct., 9 A.M.–4 P.M. Mon.–Fri., free admission) covers some of the same ground, with Calusa treasures displayed prominently. But it moves forward in time to capture moments of pioneer history, early island industries, and up into the 20th century. Both museums are really unstaffed, but a docent tour can be arranged by calling ahead. There are also maps at the museums for a self-guided tour of Marco Island's 13 historical markers, including that of the Cushing Archaeological Site from 1895, said to be one of the most historically significant excavations in North America (it unearthed the Key Marco Cat). It doesn't take long to zip through the tour, either by car or bike, and it's a good orientation to the island.

CHICKEES

What is a **chickee,** you ask? You'll see the term a lot around here. It's a Seminole word for an open, handmade structure comprised of cypress poles and a roof of palm fronds. Historically, there was an art to erecting chickees, the cypress stripped in a process called "draw knife," the fronds nailed in a particular pattern to keep out the area's heavy rains. A chickee is now more broadly defined as any open-air structure, but usually ones in which there's boozing and general merriment.

SHOPPING

Marco isn't as replete with fancy shops as Naples to the north, nor is it as retail-impoverished as Everglades City to the south. There are a few concentrated areas: The **Esplanade** (740–760 Collier Blvd. N., 239/394-7772) is a newish development with clothing and home decor stores, a few restaurants, and a fancy day spa. It's also the only place on the island with a Starbucks (and a Cold Stone Creamery). Beyond that, there's a collection of shops at the ambitiously named **Marco Town Center Mall** (on Collier Blvd. N at Bald Eagle Dr.) and a number in **Mission Plaza** (on Collier Blvd. across from the Hilton). Adjacent to the Olde Marco Island Inn at the northern tip of the island, the **Shops at Olde Marco** (100 Palm St., 239/475-3466) complex has a couple boutiques, gourmet food shops, and the inn's spa and fitness center.

But for the big kahuna of shopping you have to drive back north off the island. The **Prime Outlets** (7222 Isle of Capri Rd., just north of Marco Island, 239/775-8083, 10 A.M.–8 P.M. Mon.–Sat., 11 A.M.–6 P.M. Sun.) has more than 40 stores, most of them big names, with designer clothes and shoes, books, and housewares at up to 70 percent off retail prices.

ACCOMMODATIONS
Under $100

There's not much on Marco Island for the budget traveler. However, satisfaction is just a couple minutes away. Goodland is a little town adjacent to Marco Island, plopped on an Indian shell mound. It's about a mile square and boasts a few hundred residents, mostly rough fisherfolk, and a bunch of down-home bars. Things are changing (a sign in town now advertises 52 new luxury townhouses, the asking price upwards of $600,000), but you can still get a taste of yesterday at the **Pink House Motel** (310 Pear Tree Ave., Goodland, 239/394-1313, $59), a historic family-owned waterfront motel with boat docking, efficiency kitchens, laundry facilities, and the Marker 7 Marina and Tackle Shop. In a similar vein on Marco Island, but a little pricier, the **Boat House Motel** (1180 Edington Pl., $78–290) is a little more glamorous, two stories with a gazebo and boat docks, but still really a straightforward low-rise motel.

Under $150

Marco Island Lakeside Inn (155 First Ave., 239/394-1161, $79–290) has 17 one-bedroom and 2 two-bedroom units on a lake one mile from the beach. There is a steak and sushi restaurant on-site.

There are also hundreds of vacation rental homes and condominiums on Marco Island. Many of these rent only by the week, especially in high season, and most of these work out to less than $150 per night Several rental companies have nice websites from which you can peruse properties: **Coldwell Banker** (800/733-8121, www.marcoislandvacations .net) seems to rent largely in high-rise condos, **Holiday Homes of Marco Island** (239/389-9940, www.marco-island.com) represents a number of single-family homes, and **Prudential Florida Realty** (239/642-5400, marcobeachrentals.net) offers a wide range, from fancy high-rise condos to individual homes right on a golf course.

Over $150

Maybe it's an "if you can't beat 'em, join 'em" mentality, but if you're going to stay on Marco Island you might as well pony up the dough

© NAPLES, MARCO ISLAND, EVERGLADES CVB

Tall beachfront hotels dot the edge of the Gulf along Marco Island's four miles of white-sand beaches.

and stay at one of the "Big Three." Three beachfront resorts dominate the most coveted piece of shoreline. Each has lots of amenities, fairly good restaurants on-site, and a broad price range to accommodate different budgets.

Having just experienced a vigorous renovation ($187 million, yeesh), the **Marco Island Marriott Beach Resort, Golf Club, and Spa** (400 Collier Blvd. S., 239/394-2511, www.marcoislandmarriott.com, $135–850) may be more suited to a romantic golf-and-pampering getaway, with more than 700 rooms and lavish resort activities and facilities, the 24,000-square-foot Balinese-themed spa, a new tiki pool, and the Rookery at Marco—the resort's newly upgraded golf course.

The **Marco Beach Ocean Resort** (480 Collier Blvd. S., 239/393-1400, www.marco resort.com, $279–1,000) opened in 2001 with 98 one- and two-bedroom suites, a spa, fancy Italian restaurants (Sale e Pepe's chef is so exacting that he imports flour for pasta from his hometown in Italy), and a stunning rooftop

swimming pool with a panoramic view of the Gulf.

And the 25-year-old **Hilton Marco Island Beach Resort** (560 Collier Blvd. S., 239/394-5000, www.marcoisland.hilton.com, $99–379) is a luxury resort that consistently wins four-diamond status and so forth for its large guest rooms with Gulf-view private balconies, lighted Har-Tru tennis courts, vast amoeba-shaped pool, and other amenities. A new spa is planned for 2008.

Right out the back door of all three hotels you can rent aqua trikes, banana rides, and personal watercraft with **Marco Island Ski & Watersports** (239/642-2359) and **Holiday Water Sports** (239/642-3467), both of which also offer parasailing and dolphin-watching tours on the Gulf.

For a more historic, small inn experience, try **Olde Marco Island Inn & Suites** (100 Palm St., 239/394-3131, $90–600), a 116-year-old Victorian in the historic district. It features one- and two-bedroom suites with roomy screened lanais. There are six luxurious penthouses and a much-lauded restaurant. It's a convenient location, near beaches, shopping, golf, etc., and guests enjoy complimentary use of the inn's 38-foot catamaran.

FOOD

All the times listed below reflect peak season hours. If you're dining here during the off-season, it's best to call for hours of operation.

Casual

Originally called the Snook Hole (that has kind of an unseemly ring to it, doesn't it?) for the wealth of snook you could catch right off the dock, the **Snook Inn** (1215 Bald Eagle Dr., 239/394-3313, 11 A.M.–10 P.M. daily, $13–20) was first a sprawling, casual restaurant that catered to the Deltona Corporation's construction workers who built up Marco Island in the 1960s. Right on the Marco River, the Snook Inn is a fun indoor-outdoor joint with live music and long lines. Locals and visitors seem to come for the grouper and the vast salad bar (more than a few locals harangued me about the glories of the old-fashioned pickle barrel, its bobbing dills crisp and monstrously big). The garden courtyard is a great locale for sipping creamy seafood chowder or tackling a pile of peel 'n' eat shrimp (if you aren't wild about seafood, the jerk chicken quesadilla is commendable). There's docking available for more than 20 boats near the chickee.

Most of the island's other restaurants are lined up along Collier Boulevard. You'll see a lot of locals at **Bimini's** (657 Collier Blvd. S., 239/394-7111, 11:30 A.M.–10:30 P.M. daily, $10–20), who swear by the eatery's housemade bread and the Capt. Bimini's platter of broiled grouper, shrimp, and sea scallops, and you'll hobnob with locals while tucking into a thick-crust, heavy-on-the-cheese pie at **Joey's Pizzeria** (257 Collier Blvd. N., 239/389-2433, $10–15).

Or browse the range of possibilities at the Marco Town Center Mall: **Crazy Flamingo** (1047 1/2 Collier Blvd. N., 239/642-9600, 11 A.M.–2 P.M. daily, $10–20) is a lively raw bar with fairly good fish entrées, and **Susie's Diner** (1013 N. Collier Blvd., 239/642-6633, 7A.M.–2P.M. Mon.–Sat., 7A.M.–1P.M. Sun., $5–15) is the locals' favorite for breakfast and lunch. Go early for fresh housemade biscuits, waffles, pancakes, and omelets in the morning. Lunches come fully accessorized with included beverage and dessert.

Upscale

Marek's Collier House (1121 Bald Eagle Dr., 239/642-9948, 5:30–10 P.M. daily, $25–35) gets the nod from local publications nearly every year for fancy, romantic continental dining. It's partly due to the setting—the restaurant is nestled in Captain Bill Collier's lovely historic home—and partly because of chef/owner Peter Marek's *luxe* take on classical (read: sinfully rich) seafood dishes. This guy is a triple gold medalist at the World Culinary Olympics—yes, there is such a thing—and his lamb chops, swordfish swaddled in green peppercorn sauce, and veal scaloppini with blue crabmeat all score a solid 9.8 (except with the Russian judges, who quibble with the dismount).

The restaurant at the **Olde Marco Island Inn** (100 Palm St., 239/394-3131, 4–10 P.M. daily, $25–35) is another favorite with foodies or those who just feel like dropping a bundle on a nice bottle of wine and a perfectly prepared steak. There are five individual dining rooms, each with a slightly different feel, so try to wander through each before settling on a table (there's also an upper dining deck that looks out over the inn's gardens).

And **Arturo's Italian Restaurant** (844 Bald Eagle Dr., 239/642-0550, 4:30–10 P.M. daily, $15–25) has been nurturing Italophiles since 1994 with its justifiably famous stuffed pork chop and a range of hearty pastas. The wine list is worth a lengthy study, but for an Italian restaurant the mixologists whip up a mean Cosmopolitan and green apple martini.

Dining with a Twist

Dine one of several ways aboard the 74-foot *Marco Island Princess* (departs from the

THE PARADISE COAST

marina, 951 Bald Eagle Dr., 239/642-5415, $35–60), sister ship to the *Naples Princess*. There's the Sea Breeze lunch buffet cruise, a sunset hors d'oeuvres cruise, or a sunset dinner cruise. Head out on the luxury yacht as it glides along scenic Marco River into the Gulf of Mexico with leaping dolphins in hot pursuit. The ship itself is beautiful, as is the scenery, either by day or with a peachy sunset casting its warm glow. The food is unremarkable but pleasant (the cash bar will set you back a hefty pile if you're not careful), especially when nibbled on the open-air deck above. The ship gets busy for holidays (Valentine's Day, Mother's

Day, New Year's Eve) and is often rented out for private parties, so reserve early if you can.

Marco boasts another unusual dining experience. An evening at **Marco Movies** (599 Collier Blvd. S., Ste. 103, 239/642-1111, $8–14) is the oldest date-night one-two punch in the books: dinner and a movie, but both at the same time. A small, family-owned four-screen theater, it shows first-run movies (there's always at least one family-appropriate pick) along with very respectable Greek salad, delicious sweet-potato fries, several robust tortilla-wrapped sandwiches, beer, wine, and fancy cocktails, oh, and popcorn.

Everglades City

The way he told it, hardly anyone was innocent. He hunched low at the bar as he spoke—clamming up whenever the bartender came our way. But over the course of about an hour, he revealed the story of Operation Everglades. There were maybe 550 residents of the little town of Everglades City in the late 1970s—tough, independent-minded folks who mostly kept to themselves and made their living off the Gulf waters, shrimping, fishing, or whatnot. But, as the guy at the bar explained, there was more going on than met the eye—in those days you were likely to see a double-wide trailer or a Cracker shack with a Maserati out front and a shiny Cessna 206 parked out on the back 40.

Drug money, plain and simple. Law enforcement agents launched Operation Everglades in 1981, monitoring the sizable marijuana traffic through this sleepy town. And when the dust had settled, more than 125 residents were carted away in yellow school buses in one of the biggest stings the state had seen. Kids at the high school, carpool moms, busboys—everyone was somehow involved in the smuggling of pot up from Colombia and elsewhere through the maze of mangrove islands.

My friend at the bar—I promised I wouldn't give his name or that of the bar—paid his debt

to society. But looking back through the mist of a couple of beers, it's clear it was a wild ride. Guns, bales of fragrant dope piled on shrimp boats slicking silently through the swamps, vindictive drug lords, and a whole lot of mullet, pompano, and stone crabs—it's cinematic (why hasn't anyone made a big-budget movie of this with Tommy Lee Jones in the role of Lieutenant Charles Sanders, who made the bust, and the whole cast of *Pirates of the Caribbean* as the denizens of Everglades City?), but true.

There's a hallowed and time-honored tradition of nefarious activity and seat-of-the-pants entrepreneurship in Everglades City. The first white settlers arrived just before the Civil War, many of them evading conscription, the law, or the expectations of nagging spouses. Lots squatted, not comfortably given the heat, humidity, mosquitoes, and awkward nature of mangrove islands (no dirt, lots of knotty roots dipping down into murky, tannin-tinged water). Farming was hard-won (tomatoes, cucumbers, peppers, Florida avocados, pineapple, and sugarcane grew okay thanks to hard labor and low expectations), but the fishing was good. Mullet jumped so the waters fairly churned, the oily fish caught by net then salted down and barreled for sale in Key West.

Seminoles and the new white settlers mostly

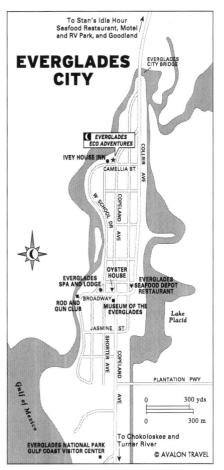

EVERGLADES CITY

To Stan's Idle Hour Seafood Restaurant, Motel and RV Park, and Goodland

EVERGLADES CITY BRIDGE

EVERGLADES ECO ADVENTURES

IVEY HOUSE INN

CAMELLIA ST

COLLIER AVE

W SCHOOL DR

COPELAND AVE

OYSTER HOUSE

EVERGLADES SPA AND LODGE

EVERGLADES SEAFOOD DEPOT RESTAURANT

ROD AND GUN CLUB

BROADWAY

MUSEUM OF THE EVERGLADES

Lake Placid

JASMINE ST

SHORTER AVE

COPELAND AVE

PLANTATION PWY

Gulf of Mexico

0   300 yds
0   300 m

EVERGLADES NATIONAL PARK GULF COAST VISITOR CENTER

To Chokoloskee and Turner River

© AVALON TRAVEL

---

it the headquarters for his Tamiami Trail road-building company in 1923. He purchased more than a million acres in southwestern Florida, promising the Florida legislature he'd complete the half-finished Tamiami Trail (linking Tampa with Miami through the swamp) in return for the creation of Collier County. Collier got to work dredging to make land and then paving over it to make the first real roads in the area, but his efforts eventually petered out and the state stepped in to finish the job.

The trail was finished in 1928, and improved access made the area's cattle ranching, commercial fishing, and produce farming more viable. For a while it was the county seat, but storms, along with Collier's decision to move his headquarters up to Naples, sealed Everglades City's fate as the sleepy mile-long mangrove island at the highway's dead end. In the 1940s many locals made their living sponge diving; after that came shrimping, stone crabbing, gator skinning, and sportfishing when wealthy outdoorspeople came to the "wilderness" for a little R&R.

Today, Everglades City's year-round population is as teeny as it ever was, its residents as self-reliant and dubious about authority. It's a locus of ecotourism, with canoe tours, airboat rides, fishing guides, and other nature-based businesses capitalizing on the mystery and majesty of the million acres of mangrove jungle just to the south. It's significantly more rustic than swanky Naples to the north—there are no Ritz-Carltons, tux-clad waiters, or turndown mints on the pillow anywhere near, but Everglades City is a must for adventure seekers. A couple days of paddling Everglades National Park, gliding past 12-foot gators giving you the hairy eyeball, delicate epiphytes (air plants) festooning the mangroves like some kind of alien Christmas trees, the birds engaged in a strenuous call-and-response—it's all enough to elicit a healthy sense of awe even in the most world weary.

EVERGLADES NATIONAL PARK

Everglades National Park (mailing address: 40001 Hwy. 9336, Homestead, FL 33034-6733,

kept to themselves, as did the descendants of the fabled Calusa in these parts. John Weeks and William Smith Allen are said to be the area's first permanent residents, settling sometime around 1870 along the Allen River (now the Barron River), the latter building himself a home on the site of the present-day Rod and Gun Club. George W. Storter, Jr. opened the first general store and trading post in 1892, in which the locals traded alligator hides, furs, and plumes for ammo and such.

The area's biggest growth spurt came when wealthy businessman Barron G. Collier made

THE PARADISE COAST

THE EVERGLADES

The Everglades proper is the mainland, about 4,000 square miles of flat prairie grass that slopes southward at one-fifth of a foot per mile. The rainfall averages fifty-five inches, June through October. In rainy season, the most southwest part near the mangroves gets anywhere from a few inches up to two or three feet under water. . . . The strip of mangrove mainland has many little rivers not much wider in the narrows than a rowboat, running all the way to the grasslands of the Glades. In rainy season these rivers slowly drain the rainwater off the Glades into the Islands. As the rainwater from the Glades mixes with the saltwater coming in from the Gulf, it becomes brackish. Most all the fish and a big portion of the wildlife, especially the saltwater birds, do most of their breeding and feeding in the brackish water here.

The fish and the wildlife all follow the brackish water line. In the driest of the season, April and May, the brackish line is at the very head of the rivers near the Glades, and so are the fish and game. As the rains come on, the brackish line slowly drifts down the rivers into the Islands and eventually to the coast.

Loren G. "Totch" Brown from *Totch, A Life in the Everglades*

He would know. He spent most of his life finding ways to eke out a life in this lush, junglelike wilderness at the bottom of the state of Florida.

THINGS THAT CAN KILL YOU IN THE EVERGLADES
Eastern diamondback rattlesnake, dusky pigmy rattlesnake, cottonmouth, and coral snake. Alligators very, very seldom attack people, even if you're thrashing about in the water. Dogs and small children are less safe from them. Keep both away from water's edge unattended. Do not, under any circumstances, feed the alligators, even if it's entertaining. It teaches them bad habits. You don't want to see a gator sit up and beg. Crocodiles, on the other hand (there are fewer of these in the Everglades, but there are some), are larger and more ferocious.

THINGS THAT CAN REALLY BOTHER YOU IN THE EVERGLADES
Mosquitoes. They are pretty fierce in the summer (always bring bug spray and long sleeves to thwart them as best you can). Information on mosquito levels during the summer is available at 305/242-7700. Also, there are a few poison plants: poison ivy, poisonwood, and manchineel tree. You might want to research these plants' leaf shape so you can avoid brushing up against them.

WHERE TO SEE GOOD STUFF
The Anhinga Trail (at Royal Palm) and Eco Pond (a mile past the Flamingo Visitor Center) are good for birding. There's also a train tour at Shark Valley that birders enjoy. Ca-

305/242-7700; in Everglades City: Gulf Coast Visitor Center, 815 S. Copeland Dr., 239/695-3311, 8 A.M.–4:30 P.M. mid-Nov.–mid-April, 9 A.M.–4:30 P.M. mid-April–mid-Nov., no entrance fee on this side of the park) is the third-largest park in the United States, outside Alaska, and has been designated a World Heritage Site, an International Biosphere Reserve, and a Wetland of International Importance. It's the only subtropical preserve in North America, containing both temperate and tropical plant communities. Really, it's the only everglade in the world.

Still, I don't think any of this conveys exactly what's so cool. The Seminoles called the park "grassy water," because it is essentially a wide, shallow river with no current, no falls or rapids, that flows very slowly southward along the subtle slope of the land, eventually meeting open water in Florida Bay 100 miles away. This

noeists like paddling into Chokoloskee Bay (Gulf Coast) and Snake Bight (near Flamingo) to see the waterbirds feeding on mudflats. For freshwater canoeing, try Nine Mile Pond. Serious canoeists tackle the Wilderness Waterway, the backcountry route linking Everglades City to Flamingo. Check at the Gulf Coast Visitor Center for canoeing maps and directions, and rentals (there's no launch fee at the Gulf Coast Visitor Center). A quick and easy way to get a sense for the immensity and majesty of the Everglades is by taking one of the 90-minute boat tours (from the Gulf Coast Visitor Center, 239/695-2591, on the half hour 9 A.M.-4:30 P.M., no reservations necessary).

CAMPING

Even if you're planning on doing primitive camping, backcountry permits are required (they're free; they just help keep track of visitors). There's established beach camping in the Everglades, chickee (little cabin structures) camping along the rivers and bays, New Turkey Key camping, Plate Creek camping, and camping at South Lostmans. Go to the visitors center to get a map and detailed description of all of the established campsites and more primitive options. Camping at park campgrounds is $16 per night, and a backcountry camping permit costs $10 per night (plus $2 per night per person, maximum 14 days).

OTHER ACCOMMODATIONS

The Flamingo Lodge, restaurant, and café are currently closed due to the damage caused

by strong winds and storm surges from Hurricanes Katrina and Wilma in 2005. For the latest status information, you may contact the park switchboard at 305/242-7700. Lodging is available in communities that border the park, including Homestead, Florida City, Miami, Everglades City, and Chokoloskee.

© NAPLES, MARCO ISLAND, EVERGLADES CVB

Everglades National Park is the only subtropical preserve in North America, and the third largest park in the continental U.S.

THE PARADISE COAST

river flows along sawgrass prairies, mangrove and cypress swamps, pinelands, and hardwood hammocks. Everywhere there are wading birds, alligators, dense and exotic tropical plantlife. But the U.S. government looked on all this as a dud, a big goose egg. In 1850, the federal government passed the Swamp and Overflowed Lands Act, which essentially gave people the latitude to manhandle this delicate ecosystem in any way they saw fit (in an effort to make the land "useful"). By the 1880s developers started digging drainage canals willy-nilly, wreaking environmental havoc with major silting problems. And in the early 1900s the first of several South Florida land booms saw the transforming of huge swaths of wetland to agricultural land crisscrossed by canals and new roads. Unsightly mangroves (essential for the maintenance of shorelines in these areas) were removed in favor of more picturesque palms.

Everglades boosters Ernest F. Coe and Marjory Stoneman Douglas (author of *The Everglades: River of Grass*) eventually prevailed, however, cajoling President Harry S. Truman to dedicate the vast swath as Everglades National Park in 1947. The park is still being rerouted, uprooted, and damaged in a variety of ways, requiring continued vigilance and stiffer environmental laws. But, in most ways, the wilderness is protected, and you have the privilege of visiting.

The Everglades region is mild and pleasant December–April, rarely reaching freezing temperatures, and mostly without a drop of rain. Summers are hot and humid, with temperatures hovering around 90°F and humidity at a fairly consistent steamy 90 percent. And, as with most places along the Gulf Coast, there are tremendous afternoon thunderstorms in the summer.

SPORTS AND RECREATION
Canoeing

Everglades National Park is America's only subtropical wilderness, a third of it given over to marine areas and shallow estuaries easily paddled by rookie or seasoned kayakers or canoers (in my experience, a kayak seems easier to navigate through these sometimes-tight quarters). The mangroves form canopied tunnels through the swamp, through which you pick in a peculiar way: Often the flat of your paddle is used to gently push off from the tangle of mangrove roots when it's too tight to actually dip into the water. In this way you pole through the tight spots, the nose of your craft sometimes hitching up in the roots, necessitating backward paddling to disengage.

Mosquitoes are surprisingly not a real problem until the summer, when you absolutely don't want to be paddling through the steamy swamp anyway (think 90 degrees with more than 90 percent humidity, no respite). Still, you'll need bug spray, water, sunglasses, a flotation device (required by law), shoes you don't mind getting wet or muddy, comfortable clothes, a hat—and a plan.

Check at the **Gulf Coast Visitor Center**

(815 S. Copeland Dr., 239/695-3311, 8 A.M.–4:30 P.M. mid-Nov.–mid-April, 9 A.M.–4:30 P.M. mid-April–mid-Nov.) for maps and directions, and you can rent canoes downstairs from the visitors center at **Everglades National Park Boat Tours** (239/695-2591, $35/day). It's fairly daunting to head off by yourself the first day, so the visitors center and Everglades National Park Boat Tours both offer guided tours on a first-come, first-served basis. For more advanced paddlers, there's a trip that departs at 9:30 A.M. on Saturday mornings that lasts seven hours; a Sunday morning trip more for beginners is only four hours.

After that, if you want to push off on your own, put in at the canoe ramp next to the visitors center or the ramp next to Outdoor Resorts on Chokoloskee Island. As everyone will tell you: Don't overestimate your abilities, and time your trip with the tides (a falling tide flows toward the Gulf of Mexico; a rising tide flows toward the visitors center). If you want to pick up a nautical chart, No. 11430 covers the Chokoloskee Bay area. There are also detailed descriptions to be had at the visitors center and other local shops of how to traverse the **Wilderness Waterway,** a 99-mile canoe trail that winds from Everglades City over to the Flamingo Visitor Center at the southeast entrance to the national park. It's about an eight-day excursion, to be undertaken only after lots of diligent preparation.

Collier County has launched Phase I of the Paradise Coast Blueway, a system of GPS-marked paddling trails in the Ten Thousand Islands region, which will eventually extend north to Bonita Springs. There is a main trail route from Everglades City to Goodland, as well as six day trip routes ranging 2–10 hours of paddling time. Visit www.paradisecoastblueway.com for route information.

◖ Everglades Eco Adventures

Everglades Rentals & Eco Adventures (Ivey House Bed and Breakfast, 107 Camellia St., 239/695-3299, $95–750) offers spectacular half-day, full-day, and overnight guided canoe, kayak, and boating adventures led by naturalist guides. I was the only customer on my five-hour kayak tour. My guide, Courtney, a lovely young woman with a clear passion for the abundant natural beauty of the area, led the way, stopping occasionally to point out an unusual orchid, a dozen striped baby alligators sunning, an eagle overhead. Paradise, really, with the dense lushness and lack of human marks that make one feel as if you've fallen somehow into a prehistoric jungle. Substitute pterodactyl babies for the osprey fledglings you see peering from that huge nest above, and the illusion's complete.

My guide and I entered the water off U.S. 41 at the old Turner River, quickly passing into narrow mangrove tunnels, then out into lagoons and past sawgrass prairies and into Turner Lake. The company runs its tours November 1 through the end of April and offers a range of specialty tours for small groups, from photography workshops to night paddles (I admit it, the swamp was eerie enough by day for me to consider this one). It also rents out equipment sans guide to the bold.

【 Totch's Island Tours

Lots of airboat companies offer competent tours with nature-focused narration, but the most historically significant is **Totch's Island Tours** (929 Dupont St., just before the Everglades City Bridge, 239/695-2333, 30-minute, 1-hour, and 1.5-hour tours, $15–40). Loren "Totch" Brown, author of *Totch: A Life in the Everglades* (a must-read if you are interested in the crusty, taciturn folks who've eked a living out of the Everglades over the past 100 years), grew up on an island near Chokoloskee during the Depression.

As a young man he fought in World War II before going home to work variously as a pompano fisherman and stone crabber (legally) and an alligator poacher and marijuana smuggler (well, illegally). You can see a picture of the local legend in Smallwood's Store, a tiny museum on Chokoloskee Island (150 acres made entirely of shells by the Seminoles), or catch a glimpse of him in the 1955 film *Wind Across the Everglades* with Christopher Plummer.

Totch died in 1996, but his tour company consists of his family members and a number of fourth- and fifth-generation Everglades residents. They'll take you out either in backcountry or open water to Totch's island to see his rustic family cottage on a tiny mangrove island. Along the way, you'll be trailed by pelicans, catch glimpses of manatees lumbering along the brackish shallows beneath you, and see alligators (big ones), wild pigs, ospreys, and incredible plantlife. The guides know a lot about the local fauna but seem to fly by the seat of their pants on the flora (my guide spouted some botanical names that sounded suspiciously ad-libbed).

Other Boat Tours

You've seen them. They're the embodiment of Newton's Third Law: Those tall boats propelled by air whooshing through their giant fans—with no outboard motor and rudder for propulsion and control, these boats can scoot through extreme shallows on their flat bottoms, perfect for swamp exploration. It's an Everglades cliché, and a loud one, but fun (although they're not allowed in Everglades National Park proper, they scoot around the edges in the Ten Thousand Islands).

One successful airboat company is **Captain Doug's Florida Boat Tours** (102 Broadway, at the Captain's Table Resort, 800/282-9194, $29.95 adults, children half price, children 3 and under free). The airboat tour groups are small and the tour is one hour of meandering through the mangrove forest backcountry and a sawgrass wetland. Back at the headquarters, visitors are treated to a free alligator show and are welcome to walk around a replica of a Native American village.

Wooten's Airboat Tours, Swamp Buggy Rides and Animal Sanctuary (32330 Tamiami Trail E., Ochopee, five miles south of Everglades City, 239/695-2781, 9 A.M.–4:15 P.M. daily, $20 adults for either tour, $15 for kids, $8 for the farm) is a little farther afield. It's fairly famous in these parts, but to my mind the 30-minute airboat ride through the mangroves and marshlands is very similar to that of the others (and it's a less intimate group, taking up to 18 people at a time). Much neater are the 30-minute swamp tours on the swamp buggy. You'll travel through spooky cypress swamp and spot alligators (as well as North American crocodiles—the Everglades being the only area you'll find these guys in the U.S.), deer, snakes, and tons of birds. Wooten's also has a little "farm" with native Florida creatures brought in expressly for your excitement (Florida panthers, bobcats).

A quieter ride, with a more overtly ecotourism piety, the **Everglades National Park Boat Tour** (at the ranger station on the causeway between Everglades City and Chokoloskee Island, 239/695-2591, every 30 minutes after 9:30 A.M. until 4:30 P.M., $16 adults, $8 children) is a wonderful two-hour motorboat tour departing from the Gulf Coast Visitor Center. The cruise is slower, following a loop through a dizzying number of the Ten Thousand Islands. Along the way tour-goers are likely to see manatees, frisky bottle-nosed dolphins, bald eagles, and loads of smirking alligators.

Everglades Area Tours (P.O. Box 670, Everglades City, FL 34139, 239/695-9107, www.evergladesareatours.com, $95 and up) provides year-round half-day guided kayak ecotours assisted by a motorboat shuttle that carries kayaks and up to six passengers. Aptly named the Yak Attack, the tour strategy allows you to quickly get to the most remote and beautiful paddling areas. All tours are guided by experienced naturalists. They also provide motorboat ecotours, sea kayaking and camping trips, backcountry charter boat and kayak fishing trips, bicycle tours, and they can arrange for aerial tours in the winter season.

SIGHTS
Big Cypress Gallery
East of Everglades City, famous black-and-white landscape photographer Clyde Butcher has a photo gallery worth the drive. **Clyde Butcher's Big Cypress Gallery** (52338 Tamiami Trail, Ochopee, 239/695-2428, 10 A.M.–5 P.M. Thurs.–Mon.) features Butcher's own work on local themes—he is to Big Cypress and the Everglades what Ansel

Adams was to Yosemite—as well as the work of other nature-inspired photographers. If you happen to be in the area around Labor Day, the gallery sponsors a huge party with a naturalist-led swamp walk, music, and more.

Museums
The dire economic climate of Reconstruction after the Civil War prompted some robust families to move to the southwest Florida frontier, a "grass is always greener" hopefulness that didn't necessarily pan out as planned. They came, cleared the land on little islands (many of them now named after the original family inhabiting them), built rough-hewn cabins of pine and cypress, and hunted, fished, and farmed to keep the wolf from the door. Stoically, they made do in the wilderness, many of them visiting their neighbors by boat only infrequently. Then Ted Smallwood opened Chokoloskee Island's first general store in 1906. There, white settlers and the remaining Seminoles alike would bring in their hides, furs, and produce in exchange for sugar, coffee, ammunition, and other of life's essentials. You can read all about the Smallwood Store and its first customers in Peter Matthiessen's riveting book *Killing Mister Watson*. It tells the story of the legendary killer Edgar J. Watson, who is said to have killed the outlaw Belle Starr and then lived a mysterious life in the wild Florida Everglades. The book is arranged as a fictionalized oral history of the intertwined lives of 10 of the area's quirky and often trigger-happy residents. Matthiessen is republishing his three-book South Florida trilogy under one title in 2008, so look for a 10-pound book in a library near you.

Today, **Smallwood Store** (three miles south of Everglades City, 360 Mamie St., Chokoloskee, 239/695-2989, open daily, $2.50) is preserved as a 1920s-era general store with its original structure and its last stock of merchandise. The small museum provides stirring insight into the hard lives of the pioneers who settled at the edge of this vast wilderness, and the isolation born of living on tiny, remote mangrove islands. The store was placed on the National Register of Historic Places in 1974 and reopened as a museum by Ted Smallwood's granddaughter in 1989.

Just off the circle in the center of Everglades City, the little **Museum of the Everglades** (105 W. Broadway, 239/695-0008, 11 A.M.–4 P.M. Tues.–Sat., $2 suggested donation) is in the town's Old Laundry, a building that dates to the 1920s, when Everglades City was Barron Collier's "company town," during the construction of the Tamiami Trail. The focus is more on the area's Seminoles and other tribes who inhabited the area before white settlers arrived. The building is of note for the history buff—listed on the National Register of Historic Places, it's the only unaltered original building in town—but the artifacts and period photographs don't quite manage to tell a rich or compelling story. You'd get a better sense of the area's unique history by chatting with the locals or gliding through the mangroves in a canoe. Still, on a rainy day it's probably worth an hour.

SHOPPING

There's a squat nondescript building in the middle of nothing near where the road ends in the Everglades. Maybe you can buy ice there, or bait, I'm not sure. It's called the Chokoloskee Mall. I'm sure it's a joke the locals play on tourists, but that about sums up the shopping options in this edge-of-the-wilderness area. Head back up into Naples if the retail bug bites.

ACCOMMODATIONS
Under $50

Camping opportunities are abundant around here, but not recommended in the hot, wet season. Too many critters with which to compete. If you do want to camp in Everglades National Park, stop off at the Gulf Coast Visitor Center for an overnight pass, and always make sure someone has a fairly good idea of where you're camping.

RV campers have an appealing option at **Outdoor Resorts of America** (at the entrance

The Ivey House Bed and Breakfast is a welcome refuge for recreation enthusiasts.

© NAPLES, MARCO ISLAND, EVERGLADES CVB

THE PARADISE COAST

to Chokoloskee Island, 239/695-2881, $49–69). Tent and van camping are prohibited, but the RV campsites are lovely and the campground offers cabin rentals along with kayak rentals (at the dock), showers, laundry, and a small convenience store. It may be the quickest route from under the covers to steering through the magical Ten Thousand Islands. Pets welcome.

$50-150

There are three wonderful places to stay in Everglades City—none glamorous, but all significant pieces of local history and legend. The white clapboard **Rod and Gun Club** (200 Broadway, 239/695-2101, $85–125, no credit cards) was built in 1850 on the site of the first homestead in Everglades City. It has hosted movie stars, U.S. presidents, and lots of other celebs needing to get away from it all. The Rod and Gun Club was for years where local and visiting sportspeople gathered to tell big fish stories or share hunting information. A long, low lodge, it contains 17 comfortable rooms, a waterfront restaurant, and dock space. The **Everglades Spa and Lodge** (200 Riverside Dr., 239/695-3151, www.banksoftheeverglades.com, $100–125) is right next door to the Rod and Gun Club and is another piece of local history. It was built as the Bank of the Everglades, the first bank to serve Collier County in the 1920s, and has now been converted to a small bed-and-breakfast and day spa. The refurbished building has six rooms with names such as the Mortgage Loan Department and the Dividends Department, and breakfast is served in the vault. And the ❰ **Ivey House Bed and Breakfast** (107 Camellia St., 239/695-3299, $70–155), my favorite, was first built as a recreation hall for workers on the Tamiami Trail. The building was subsequently moved and converted to a boarding house—it's not fancy, with cinder-block walls and simple room furnishings, but the restaurant is wonderful (a delicious à la carte breakfast is included). The inn's staff is a wealth of information on the area, there's a small Everglades library on-site, and the complimentary bikes make familiarizing yourself

with the area a snap (take a bike and ride all the way to Chokoloskee Island for a coffee at Big House). The Ivey House is also the headquarters for Everglades Rentals & Eco Adventures, with charter trips and canoe and kayak rentals.

FOOD

Dining in Everglades City is unilaterally casual, but with no fast food and very few ethnic restaurants. All the times listed below reflect peak season hours. If you're dining here during the off-season, it's best to call for hours of operation. Several spots are outstanding, both for the food and the convivial ambience. ❰ **Big House Coffee and Gumbo Limbo Gallery** (238 Mamie St., Chokoloskee, 239/695-3633, 10 A.M.–4 P.M. daily, Thurs. until 10 P.M., call for summer hours, $10–15) has a bohemian vibe, not exactly hippie, but a free-spirited something like that. The cute little coffeehouse and shop (great array of books on the Everglades and lovely local handicrafts) was established circa 1890 as C.G. McKinney Store and looks today like a sprawling, comfortable house with extra tables set up in the side yard under a papaya tree. This is the place to go in the Everglades for Internet access and a peek at newspapers and periodicals. Enjoy homemade key lime pie, brownies, and coconut cream pie with a cup of organic coffee or a glass of fresh limeade.

The **Oyster House** (901 S. Copeland Ave., 239/695-2073, 11 A.M.–9 P.M. daily, Fri. and Sat. until 10 P.M., $10–19) is fun, but don't be a stickler on the culinary details. A sprawling, goofy place with model boats, murals, mounted largemouth bass, swordfish, and assorted taxidermatological handiwork. The safest bet is a fried fish platter and a beer (if you order something fancy like a glass of chardonnay there's no telling when that bottle was opened). Stone crabs are also a house specialty—eat them like the locals, chilled (it's gauche to ask for them hot) with mustard sauce—as is fried gator tail. And here's a must after lunch or dinner: If it's still open (some talk of it closing to the public), take the walk up to the top of the Ernest Hamilton

Observation tower right behind the restaurant. This is a 75-foot-tall structure built in 1985, with a panoramic view of Chokoloskee and the Ten Thousand Islands.

Beyond these three, a few other places will feed you satisfactorily (maybe not precisely with gourmet aplomb) and perhaps introduce you to something new. At the **Everglades Seafood Depot Restaurant** (in the old train depot opened in 1928, 102 Collier Ave., 239/695-0075, 10:30A.M.–9P.M. daily) try the deep-water lobster or stone crabs (their season is Oct. 15–May 15), and at the **Rod and Gun Club** restaurant (200 Broadway, 239/695-2101, 11 A.M.–2:30P.M. and 5–9:30P.M. Mon.–Sat., $12–25, no credit cards) set your sights on the conch fritters, gator nuggets, hushpuppies, or blue crab claws.

Anyplace that's known for a dance called the Buzzard Lope and that throws the biggest annual party around in honor of the lowly mullet is worth some investigation. **《 Stan's Idle Hour Seafood Restaurant** (221 Goodland Dr. W., Goodland, 239/394-3041, 11 A.M.–10 P.M. Tues.–Sun., $14–25) is on the tiny island of Goodland, in between Marco Island and Everglades City, connected by causeways. Sunday afternoons are the time to go to Stan's—heck, anytime's a good time to go to Stan's—when a fair percentage of the island's 200 or so residents show up for some live music, pitchers of beer, peel-and-

eat shrimp, and fried oysters. (For fisherfolk, Stan's also has a "you caught 'em, we cook 'em" policy.) Stan is a real guy, a hellion dubbed the Buzzard King and the author of the "Buzzard Lope Song," which goes something like this:

Going down the highway feeling fine
Doing 55 and right on time
Look up ahead and saw something in the highway, looks dead
A bunch of buzzards standing around
They all step back, with a lot of hope
Start doing the Buzzard Lope . . .
Flap your wings up and down
Take a few steps back
Go round and round . . .

Enough said? The weekend after the Super Bowl every January brings the Mullet Festival to Stan's, with lots of hilarity and hijinks.

Everglades Seafood Festival

The annual Everglades Seafood Festival in Everglades City draws thousands the first weekend in February with the promise of stone crabs (they say Everglades City is the world's capital, with more than 400,000 pounds of crab claws harvested Oct. 15–May 15), fish chowder, gator nuggets, fresh Gulf shrimp, grouper, and fish of all local vintage, along with live country music, rides, and arts and crafts.

THE PARADISE COAST

Information and Services

Naples and environs are located within the **Eastern time zone.** The telephone area code is **239,** but it used to be 941 (unfortunately, some guides and brochures still list the old area code, and the automatic call-forwarding expired in 2003).

Tourist Information

The *Naples Daily News* (239/262-3161, www.naplesnews.com) may be the best way to find out about local events and entertainment

(it also produces the *Bonita Daily News,* the *Marco Island Eagle,* and the *Bonita Banner*). Kiosks are pretty much everywhere, and it will run you $0.53. For visitor information, stop in at the **Chamber of Commerce Visitors & Information Center** (2390 Tamiami Trail N., Naples, 239/262-6141) to pick up brochures, maps (there's a good city one that's worth the couple of bucks they ask for it), and lots of coupons. The **Convention and Visitor Bureau** (800/688-3600) maintains a tremendous visitor information website at www.paradise coast.com.

Golfers have lots of local publications at their fingertips, such as the freebie *Golf Naples Times* (www.golfnaplestimes.com).

Marco Island events and information can be found easily in a copy of ***Marco Island Sun Times*** (239/394-4050), the widely distributed free community paper. And for Everglades City information, call the **Everglades Area Chamber of Commerce** (800/914-6355, www.florida-everglades.com), or visit it at the junction of U.S. 41 and County Road 29, where there's a nice little gift shop and lots of good books on the area.

Police and Emergencies

As always, if you find yourself in a real emergency, pick up a phone and dial 911. For a nonemergency police need, call or visit the **Naples Police Department** (355 Riverside Circle, 239/213-4844, www.naplespolice.com). The **Marco Island Police Department** can be reached at 239/389-5050, and the sheriff in **Everglades City** can be reached at 239/695-3341. In the event of a medical emergency, stop into the **Naples Community Hospital** (350 7th St. N., 239/436-5000) or **Marco Healthcare Center** (40 S. Heathwood Dr., Marco Island, 239/394-8234). To fill a prescription there are nine CVS pharmacies in the Naples area, the most central to downtown

being at 294 Ninth St. S., 239/261-8610. The **Island Drug** (1089 Collier Blvd. N., #409, Marco Island, 239/394-3111) has met Marco Island's pharmaceutical needs for 30 years.

Radio and Television

For when you feel like cranking a little music around here, turn to **100.1 FM** for smooth jazz, **96.1 FM** for classic rock, **99.3 FM** for new music, **102.9 FM** for an eclectic "we play anything" format. Turn to **770 AM** for sports talk, and either **1240 AM** or **1270 AM** or **98.9 FM** for news talk.

And on the television, **WBBH Channel 2** out of Fort Myers is the NBC affiliate, **WEVU Channel 8** out of Naples is the UPN affiliate, **WINK Channel 11** out of Fort Myers is the CBS affiliate, **WZVN Channel 7** out of Fort Myers is the ABC affiliate, and **WGCU Channel 30** out of Fort Myers is the PBS affiliate.

Laundry Services

If you're staying at one of the upscale hotels, condos, or inns on Marco Island or in Naples, most offer their own laundry services to guests. There's also a cool **24 Hour Laundromat** (4045 Golden Gate Pkwy., Naples, 239/352-2349) that doesn't use coins. You stick in bills and it issues you a card, which you then stick in the washer or dryer. In Everglades City it's a little trickier—the Ivey House and a few other accommodations have launderettes for their guests.

Getting There and Around

BY CAR

Main driving access to the area is via I-75, either from the north or straight west across the bottom of the state (this section of I-75 is known as Alligator Alley, with ample cause). From I-75, you may take Exit 101 to Highway 84, which leads to downtown Naples (best if your aim is to do a little shopping or dining along 5th Avenue South or 3rd Street South, or if you want to amble along the Naples Pier). The new Exit 105 is best to reach Naples Zoo and Naples Municipal Airport. Exit

107 (Pine Ridge Rd.) takes you directly to U.S. 41, otherwise known as the Tamiami Trail, the best exit for reaching Clam Pass and Vanderbilt Beach parks and beaches. National Audubon Society's Corkscrew Swamp Sanctuary is easiest accessed by Exit 111 (Immokalee Rd.), which also takes you to North Naples.

To get to Marco Island, take Exit 101, then follow Collier Boulevard (Hwy. 951) west to the island. And to reach Everglades City, continue south from Naples on U.S. 41.

If you're coming from Miami, take U.S. 41 the whole way. The Tamiami Trail is a little slower than I-75, but it offers more sightseeing possibilities, as it has been designated a National Scenic Byway and Florida Scenic Highway. The route celebrated its 75th anniversary in 2003 and takes you right through the Everglades and Big Cypress National Preserve.

BY AIR

By air, the closest large airport is **Southwest Florida International Airport** (239/768-1000, www.flylcpa.com), 40 minutes to the north in Fort Myers. Most major domestic airlines serve the airport, and there are international flights from Germany and Canada. The airport has enjoyed enormous growth recently, finishing an expanded terminal and new runway opening in 2005. There is a little commuter airport in Naples, the **Naples Municipal Airport** (239/643-0733, www.flynaples.com), which offers nonstop jet service from Atlantic Southeast Airlines as well as regular flights to Key West on Yellow Air Taxi. Private jets constitute much of this airport's daily traffic. Private planes can also fly into Marco Executive Airport, Immokalee Regional Airport, and Everglades Airpark in Everglades City.

Alamo (800/327-9633), **Avis** (800/831-2847), **Budget** (800/527-0700), **Dollar** (800/800-4000 domestic, 800/800-6000 international), and **National** (800/227-7368) provide rental cars from Southwest Florida International Airport. From the Naples Municipal Airport, there is a convenient **Naples Airport Shuttle** (888/569-2227).

BY TRAIN AND BUS

Amtrak (800/USA-RAIL) offers train service as far south as the Fort Myers station, 40 miles or so north of Naples, but you'll have to drive from there. Also, Greyhound Bus Line (239/774-5660) provides regular service into Naples, and Collier Area Transit operates a reliable network of city buses ($3 for a day-long pass). One of the most pleasant sightseeing opportunities in Naples is the **Naples Trolley** (1010 6th Ave. S., 239/263-7400, day passes $18 for adults, $8 for children 4–12, free for children under 4, free reboarding). The narrated tour covers over 100 local points of interest and a nice historical overview of the area. You can disembark whenever something captures your interest, then hop the next trolley shuffling by.

THE PARADISE COAST

MOON SARASOTA, NAPLES &
THE PARADISE COAST
Avalon Travel
a member of the Perseus Books Group
1700 Fourth Street
Berkeley, CA 94710, USA
www.moon.com

Editor: Shaharazade Husain
Series Manager: Kathryn Ettinger
Copy Editor: Emily Lunceford
Graphics Coordinator: Tabitha Lahr
Production Coordinator: Tabitha Lahr
Cover Designer: Tabitha Lahr
Map Editor: Kevin Anglin
Cartographers: Chris Markiewicz, Hank Evans,
    Kat Bennett

ISBN: 978-1-59880-536-9

Text © 2008 by Laura Reiley.
Maps © 2008 by Avalon Travel Publishing, Inc.
All rights reserved.

Some photos and illustrations are used by permission
and are the property of the original copyright owners.

Front cover photo: mediterranean hallway at the
Ringling Museum, Sarasota © istockphoto.com
Titlepage photo: Flamingo © dreamstime.com

Printed in the United States

ABOUT THE AUTHOR

© MAX SHAFIQ

Laura Reiley

Laura Reiley entered the world of work on the heels of a two-year culinary school program. As a professionally trained chef, she was now qualified to draw discriminating and effete conclusions about meals eaten and wines consumed. She did so with gusto, reviewing restaurants and writing about food for magazines and newspapers in Baltimore, San Francisco, and most recently St. Petersburg, Florida.

A food writer must keep one eye on food, but it is somewhat inevitable that the other eye drifts to the anthropology of food — the folkways of the eaters and drinkers. After moving to Florida's Gulf Coast in 2003, Laura began to admire how Harriet Beecher Stowe once described her home state: "a tumble-down, wild . . . general happy-go-luckiness which [is] Florida." There was no better way to explore her wild new home than writing the first edition of *Moon Florida Gulf Coast,* for which she won first prize from the North American Travel Journalists Association. From there, she set her sights on Central Florida for *Moon Walt Disney World & Orlando.*

Laura is now back to reconnecting with the Gulf Coast. She currently lives in Tampa with her husband, a psychologist; her daughter, a twelve-year-old; and her dog, a balding schnoodle. She can be reached via email at lreiley@tampabay.rr.com.